SEXUAL TURNING POINTS

SEXUAL

MACMILLAN PUBLISHING COMPANY

New York

COLLIER MACMILLAN PUBLISHERS

London

TURNING POINTS

The Seven Stages of

Adult Sexuality

LORNA J. SARREL, M.S.W.

PHILIP M. SARREL, M.D.

Macmillan Publishing Company
866 Third Avenue, New York, N.Y. 10022
Collier Macmillan Canada, Inc.

Library of Congress Cataloging in Publication Data
Sarrel, Lorna J.
The seven stages of adult sexuality.
Bibliography: p.
Includes index.
1. Sex (Psychology)   2. Sexual disorders.   3. Sex
therapy.   I. Sarrel, Philip M., 1937–   .   II. Title.
BF692.S22   1984   155.3   84-739
ISBN 0-02-606910-5

10   9   8   7   6   5   4   3   2   1

Designed by Jack Meserole

Printed in the United States of America

Macmillan books are available at special discounts
for bulk purchase for sales promotions, premiums, fund-raising,
or educational use. Special editions or book excerpts
can also be created to specification.
For details, contact:
Special Sales Director
Macmillan Publishing Company
866 Third Avenue
New York, New York 10022

This book is not intended as a substitute for the medical advice
of your own physician. The reader should regularly consult a
physician in matters relating to his or her health and particularly in
respect of any symptoms which may require diagnosis or medical
attention.

To Our Mothers and Our Children

Contents

We want to thank Sey Chassler and Anne Mollegan Smith for their support and encouragement. We also want to thank William Masters and Virginia Johnson for training us in the field of sex therapy. Thanks, too, to our very helpful editor, Arlene Friedman.

SEXUAL TURNING POINTS

Introduction

We have been writing about sex for women's magazines for almost fifteen years. That is a lot of words, a lot of ideas, about sex. And yet we never seem to run out of things we want to say that we believe are important to communicate. The wellspring of our ideas is our day-in, day-out work with couples and individuals who come to us to talk about sex; sometimes about very serious problems, sometimes about simpler matters, like birth control or a question about sexual response. We direct the Sex Counseling Service (SCS) at Yale University. Students, employees, and faculty are our "patients." Since we began the SCS, in 1969, we have seen approximately 5,000 people. These people—their stories, their struggles, and their progress—have been our primary teachers.

We have been working as a team since the late 1960s, when we were both involved in a sex education course for students at Mount Holyoke, Smith, and Amherst colleges. Phil is an obstetrician-gynecologist by training, Lorna a social worker. At first, our different disciplines meant we approached the subject of sex differently. Phil, naturally, focused on the biological, Lorna on the psychological. We mirrored perfectly the tendency of our culture to split the mind and the body. As a result, when we first began seeing counselees and patients together, we sometimes seemed to be speaking different languages with them.

Then, in 1971, we went to St. Louis to be trained in sex therapy by William Masters and Virginia Johnson. This training was rigorous, intense, of a very high standard, and, for us, revolutionary. We were told that our division of labor into mind/body wouldn't work because the co-therapy approach required that the male therapist focus on and be the primary therapist for the male "patient" and likewise the female therapist for the female "patient." This meant that Phil would have to deal with male psychology and Lorna would have to learn about female physiology, be present when the woman was being examined, and be able to interpret her body responses as she reported them during therapy.

Masters and Johnson also insisted that we function as equals in the co-therapy team. No more dominance-submission patterns based on male/female or doctor/social worker status differences. But that's another story.

We returned to Yale deeply enriched by our training in St. Louis. It began to seem obvious to us that a mind/body dualism wasn't helpful. Sexual experiences and sexual problems involve the whole person. It is impossible to say where biology ends and psychology takes over. This psychosomatic perspective has permeated our clinical work, our teaching, and our writing.

We were also fortunate to work in a unit at Yale called the Mental Hygiene Department, a slightly quaint term for a psychotherapy service. This department has an excellent group of psychiatrists, psychologists, and social workers whose orientation is psychodynamic and developmental. The focus of the department is its work with Yale students. We learned a great deal in this environment, most important, an emphasis on normal developmental phases.

Meanwhile, across town, in another division of the Yale Psychiatry Department, Dr. Daniel Levinson was carrying on the pioneering research that culminated in his book *The Seasons of a Man's Life*. Levinson's work and the book *Passages* by Gail Sheehy underscored earlier works by Erik Erickson, Theodore Lidz, and others which make it clear that psychosexual development doesn't stop at age twenty-one. Adults continue to grow and change throughout the life cycle.

Working in the context of these intellectual influences, we started to pay more attention to the normal developmental hurdles in our patients' lives. We had always placed considerable emphasis on a detailed medical history. Now we explored this in even more detail. What we found was fascinating. Among the people coming to us for serious sexual problems, an unusually high proportion had been very ill during infancy or adolescence. When it occurred in the first year of life, the illness and prolonged hospitalization seemed to interrupt normal child-parent bonding. These infants were also deprived of the touching, holding, and fondling upon which is built the later adult capacity to relate sexually.

We also began to pay more attention to the meaning of illness in adult life. We found that many of our older patients who had never had a major sexual dysfunction developed a problem in the months following a serious illness. This is not surprising when the illness is something like a heart attack and the person may be frightened that sexual excitement could cause another heart attack. But we found that the disrupting illness could be virtually anything, from pneumonia to a mild stroke. It was the *meaning* of the illness to the individual and the sexual partner that mattered.

The more attention we paid to what we began to call turning points or life-cycle crises, the more important they seemed; so many couples dated the onset of their sexual problem to a turning point in their lives. An event, or a biological change, had occurred that unsettled their equilibrium, and they developed a sexual problem: One newly married woman remarked, "I had no problem responding—in fact I really liked sex—until the day we got married. My husband thinks I used to fake pleasure so I could trap him, but I know that's not true." Or, as a new mother told us, "After the baby was born, neither of us seemed very interested in sex. The baby cried a lot at night and we were both so tired. When we did have intercourse, I was tight and it hurt, even after the doctor said my episiotomy was healed. That was a year ago, and we've only had intercourse three times since then." Or, "I never had a problem with premature ejaculation until after my wife left me." Or, "Since my wife's menopause, I seem to have lost interest in sex. Does that make any sense?"

Contrary to popular mythology, we don't get our sexual act together in adolescence and live happily (or unhappily) ever after in the same groove. Our bodies change, our world changes, and, consequently, our sexual behavior and feelings change. Not all the change is for the worse. When a spouse departs, we may discover a new partner and exciting new experiences—sexual and otherwise. Menopause may usher in a revival of erotic intensity. As Gail Sheehy wrote in *Passages*, "Times of crisis, of disruption, are constructive; they are not only predictable but desirable. They mean growth."

These major shifts in our lives can be compared to the movements of the tectonic plates beneath the continents. The movement occurs usually imperceptibly, underlying everything else; and every once in a while, a small seismic event—or a giant quake—reminds us that our base is continuously shifting.

In using the term *sexual turning points*, we are referring to the specific and predictable life events experienced by most people that tend to produce alterations in sexual behavior, attitudes, and feelings. These life events often are the expected biological changes of the life cycle: puberty, pregnancy, menopause, illness, and aging. Or they may be interpersonal and social changes: having a boyfriend or girlfriend, getting married, parenting, breaking up, becoming a widow.

Why write about life's sexual turning points? One reason is that people are interested. When it comes to sex, people are curious about others' experiences—not with a prurient interest but a real hunger to understand and compare themselves to others. Even though ours is supposedly a nation obsessed with sex (probably no more than others in the past), there aren't many opportunities to really find out the details or the deepest meanings of sex in others' lives. Even close friends rarely talk about the nitty-gritty of their sex lives. In group-therapy sessions focused on sex, both men and women are infinitely relieved to hear what others have to say. It is as if a murky, anxiety-causing area becomes clear and calm. It is comforting to recognize that some of our most private experiences are shared by others. It is also helpful to look ahead and be forewarned about the bumps and curves waiting down the road.

But the most important reason to write about sexual turning points is that so many of the problems our patients have described could have been prevented—if only they had known some facts, if only they had understood what constituted "normal" human experience, if only they had been able to share their anxieties and confusion with someone else. We want people to understand the basic facts about sex. Beyond that, we want to give people a sense of what sexuality can mean to them at different times in their lives.

—LORNA SARREL, M.S.W
—PHILIP SARREL, M.D.

London, 1983

STAGE *One*

Sexual Unfolding—

Taking the First Steps

toward Adult

Sexuality

WE OFTEN BEGIN a sexuality discussion group by asking the participants to think back to their own childhood and adolescent experiences with sex; how they learned about sex and how they felt about it. After allowing for a few minutes of silent recollecting, we say to the group, "Now that you've had a chance to think about your own experiences, ask yourselves, 'What would I want my kids to experience?' "

This is how we'd like you to read this section of the book—backward first, into your own memories, and then forward, thinking how you can use what you read to help your teenage sons and daughters have a smoother, less anxious and confused transition into adult sexuality than you had.

Did you notice that we immediately assume that your memories of adolescent sexual learning aren't just memories of excitement and pleasure but include memories of confusion and pain? Because that is what most—not all, but most—people tell us; and not just the patients who come to us with sex problems, but the parents and teachers who attend discussion groups about sex education in the schools, the college and medical students we teach, and the professionals we train.

When we began working in the field of sexuality, in the mid-1960s, the extent of people's pain regarding sex was a surprise to both of us. We discovered that our own adolescent experiences had been storybook and idyllic by comparison with most. We both grew up in fairly liberal homes (around the corner from each other) where sex jokes and references were common, where facts were supplied, and, in Lorna's case, sex was described as beautiful.

Phil's father was a gynecologist, and his house had more technical information available than the local library. Phil was curious about sex, and when the first Kinsey book, *Sexual Behavior of the Human Male*, appeared in 1948, he read it from cover to cover a few times. Then we read it together, at a time when we were "just" best friends. So, at eleven and thirteen, respectively, we could talk about masturbation, fellatio, and orgasm, and theorize abstractly about mammalian sexual behaviors. We didn't know then how lucky or how unusual our experience was. The way kids do, we assumed that everyone else learned about sex the way we did. We were also lucky to fall in love (with one another) early and learn about sex together, gradually, over a span of years.

Perhaps we had been too influenced by our own histories, but as we listened to literally thousands of tales describing sex during adolescence, we noticed that the basic elements that had been present in our lives were very often missing—the positive attitude toward sex as something important (although sometimes humorous), the comfort in talking about it, the knowledge, the chance to explore without fear or guilt. We evolved a philosophy about adolescent sexuality in which we believe that these elements *should* be present, if it is possible. Eventually our ideas wound up as a book written for professionals, *Sexual Unfolding: Sexual Development and Sex Therapies in Late Adolescence*. That book focused on late adolescence because most of our clinical experience, through working at a university, is with that age group. *Sexual Unfolding* began with puberty, a logical starting place, and the place at which we want to begin this section.

First, a few definitions:

puberty   The period of biological change in which the transition from boy to man and from girl to woman occurs.
pubarche   The beginning of puberty.
menarche   The time of the first menstrual flow.
semenarche   The time of the first seminal emission.
sexual unfolding   This is a term coined by us that refers to the process, set in motion by puberty, of learning whom you will become as an adult sexual being.

Certain developmental "tasks" must be tackled, questions answered, and life experiences assimilated if one is to function as a sexual adult. Working with students over a span of four or more years, the nature of this process of becoming a sexual adult became clear to us. As a way of understanding and communicating, we have divided sexual unfolding into ten steps or categories. We'll tell you what they are and then discuss each one in turn.

1. adapting to the bodily changes of puberty
2. overcoming guilt, shame, fear, and childhood inhibitions about sex
3. shifting primary emotional attachment from parents to peers
4. answering questions about one's sexual orientation
5. learning and communicating what we like and dislike
6. first intercourse
7. coping with sexual dysfunction or compulsion
8. understanding the place and value of sex in our lives
9. becoming responsible about sex
10. intimacy—combining love and sex

Adapting to the Bodily Changes of Puberty

When our daughter was ten, she needed a ladies' size 8 shoe. This was a problem. Little-girl shoes aren't made in that size, and women's shoes look ridiculous on a ten-year-old. She was not unusually tall or physically precocious. What had happened to her happens to many girls at that age: Their hands and feet have a growth spurt. It is the earliest physical change of puberty, and it usually happens to girls a year or more before it happens to boys.

Even this innocuous event has sexual implications. For girls, it ushers in an awkward few years when they are neither here nor there; they are *preteen*. The discrepancy between the earlier-growing girls and their littler boy friends makes some girls feel "unfeminine" and some boys feel inferior and intimidated.

One young man who came to talk with Phil about his shyness and extreme sexual insecurity related his problem to this preteen girl-boy discrepancy. He had been a star athlete as a young boy, a Little League baseball player and a good runner. Being an athlete was his main source of pride. One day in his fifth-grade gym class, they introduced rope climbing. Two girls, before him, easily climbed the rope. He walked up to the rope, wrapped his "little boy" hands around it, gave a pull—and nothing happened. The necessary parts had not yet developed. The impact of the event was humiliating. He felt that no matter how well he honed his body to perform athletically, he had basic defects that diminished his manliness—and attractiveness—in the presence of females.

We think of this story as a classic example of the pain engendered by the normal changes of sexual development and the differences between the sexes. Years later, when this student came to see us, he appeared, physically, to meet a cultural ideal—tall, strong, athletic. In his mind's eye, however, he was still that little boy who couldn't climb the rope. He expended enormous energy on keeping his body in shape, running five to ten miles a day, then adding one hour of lifting weights and half an hour of swimming. He did have a girlfriend who said to him one time, "I'm embarrassed to undress in front of you. My body is less than perfection and that seems to be what you need most." How perceptive she was, and helpful as well, for her remark led to his going for counseling, which eventually helped him get to the roots of his sense of inadequacy. As he became more comfortable with who he was—as a person and as a body—he needed less time to "keep in shape." His grades, which were very good to begin with, became outstanding, and he was accepted into one of the finest postgraduate schools.

Boys experience the changes of puberty at widely differing ages. Some boys have gone through all the stages—hand and foot growth, skeletal and muscle-mass growth, hair development, penile and testicular development, and ejaculation and voice change—before others have even begun. Thus some seventh graders are starting to shave when some of their classmates have not even entered the earliest stages of puberty.

One man who came to us for sex therapy, Mr. P., presented an extreme example of late sexual development. His puberty didn't begin until he was fifteen, he shaved for the first time at seventeen and a half (although it wasn't really necessary), and he had experienced his first ejaculation at nineteen. At eighteen, however, he had been tall enough to enlist in the military, and it was there that the differences between himself and other men were accentuated. This was especially true with regard to sex. He felt himself a "little boy among men"—and that feeling persisted into his early thirties.

Eventually he matured and became a fully functioning man. He married, fathered two children, built his own house from the ground up, and became a foreman in charge of more than two hundred men. Although he felt sexually insecure, he had no marked sexual problems.

Then Mr. P. developed hepatitis, a liver infection, and was quite ill for several months. His doctor mentioned that impotence sometimes occurs with liver disease, and although Mr. P. recovered completely and was able to resume all his usual activities, impotence did indeed develop. Mr. P.'s confidence in himself and in his body, never very secure, was now badly shaken.

In sex therapy, the first clue to his underlying feelings about his body emerged in his drawings. We routinely ask people to draw one picture of a whole person and one, specifically, of a person of the other sex. Mr. P. drew a large, mature-looking female, but his male looked like a young boy. The illness had brought to life all his old fears and uncertainties about his bodily adequacy. Once again he felt he didn't measure up to other, "normal" men.

As it turned out, there was no physical limitation to his sexual functioning, and he and his wife were gradually able to reestablish their sexual relationship.

Another man in his thirties also had a sexual problem rooted in this later-than-normal pubertal development. Joe S. is thirty-three years old. He was married for twelve years and has been divorced for the past two. He is a successful businessman. He is six feet two inches tall, weighs 180 pounds, and jogs four miles each day; and most people, we think, would consider him a handsome man. Following his divorce, he dated a bit, and then, about six months ago, met his present girlfriend, Arlene. She's in her late twenties, vivacious, bright, and attractive. She seems genuinely attracted to him, though he finds this difficult to accept. It is particularly hard for him to believe that she is sincere when she says she really likes his body; no one ever told him that before.

Joe came to see us because of his worry that he would not be able to meet Arlene's sexual needs. He believes that the man is the provider; that he is responsible for sexually satisfying his woman. He felt this way during his marriage, and when, after two years, his wife had not had an orgasm, he asked her to go with him to get professional advice. She refused. She eventually had an affair, which so upset Joe that he insisted on a divorce.

Before meeting Arlene, he had made several attempts at intercourse with different women, but he always felt his partner was left unsatisfied. He wouldn't see the woman again after such an experience. With Arlene, he felt more comfortable. But they had just petted and had not tried intercourse. Wishing to avoid another failure, he sought our help.

A crucial question turned out to be, "How do you feel about your body?" Joe didn't regard his physical self in any positive way whatsoever. Most important, he always felt he had a small penis, and when he developed an erection, it always curved slightly to one side until fully erect. He felt the size and curvature of his penis were abnormal.

It turned out that Joe's feelings of inadequacy had been established around the time of puberty. "What did you look like then?" we asked him. He had been a little on the chubby side, and at times his penis had seemed so small, he could hardly see it. He had also been very embarrassed about having some breast enlargement—which occurs temporarily in about 75 percent of boys at puberty and is usually normal. He remembers looking like a little boy until his late teens, when he finally reached his present height, hair developed on his chest, and the breasts seemed to disappear. Although he then realized his penis wasn't terribly small, he still felt it was smaller than other men's, and he did connect it to his former wife's nonorgasmic response. "If I were bigger, maybe she would have had orgasms."

Many men have feelings similar to Joe's, which are rooted in their feelings about their bodies during adolescence. If a boy doesn't know, for example, that some breast enlargement is normal, imagine the psychological impact of such a phenomenon just when a boy is feeling a strong need to be different from girls and to be like other boys, and social roles are starting to demand "masculinity."

All boys develop a pubic fat pad. This pad of tissue surrounding the base of the penis has the effect of making the penile shaft appear smaller, especially if one is looking down at it. If the penis is observed in a mirror or from the side, it doesn't appear as small as when viewed from above.

Another source of misunderstanding about penis size stems from the fact that boys don't often have an opportunity to see other boys' erect penises. In the nonerect condition, there can be major differences in penile length, but as Masters and Johnson have found, when fully erect, there isn't much difference. Still, boys and men learn about themselves, vis-à-vis others, in the non-erect state.

Another factor in judging comparative penis size is that, in showers or locker rooms, where males are naked together, it is not unusual for some to experience a low level of sexual arousal, with accompanying partial engorgement of the penis. A full erection does not usually develop, but there can be an increase in the size of a boy's or young man's penis compared with those of others who do not experience the scene as sexually stimulating. Since about 40 percent of boys have adolescent homosexual experiences, size comparisions at such times may also be a source of later insecurities about having a small penis. Whatever their origins, feelings about penis size are often an important part of a man's image of his sexuality.

Eric Berne, the father of transactional analysis, wrote in *Sex in Human Loving* a chapter entitled "Sex is Wet." Wetness introduces both boys and girls to their own "adult" sexuality: boys through ejaculation (more about that in a moment), girls *not* through menstrual blood, as most people would think, but through vaginal discharge. One or even two years before menarche (the onset of menses), as the level of circulating estrogen increases, the vaginal walls change and normal vaginal secretion is produced rather copiously, sometimes more copiously than it will ever again be in that young woman's lifetime. Since the average age of menarche in the United States is twelve and a half, the average girl will be discharging white or clear vaginal fluid from the age of ten, and many will begin at eight or nine. This is one of the best-kept secrets about puberty. The average pediatrician is only dimly aware of it, if at all. Hardly any eight-year-old girls are taught about it.

Why is it important? Often it's not. The girl either accepts the new wetness in her underpants or she asks her mother, who provides a vague but reassuring response. Sometimes, however, it is confusing, repulsive, or frightening. Women recollecting the experience may say, "I thought I must have had some kind of infection and I kept waiting for it to get worse or better," or, "I thought I'd made it happen from touching myself," or, "The only white discharge I'd ever heard of was semen, so I assumed I must have a penis inside me and they'd eventually find out I was a freak—a boy/girl." One patient of ours was taken to a doctor at age ten or eleven because her mother thought the girl had vaginitis (a vaginal infection). The examination by her mother's gynecologist was embarrassing and scary. The doctor prescribed some medication to be inserted into the vagina, but the girl couldn't bring herself to stick anything inside herself, so the mother inserted the medication. Her memory focuses on the messiness. To this day, she is repulsed by her own vaginal secretions and by seminal fluid leaking out after intercourse.

This case may sound extreme, but it isn't an unusual story. The point of the story, and the point of learning about vaginal discharge, is to normalize it—to help women recall their experiences and to understand both that the discharge is normal and that an early negative reaction is typical. It is also important to stress the need for girls to be taught about their bodies and to know that curiosity about one's own sexuality is healthy. If we really want to encourage a girl to feel good about her awakening sexuality, perhaps we should tell her that this discharge is important and valuable because later on in life, when she has sexual intercourse, her wetness will help make it more pleasurable.

Not too long after the vaginal discharge begins, breasts start to grow. No one has captured the emotional agony of being a late developer, or the flattest girl in the eighth grade, better than Nora Ephron in her book *Crazy Salad.*

I started out with a 28 AA bra. I don't think they made them any smaller in those days . . . ; trainer bras they are called. My first brassiere came from Robinson's Department Store in Beverly Hills. I went there alone, shaking, positive they would look me over and smile and tell me to come back next year. . . . "Lean over," said the fitter. . . . I leaned over, with the fleeting hope that my breasts would miraculously fall out of my body. . . . Nothing.

"Don't worry about it," said my friend Libby some months later, when things had not improved. . . . "When you get married your husband will touch your breasts and rub them and kiss them and they'll grow."

That was the killer. Necking I could deal with. Intercourse I could deal with. But it had never crossed my mind that a man was going to touch my breasts, that breasts had something to do with all that, petting, my God, they never mentioned petting in my little sex manual about the fertilization of the ovum. I became dizzy. For I knew instantly—as naive as I had been only a moment before—that only part of what she was saying was true: the touching, rubbing, kissing part, not the growing part. And I knew no one would ever want to marry me. I had no breasts. I would never have breasts.

Here are some things I did to help: Bought a Mark Eden Bust Developer, Slept on my back for four years, Splashed cold water on them every night. . . . Ultimately, I resigned myself to a bad toss and began to wear padded bras.

Buster Klepper was the first boy who ever touched them. He was my boyfriend my senior year of high school. He wasn't dumb. He just wasn't terribly bright. There was necking. . . . Incredibly wonderful, frustrating necking, I loved it, really, but no further than necking, please don't, please because there I was absolutely terrified of the general implications of going-a-step-further . . . terrified of his finding out there was next to nothing there (which he knew, of course; he wasn't *that* dumb).

Nora Ephron and I (Lorna) are contemporaries. I have my own painful memories. By the time Nora and I grew up and began writing, attitudes toward breasts had changed. Twiggy ushered in the skinny, boyish look; bras were being burned; almost every female under thirty-five went braless at least part of the time; and the women's movement told us that we were wonderful no matter how uncenterfold our bodies were. This was the late 1960s and early 1970s: very liberated. That is why I was so amazed to receive the kinds—and the quantities—of letters we did from readers of our column, "Sex and Health" (then in *Glamour* magazine). Second in number only to questions about orgasm came an avalanche of letters complaining about small breasts. They were often long, long letters, detailing a sense of inadequacy, fear of dating, envy of other girls and women. The letters came from girls of thirteen, fourteen, and fifteen, but also from women in their late teens and early twenties. We still get such letters.

Breasts, apparently, have an enduring symbolic value in our society. They are equated with feminity, attractiveness, sexiness. Girls lacking in breast tissue fear they will lack the associated attributes.

Time often heals this wound. You discover that some boys, and later men, like your body. You breast-feed your baby and feel good about that. Maybe you are finally able to believe that your value as a woman, as a person, doesn't rest in your shape.

Not everyone gets over it. For some, the early self-image of being sexually inadequate is carried lifelong. In an attempt to feel better, some women even undergo breast-augmentation surgery. In sex therapy, we hear about the residues of teenage feelings. One fifty-year-old woman had never had any pleasure in having her breasts touched or looked at because she was so self-conscious about being "flat." She was sure that her lack of intense arousal from nipple stimulation related to her "underdevelopment" and was amazed to hear that according to Kinsey, only about 50 percent of women find that their nipples are very erotically sensitive. A lot of the therapy, in this woman's case, involved reconstruction of her self-image—an alternative to the surgical approach.

Another woman was not so fortunate. She equated her small breasts with a lack of feminine sexuality and sought breast augmentation as a means for achieving orgasm. By the time she underwent sex therapy, she had put herself through three operative procedures, each making her breasts larger and larger. She responded well to sex therapy when the focus became her underlying lack of self-esteem, and the therapy helped her decide what she really wanted and needed for herself.

Girls with larger-than-average breasts can also suffer embarrassment, but of a different kind. "In high school, I always wore big sweaters or layers of clothing to hide my big breasts. They seemed to call attention—not to me as a person, but to my sexuality. I wasn't ready to be seen as sexual." Boys often read large breasts as a sign of sexual readiness, and some women tell us they actually got the reputation of being "fast" simply on the basis of their anatomy.

One of our patients was particularly bitter about always being a sex object. "From the time I was eleven and, it seemed overnight, developed huge tits, men would whistle and comment; boys wanted to date me and get their hands on me. I got so I hated my breasts and I hated men. I really didn't trust guys. They just wanted to be seen out with the biggest pair in the school. I think to this day I don't really trust men, and I know I don't like my body."

Breast growth alerts the world that a girl is approaching menarche. It's the eleventh hour, but still not too late to tell her about menstruation. "But don't all girls today know about that by fourth grade?" people ask. Shockingly, the answer is no. A study sponsored by Tampax in the early 1980s found that one-third of the girls in America didn't know what was happening to them when they got their first period.

Retrospectively, the first period stands out as a developmental marker. In spite of the other signs of transformation into a woman, menstruation is still *the* event. Girls who experience it early feel pushed into adulthood and are shy about it. Girls who experience it later than their friends feel left out. Sociological studies indicate that girls whose developmental timetable is about average are more self-confident and popular. As women recall these years, no one ever seems to feel that she was this happy average. There was always something not quite right. Where have all the happy average developing girls disappeared to?

Of the women college students we surveyed, almost 80 percent were using tampons one year after menarche, 90 percent by two years after. Inserting a tampon is usually a girl's first experience with vaginal penetration. It is an important moment, because her feelings about vaginal penetration will color her sexual experiences for the rest of her life.

There appears to be a natural reluctance to let something penetrate our body boundaries and enter our interior space. We cross these boundaries regularly when we eat, less regularly when we clean our ears or stick a finger up a nostril. Experiences with needles or with having a doctor take a throat culture usually reinforce the reluctance. But in order to have intercourse, the female has to allow a fairly large object to penetrate inside her, and using tampons can be an excellent psychological preparation for that experience—that is, if there is no difficulty using the tampons. The women we counsel who, as adults, have a fear of vaginal penetration and whose vaginal muscles tense often have tales to tell of troubles using tampons. Not infrequently, they have never been able to insert one.

Most girls can learn to use tampons, although it may require coaching from outside the bathroom door by a mother, sister, or two or three best friends. Those who can't learn are usually very scared, and so their muscles tense and make the opening small; or they may have a physical problem, such as a strand of hymenal tissue partially blocking the way.

We need to digress for a moment to say something about the hymen. We know that most people—men and women alike—do not have an accurate picture of what and where the hymen is. Many think it is located deep inside their vagina. Most people imagine that the hymen is a solid, closed membrane. The popular image is that this solid membrane must be broken through somehow and then it is gone forever.

What are the facts? The hymen consists of tissue at the opening to the vagina. This tissue does not close off the opening completely, although it usually makes it narrower than it will become later on (after it has been stretched by intercourse or other means). The opening is important. It allows normal vaginal secretions and menstrual blood to flow out. The normal opening also makes it possible for a virgin to insert tampons. Women have hymenal tissue at the vaginal opening all their lives, even after childbirth. You can look in a mirror and see it. With the smaller inner labia (lips of the vulva) parted, you can usually see the vaginal opening. There is pink tissue here that looks fleshy and has irregular edges. That is your hymenal tissue.

The hymen will ordinarily permit insertion of a tampon, since the opening is wide enough, in a virgin, for the tampon to pass through. However, in a small percentage of girls, there is a strand of hymenal tissue dividing the opening. This may make tampon insertion impossible and attempts at insertion painful. Some girls manage to ram the tampon in, but when they try to remove it, it gets caught behind the strand of tissue. They may then yank hard and tear the strand. Whenever pain, fear, and failure have been repeatedly associated with vaginal penetration by a tampon, there are likely to be problems with intercourse later on.

It is ironic—and mildly disturbing—to realize that the girl's first period (menarche) is the biological counterpart of first ejaculation (semenarche) in the boy. We have coined the term *semenarche* because there is no word for first ejaculation. Both menarche and semenarche are the result of maturation in the central nervous system, the hypothalamus (part of the brain), and the pituitary gland, which stimulates gonadal function and sex-hormone production. Some women become irritated when they hear this analogy because they associate menstruation with pain and nuisance, while they imagine first ejaculation to be a pleasurable experience. They think it's unfair. It may be cold comfort, but the fact is that first ejaculation is not an entirely pleasurable experience for about 50 percent of boys. It occurs, typically, between age twelve and age fifteen. Our data show that only 31 percent of the boys knew exactly what was happening to them. A full 42 percent say that the experience left them confused, embarrassed, or fearful, and not solely with a feeling of pleasure.

Menarche is not usually a totally private event. Girls are likely to tell their mothers and/or close friends. Boys, on the other hand, are intensely private about semenarche. According to our findings, only 12 percent tell another living soul. We know from a study of sexual learning done a few years ago in Cleveland that 99 out of 100 parents never discuss ejaculation or wet dreams with their sons.

As with menarche, semenarche is a symbolic milestone, *the* turning point in adolescent male sexuality. Kinsey, whose researchers had personally interviewed 291 boys and young men, said the first ejaculation is the single most important psychosexual event of male adolescence. It sets a stamp upon the boy's feeling about ejaculation and about his sexuality. From Kinsey, we know that it almost always leads to a fairly regular pattern of masturbation and/or wet dreams within just a few months.

The vast majority of grown men can recall their first ejaculation in vivid detail. A seventy-five-year-old man who saw Phil because of his intermittent erection problems reached back into his memory more than sixty years to describe his first ejaculation. He was a poor boy and lived on an island in a humble cottage (no electricity) with his parents and his grandmother. In his words: "Grandma and I shared a small room. In the middle of the night once—I was about twelve at the time—I awakened suddenly and felt I was bleeding from my penis. I was panicked. I jumped out of bed and lit a candle to see. My grandma woke up and saw what had happened. She told me what it was, in a very calm way. She said it was natural and a sign that I was becoming a man. She congratulated me. I've always been grateful to her for that night. I think it helped me to have the positive feelings about sex that I've had all my life."

This story stands almost alone in its positive tone among the approximately one thousand descriptions of the first ejaculatory experience told to us by men with whom we have worked in sex therapy.

In a questionnaire study conducted by us, and in our clinical practice, 15 percent of men could not recall their semenarche. However, in the course of therapy, when psychological defenses were lowered and the men started to feel more comfortable with their sexuality, only about 3 percent could not recall the details of what had happened. Sometimes the story is of a mostly negative experience. "I thought I was having a heart attack"; "I thought I had wet the bed and couldn't control myself"; or, "I couldn't urinate afterward and was sure I had damaged myself"; or, "I was the youngest and the baby-sitter manipulated me. She knew what was happening, but I didn't. I was just scared"; "The game was to hit the cookie in the middle of a circle and to see who came fastest"; or, "I was in the bathtub and saw the sperm floating on the water. I thought, 'I'm too young to be a father'"

Menarche and semenarche have this in common, then: Both mark a special moment in time when, biologically, we change from girl to woman and from boy to man; and both are complex psychosocial events, which may leave a permanent stamp on our sexuality. As for adequately preparing our children for this step in sexual unfolding, we have barely begun.

Overcoming Guilt, Shame, Fear, and Childhood Inhibitions about Sex

In some societies, erotic feelings and overt sexual behavior are permitted and are expressed throughout childhood. On Mangaia, a Polynesian island, as reported by the anthropologist Donald Marshall, children observe adult sexual activity throughout their lives, since the one-room huts hold families of five to fifteen people. Both boys and girls masturbate as an accepted practice. Outside the family, children hear lots of stories and jokes about sex, and the language is rich in sexual words. At the age of twelve or thirteen, boys and girls are fully initiated into the world of adult sex. For boys, there are two weeks of intensive instruction in "cunnilingus, the kissing and sucking of breasts, and a means of achieving simultaneous mutual climax, as well as how to bring the woman to climax several times before the male." The newly expert young male then initiates and teaches one or more young females. It is said that on Mangaia, all the women have orgasms.

Clearly, teenage Mangaians are not faced with the same psychosocial issues as are Western teens. They seem to have virtually no guilt, shame, fear, or inhibitions to overcome. By contrast, American children have a dozen or more years of learning during which, typically, sex is shrouded in shameful mists; hands are removed from genitals with outraged glares, and information is withheld or parceled out grudgingly. Perhaps one reason we need a prolonged adolescent-youth phase in our culture is to allow enough time to rid ourselves of all the negative messages we have received over the years concerning sex.

A large share of guilt and shame about sex comes from childhood learning about masturbation. We are just beginning to emerge from a dark age of incredible misbelief about and terror of masturbation. Nineteenth-century books on the subject now sound absurd, with their dire warnings about "self-pollution" causing everything from insanity and epilepsy to sallow complexions. But these ideas have persisted into our century. Until about 1920, there were still neuropsychiatric centers where people with nerve-degenerative diseases and other as yet unclassified ailments were treated in "Masturbation Clinics."

Today we are more enlightened, but such deeply embedded myths still influence our thinking. In Cleveland in the late 1970s, a study of eleven hundred families with children between the ages of three and eleven showed both enlightenment and the persistence of irrational fears. Between 80 and 90 percent of the parents believed that most children masturbate (which is true). However, 40 percent believed that masturbation is immoral, sinful, and harmful. Their fears ranged from the idea that children could get sick from germs getting onto their hands, to the concern that it would make the penis too large (believing that, like any muscle, exercise it too much and it will be overdeveloped). Just to be sure *we* aren't perpetuating any myths, we should mention that these ideas are false and that the penis is not a muscle; it becomes hard as the result of blood flowing into and remaining in its blood vessels.

One of the mothers in the Cleveland study thought she was being very up to date and reassuring when she told her six-year-old, "It's fine as long as you don't overdo it or get sick." Thus, in subtler form than our grandparents, we perpetuate sexual anxieties.

In spite of direct threats or subtle injunctions, children do masturbate. In examining the sexual histories of adults, we hear how wide a range of experience this can be. Some people say they have always masturbated since their earliest, dim recollections of early childhood. This was often a casual sort of self-pleasuring and play, but tinged with a sense of the furtive and kept secret. Many men and women tell us they knew the word *masturbation* for a long time before they connected it with their own self-pleasuring. Others remember masturbating until they were discovered and scolded or until they stopped for unknown reasons. Still others have no memory of masturbation.

At puberty there are hormonal, anatomical, and physiological changes—not to mention psychosocial changes—that affect masturbation behavior. As we have already stated, boys begin to ejaculate and are likely, soon afterward, to start a pattern of regular masturbation. In girls, the clitoris enlarges from its prepubertal size and may focus a girl's attention. Even with pubertal changes, though, not all adolescents masturbate. At the time they enter college, about five out of six males are masturbating. The freshman year apparently provides a strong impetus, so that half of those who had never masturbated before will begin to do so in that year. Eventually only one male in twenty does not masturbate.

In 1969 and the early 1970s, the data we collected on the sexual knowledge, attitudes, and behavior of women students showed that about one-third of them masturbated—a statistic that exactly agreed with the Kinsey findings for this age group. Starting in 1973, there was a sudden and steep rise in the number of women students who said they masturbated. To some degree, the change may simply have reflected a greater willingness to admit to masturbating, but there has undoubtedly been a marked change in young women's actual behavior. From 1976 on, the statistic has been fairly consistent, and now about 70 to 80 percent of college women say they are masturbating.

More college women today accept the idea that masturbation is healthy. In 1970, 66 percent of them agreed with the statement, "Masturbation is acceptable when the objective is simply the attainment of sensory enjoyment." By the 1980s, more than 82 percent agreed.

What role does masturbation play in a young person's sexual unfolding? The answer will obviously vary from one person to the next. It can be a very important, positive force when there is not a great deal of guilt or conflict. Masturbation can provide important lessons for each of us about our own sexuality. When we masturbate, we experience the physiological changes of sexual response, and these become familiar. We learn what kinds of stimulation are pleasurable. At orgasm, we discover that we can let go and lose control without any terrible consequences. We learn to integrate fantasies with arousal from touching. All of this can be important preparation for sharing sex with another person.

Unfortunately, masturbation is seldom completely conflict free. This may be because parents, including even the most progressive, still incubate negative ideas about it, or it may be for deeper reasons. Some mental-health professionals believe that masturbation will always be connected with guilt and ambivalence because it involves primitive fantasies that are unacceptable to the civilized, adult mind. Whatever the explanation, the stories we hear about masturbation, like the young woman's story to follow, tend to include fear, guilt, and struggle.

"Before the age of thirteen or fourteen, I had no clearly sexual fantasies and I didn't masturbate. What fantasies I had took place in a big castle. I was a prisoner, and the men running the castle had the right to do things to me. This would involve anything from suspending me over hissing snakes to watching as I went to the bathroom. Though these thoughts gave me no outward pleasure, they were not recurring dreams or nightmares but set scenes I would think up as I was falling asleep. When, at thirteen or fourteen, these fantasies became overtly sexual, the gist was about the same; they were still centered around my being bound or passive while men watched or manipulated me in some way. The usual participants were—and still are—middle-aged men, only occasionally boys my age or women. These men were sometimes indifferent or too busy with other things to notice me or the things they were doing to me, and at other times they were mocking and cruel.

"I began masturbating around this time, an idea I got from a book. I masturbated quite often until I was about sixteen, always feeling guilty and dirty. I sometimes read dirty books as stimulation. I would get these books from my parents' bedroom when I thought everyone was asleep and bring them to my room. After I finished, I would return the books. One night as I was just creeping back to my room I rounded the corner to my room and ran right into my parents. Even as I was thinking, 'It's okay, keep cool,' I screamed and the sound of my own scream made me scream some more. I lost control completely and fell down at their feet crying. They, of course, were completely baffled. I made up a reason for my hysteria when I finally regained my composure. This incident was my first run-in with the power lurking behind things sexual. I realized for the first time the dimensions of my guilt and fear about masturbating and resolved, once again (for I had resolved the same many times before), to stop masturbating completely."

Ironically, the liberation of masturbation from irrational fears and the modern attitude of acceptance have generated a new set of problems for some young men and women. They now feel that they should or must masturbate. A thirteen-year-old had this experience. His Boy-Scout troop heard a lecture on sex in which they were repeatedly reassured about the normality of boys masturbating. He had never masturbated and, in fact, the idea wasn't very appealing to him. He went home and talked to his father, who told him, "Of course, all boys do." Five years later, this boy came for help because he was unable to masturbate to the point of ejaculation. Most of his problem was simply his goal orientation. He was trying so hard to do the thing "all normal boys do" that he was anxious every time he stimulated himself. The anxiety interfered with his sex response. (This anxious self-observation is called *spectatoring*. It is a concept we will refer to often because it is a major factor in all sexual dysfunctions.)

Young (and not so young) women also come under some pressure to masturbate. There must be thousands of women across the United States who have read something in a magazine or book or seen something in a movie that encourages them to try masturbation. Unfortunately, they also get the idea that it should "work" immediately, or at least very quickly. When there isn't some readily observable result, these women feel they have failed, and their sexual self-image goes down a few notches. Of course, once they begin trying to force a "result," they are likely to become anxious self-observers and then erotic response is almost impossible. For many women, learning to experience sexual arousal and orgasm is a very slow process that can't be rushed. Patient but persistent exploration is the most helpful attitude. It is also important to understand that a person doesn't *have* to masturbate in order to be fully sexual.

We have stressed conflict about masturbation because that is an important, almost universal theme, but there are many other sources of guilt, shame, and inhibition young people struggle to outgrow. There are painful memories of being caught playing doctor or reading *Playboy*; of an adult grabbing a towel when you entered unexpectedly; of Daddy's anger the time you asked what *fuck* meant. There is the less specific but still powerful sense that sex was a burden for your mother and a painful, unapproachable topic. There is the lingering shame over the erection that happened in front of the class and the sound of everyone giggling. There are all the *don'ts* ever said to you: Don't let a boy touch you there. Don't get carried away. Don't let a boy use you. Don't be a tramp. Don't disappoint us. Don't get a girl pregnant.

Painful memories fade and, often, negative attitudes are replaced. Unfortunately, negative attitudes toward sex tend to persist even when new ideas have been accepted intellectually. A young woman patient who described herself as "emancipated from my sexually repressive background" found that her mother's injunctions about not letting anyone touch you "down there" would suddenly come into her mind when she was in bed with her boyfriend. She said it was like having her mother sitting on her shoulder. In the course of sex therapy, she had a dream in which "a little person, looking a lot like you, Lorna, was sitting on my shoulder, telling me it was okay." After this dream, she found that she could enjoy sex without nagging guilt. Her "emancipated" ideas had gotten through from her head to her gut.

Another woman was amazed to realize, during the course of therapy, that she had negative feelings about her genitals. She couldn't really relax when her husband touched her clitoris or stimulated her genitals with his mouth (cunnilingus). One day, as we talked about her early experiences with that part of her body, she remembered something she had forgotten—that as a child she always had two towels, one for her face and body and one for "down there." Remembering this helped her recognize the extent to which she had been conditioned to think of her genitals as a dirty and shameful part of her.

There are tremendous pressures on young people today to be sexually sophisticated and experienced—whether they want to be or not. Some plunge into sex with the idea that once they do it, all their fears and ambivalence will magically melt away. A few months later, they appear in our office in a state of confusion. The fears and ambivalence are worse than ever.

One sophomore woman, Susan, had been a virgin and, in fact, had never done more than kiss and hug in a car until she met a twenty-four-year-old medical student, Michael, and fell for him in a big way. He seemed to assume that there would be an immediate, full sexual relationship between them. She thought she would seem hopelessly childish or hung up if she refused. In the one month they were together, she had her first experiences with mutual nudity, genital touching, intercourse, cunnilingus, and fellatio. Then Michael left for medical school two thousand miles away. She started to have difficulty concentrating. Images would flood her mind—images of an ax mutilating her breasts or a razor slashing at her genitals. When Susan first came to see Lorna about these disturbing images, she had no conscious guilt or conflict about what she had done sexually. It took several weeks for her to recognize that she had suppressed all the doubts and fears she had had about sex because she wanted so desperately to hold onto this man. I (Lorna) urged her to tell him her real feelings. She finally did, in a letter. He wrote back a sympathetic response. After this her images stopped appearing. When Michael came to visit for a week, they had a pact—nothing beyond kissing and hugging until she felt *really* comfortable with the next step. She needed to go slowly and to respect her own feelings—all her feelings, not just the ones she thought would please Michael.

Most young people are like Susan in their need to take things gradually. The slightly out-of-date courtship rituals of times past served the purpose of pacing: they called-for one month at the good-night-kiss stage, one month of breast touching outside clothing, one month of bare-breast touching but nothing below the waist, and so on, until you reached "third base" or maybe "went all the way." You had a chance to become comfortable with each step before you went on to the next. You even had a chance to get to know each other! Is it the distortion of nostalgia that makes that sound so good?

About 80 percent of college students have intercourse before they graduate, and most have gone a long way toward putting their sexual inhibitions and fears behind them. It is very upsetting to see how years of psychological growth can be wiped out overnight by one trauma. The kinds of trauma we are talking about are a pregnancy scare, an unwanted pregnancy, an abortion, being raped, or getting a sexually transmitted disease. Any of these can be experienced as a punishment for sexual behavior, and the guilt, fear, and shame associated with sex can come flooding back.

This sort of regression can be illustrated by Nina, a young woman who came for counseling after she had been raped by an acquaintance. Nina was in her junior year in college and had a steady boyfriend, Joshua, with whom sex had been pleasurable and satisfying. After the rape she could only tolerate hugging with clothes on.

Her upbringing, in a small New England town, had been conservative. Her mother had repeatedly told Nina, "Sex is the girl's responsibility. Nothing wrong can happen if *she* does the right thing." Nina tended to blame herself for the rape. She went over and over the details of the interactions between herself and the acquaintance (rapist), trying to discover unintended signals of sexual interest that she might have given him. She kept saying, "But he's such a nice guy, really sweet—I think." She refused to press legal charges because she didn't want her family and her hometown community to know about the rape. "I'd be more ashamed than if I flunked out of school."

Nina's primary emotions were shame, anxiety, and guilt. She wasn't able to express any rage at the young man who had raped her. When Lorna asked why she wasn't angry, Nina said, "I wondered that too. Maybe because he wasn't brutal. I mean he forced me, but he didn't hit me or use a knife so it makes it seem more like regular sex. I have to keep reminding myself it *was a rape.*"

It took several months before Nina could begin to feel appropriate anger at her assaulter instead of at herself, and it took several more months, before she could get over feeling too anxious and ashamed, to relate sexually to her boyfriend.

Nina did eventually tell her family about the rape. While they were solicitous and caring, some of their comments reinforced Nina's worst fears, that somehow she was responsible. Her mother kept reminding her never to be alone with men she couldn't really trust. Nina asked, "How am I supposed to know who to trust?" Her father said he was glad she hadn't gone to the police because she probably couldn't have proved it was rape since there were no signs of trauma.

Nina was lucky to have a loving and patient boyfriend who helped her to recover her ease and pleasure in sex. She said, "I can't imagine how I would have gotten back to sex without Josh. I felt so bad about sex I think I would have stayed away from it for a *very* long time."

Shifting Primary Emotional Attachment from Parents to Peers

This process can best be illustrated by a brief case history. A young woman named Sheila, who had transferred from a local community college to Yale University in her junior year, came to us at the Sex Counseling Service because she had been having recurrent nightmares about forgetting to take her birth-control pills. She had been taking the pill for about four months, ever since she had become serious about a fellow student named Gary, and she had never actually forgotten to take it. The nightmares were upsetting and led her to wonder what was going on inside her to cause them. Was it an omen?

This was not Sheila's first sexual relationship. She and a boy-friend had had intercourse for almost her entire sophomore year. She had taken birth-control pills then, too, but had never had the nightmares. She said she had never felt guilty about having inter-course. In fact, she had told her parents about it. This was not contrary to their values and had not been a source of conflict or tension.

The obvious question seemed to be: what was different now? What in Sheila's current life experience could account for the conflict symbolized by the dreams? There seemed to be two im-portant things in her life that were new: (1) she was living away from home for the first time; and (2) she realized that this was the first time she was really in love.

Sheila was very close to both parents and to a younger sister, who was extremely dependent on her. Since she had fallen in love with Gary, about two months into her junior year, she had not been writing or calling her family as often as she thought she should. In addition, although her parents had met Gary, she couldn't bring herself to tell them how deeply she cared for him. She realized that she felt guilty about possibly loving Gary more than she loved her parents or her sister. Once Sheila recognized the source of her conflict, she was able to tell her parents about her feelings for Gary. She began to feel better about her rela-tionship both with her family and with Gary. The nightmares gradually faded and then disappeared.

The primary emotional attachment being displaced is not necessarily an attachment to a parent. During his first year in college, Bill had intercourse for the first time without any difficulties. His girlfriend at that time was sexually experienced. She and Bill were good friends, but at all times it was understood that they were not "lovers." Toward the end of one year, they stopped having sex with each other and remained friendly classmates.

During the summer, Bill returned home. Home was a ghetto area of a large East Coast city. Bill spent the summer doing church work and renewing his close friendship with his parish priest. Bill's priest was a man who had recognized Bill's potential for academic excellence when Bill was a preteen. Throughout those years and his teenage years, the priest nurtured and encouraged Bill to reach for and attain goals in school and in sports. "Father" became a father substitute and was, indeed, the most important person in Bill's life. His influence was the major factor in Bill's going on to a prestigious academic career.

On returning to college for his sophomore year, Bill met Linda. They were in the same math class. Gradually over the course of the first semester, they became close friends and then began experimenting with sex together. Linda had no previous experience with intercourse. Bill's earlier experience faded and seemed to disappear. This was an entirely new kind of relationship for both of them. They were in love. After several months of petting and sleeping together, they decided to have intercourse. Linda came to see us with Bill. She was fitted with a diaphragm. Talking about their relationship indicated, to us at least, that they were a couple for whom sexual intercourse seemed very right and very appropriate.

We had not heard about Bill's relationship with his priest. Only when Bill was unable to have an erection did his feelings about abandoning his priest come to the surface. Fortunately, Bill and Linda had a return appointment scheduled with us. (Whenever we prescribe any contraceptive method, we ask our patients to return within a month to six weeks for a follow-up visit, just to let us know how they are doing and to see if there are any further questions.) They did not seem too upset by the failure to have intercourse. An appointment was made for Bill to speak alone with Phil.

At the appointment, Bill was able to talk about his relationship with his priest. The subject came up in response to my (Phil's) question: "Is there anyone else with whom you have a deep emotional attachment whom you have not told about your relationship with Linda?" Bill had told his mother. He hadn't said anything to his father, as he felt he really didn't have much of a relationship with him. He had avoided the subject with his priest.

After hearing more about Bill's priest and the man's values and concerns, I encouraged Bill to go home and tell the man about Linda. He did that, and the priest was fully accepting of Bill's falling in love and having a significant relationship with a female peer. "Father" was also accepting of Bill's sexuality—somewhat to Bill's amazement. For the next two years, when we periodically had opportunities to talk with Bill and Linda, there were no sexual difficulties.

Answering Questions about One's Sexual Orientation

Throughout adolescence and into our twenties, we are all seeking an identity, making choices, and labeling ourselves. In the area of sexuality, one of the major identity issues is, Am I homosexual, heterosexual, or perhaps bisexual? Some people seem to feel sure about their answer to this question even from preadolescence, but some young people have a degree of uncertainty.

There is agreement among most authorities today that all of us incorporate elements of masculinity and femininity in our personalities, and also a degree of bisexual potential. Early adolescent sexual experiences with friends of the same sex are not uncommon. And even when there is no overt sexual activity, there is likely to be the awareness of attraction and perhaps fantasies. In their book *Homosexuality in Perspective*, sex researchers William H. Masters and Virginia E. Johnson state that people who are basically heterosexual often have homosexual fantasies and that people who are basically homosexual often have heterosexual fantasies. Learning to accept the complexities of our own sexual nature can help us in the process of sexual unfolding. We can be more comfortable with our heterosexuality or our homosexuality if we are not constantly trying to prove to ourselves and to the world that we are 120 percent one or the other.

Just as women like to look at women's bodies, we have found that many men admire other men's bodies. Because men don't talk about this, it is not unusual for a man to feel there is something peculiar about himself if he is interested in the way other men look. The sexual issue raised is usually one of sexual orientation, that is, If I like to look at other men, doesn't that mean I'm homosexual?

TR is nineteen years old. He saw us because he felt shy and had not been dating women at all since entering college. A tall, attractive, athletic young man, he "confessed" that he occasionally liked to look at other men's bodies and, although he had had no homosexual experience, was worried that this was a sign of "being gay." In high school, he had had a girlfriend and found sex with her exciting and satisfying, but he had not had sexual feelings for other girls and wondered if his lack of interest might be yet another sign of being gay.

We talked for several hours over the course of about a month. During that time, he began to open up about his feelings toward his roommate and some other friends. To his surprise, he found that most of them shared his feelings, although none of them was gay. He said he also began to notice that in a museum, "almost every man stopped to look at the statues of men as much as the statues of women." Over the summer vacation he saw his former girlfriend and realized that not having sexual feelings for other women had more to do with his feelings toward her than with his sexual orientation.

The need to be 120 percent heterosexual is something men seem to worry about much more than women. In our counseling work, we frequently see young men who are in a panic about possibly being homosexual. Almost any sexual experience that seems peculiar or below par can raise the specter of confused sexual preference. Experiences that have led predominantly heterosexual men to wonder about their sexual orientation include:

1. Early adolescent or preadolescent same-sex sex-play experiences. We have seen a carryover impact in college students, especially when the early homosexual play led to the first ejaculatory experience. Homosexual imagery from the experience may persist in fantasy, and subsequent heterosexual experiences may not be as physiologically intense. An extra heterosexual performance pressure may develop in an attempt to dispel homosexuality, which in turn may lead to sexual dysfunction.

2. Delayed sexual maturation and onset of sexual behavior. Not being average is often equated, particularly by males, with homosexuality. "I didn't start pubertal changes until I was almost sixteen. I knew I wasn't a girl. But then I also knew I wasn't a man. I concluded I must be homosexual." Students who don't masturbate and discover that "all" the others do have seen us, thinking their lack of masturbation was a sign of homosexuality.
3. Being turned off by particular kinds of behavior, e.g., cunnilingus.
4. A more intense sexual response from self-stimulation as compared with intercourse.
5. Being a virgin at an age when he thinks everyone else has had intercourse.
6. Sexual inadequacy. Many male students who have consulted us about a sexual dysfunction have at some time expressed the idea that the root of the problem might be homosexuality.

Young women seem to be less troubled than young men by homosexual feelings. Statistics show that they probably have distinctly homoerotic feelings less often than young men. When they are attracted to another female, have homosexual fantasies, or "fall in love" with a female friend, they often accept their feelings as natural. They are much less likely to walk into a professional's office panicked about being homosexual.

This is not to say that some young women don't feel confused by their sexual attraction to women—just that they tend to be calmer about it. We have talked with quite a few students who wonder if they should act on their homosexual feelings. Sometimes it has been hard to sort out how much is spontaneous attraction and how much is feminist ideology ("I really love my friend Cynthia. It would be natural for us to make love").

We have been impressed by the apparently effortless transition some young women have made from heterosexual relationships into homosexual relationships and occasionally back to heterosexuality. Such easy shifts of sexual orientation would have been much more difficult in the past. A wider acceptance of the concept of bisexuality probably allows for more experimentation. We think no one yet knows what, if any, long-term effect this might have on an individual's sexuality. Perhaps, in fact, this is not as new a phenomenon as it appears. Kinsey noticed in his studies that sexual orientation did shift in some people as they moved through life, through shades of homosexuality, bisexuality, and heterosexuality.

For either sex, the process of sexual unfolding toward a primarily homosexual orientation can present some special problems. The homosexual world has its own sexual myths, its own codes and expectations. Until very recently, each individual had to find his or her own path without much guidance. Now that there are gay alliances, gay support groups, gay magazines and newspapers, and books about the gay world, information is much easier to come by. There are still, of course, the sexual, interpersonal, and social issues to be grappled with.

We will include the story of one young man to illustrate both the differences from and the similarities to heterosexual unfolding. Andrew is an undergraduate who sought sex counseling. He was a very articulate and perceptive young man. At the end of the counseling process, Phil asked if Andrew would be willing to write his story briefly. This is what Andrew wrote.

Now that I'm twenty-one and look back on the past few years, I can see that I was working toward something, toward accepting my own homosexuality and finding someone to love and love me, but when I was going through it all, I felt lost and confused. I didn't have a clue where I would end up, or even what I wanted. That was very frightening.

I think my special awareness of males dates back pretty far, but it's most vivid to me starting about my senior year in high school. I got real "crushes" on guys, liked to look at male bodies and my sex fantasies were mostly about being seduced by some perfect guy. I wasn't particularly attracted to any girls. I had some fantasies about intercourse, but not very often. I began to think that I was gay, but I didn't have any actual sexual experiences with a guy, so I wasn't certain.

Starting in seventh grade, I had wet dreams. When I would wake up during or after the orgasm, I could usually recall a vivid dream of sex with a man, though an occasional erotic female figure did drift into my dreams.

In my sophomore year in college, I decided to date girls. I wanted to settle the question in my own mind about my sexual orientation. I think I expected no arousal, but when I finally got up the nerve to date a girl and we ended up in bed, I was surprised to find I got an erection pretty easily. Eventually I had intercourse. It felt nice, but I always had fantasies of men during it. I found it a very schizophrenic sort of experience. I mean, in the sense of feeling split. It was so distracting that I couldn't ejaculate. In fact I never ejaculated with either of the two girls I slept with. By the end of these experiences, I felt sure I was homosexual and what's more, I wanted to relate to guys. I was scared, however, because I thought I'd have the problem of not ejaculating and, from what I had read and heard, a gay partner absolutely expected you to come. You'd be rejected if you didn't. I thought learning to masturbate would help. That was when I came to you, Dr. Sarrel, for some advice. You helped me not to focus on achieving ejaculation, and I was able to masturbate.

After that, I dared to venture into the gay world. I had a few casual relationships in which I couldn't ejaculate. The reactions weren't so terrible, but I was still nervous about it when I met Jim. Our relationship started out as friends. It was only after a few months that it became sexual. Neither of us ejaculated, although we seemed to like each other and be mutually attracted.

This was when Jim and I came to see you together, Dr. Sarrel. You got us to talk about the meaning ejaculation had for each of us. I remember Jim saying that he had never before had a problem. Ejaculation had always happened as a kind of mechanical release, but he had never felt emotionally satisfied. He said he thought maybe he was holding back because he didn't want our sex to be like that.

I remember saying that letting go and ejaculating with Jim felt like a big step for me. It would be a final commitment to him and also to my own gayness. You helped us to focus on what we wanted from the relationship and to let the question of ejaculation take care of itself—and that's what happened.

Jim and I love each other and feel very fulfilled in the relationship. Now my only problem is what to do about coming out of the closet. I'm worried it will hurt my family and I don't know if it will affect my career (in law).

I hope this account may be useful to others in understanding what it's like to go through the sexual unfolding process when you are homosexual, but I think each person's story is unique and I wouldn't want anyone to generalize from my experiences.

Learning and Communicating What We Like and Dislike

A friend and fellow sex therapist told us this story. Her six-year-old daughter had just finished looking through a sex education book (which to our minds is distinctly too detailed and graphic for young children). She looked up and asked, "Mommy, does everyone do all the things they show in here?" What she was really asking, we think, was, "Do you and Daddy do those things?" but never mind that; we want to focus on the question she verbalized.

Her mother, being well schooled in these matters and also a wise person, said, "People do what they like—what feels nice. People don't do things if they'd rather not." The daughter breathed a small sigh of relief. Her mother (remember she *is* a therapist) said, "You sound relieved." The girl responded, "Well, I don't think I want to do what they show on page 36!"

This six-year-old is way ahead of the thousands of high school and college students who seem to think they *must* do everything sexual there is to do. Not only that, they must like it. We think they mistakenly interpret the concept that sex is normal and natural as meaning that sex is automatic and simple. It isn't. For most people, it takes some getting used to and practice. What happens to each person along the way to discovering what she or he likes and doesn't like is very important.

Rather than discuss it in the abstract, let's take one young woman, Barbara, and follow her through this process in her sexual unfolding. At fifteen, Barbara had her first experience with genital petting. She found the erect penis startling at first but then learned to enjoy giving her boyfriend pleasure by stimulating him to orgasm with her hand. She became very excited by his touching her clitoris and usually had an orgasm when he kept up the touching long enough. When he stopped before her orgasm, she was too shy to ask him to continue.

Her next boyfriend, Zachary, seemed obsessed with fellatio, so she tried it. She didn't enjoy it, but it was all right since it pleased him so much. On a few occasions he "slipped" and ejaculated in her mouth. She didn't like the taste of the semen and gagged. But she continued fellatio with him for another three years. She did have orgasms with Zachary by his stimulating her with his hand.

When that relationship broke up, she met Tim (later to be her husband). They had intercourse on the third night they were together. Barbara found that intercourse was nice, but she never had an orgasm. Tim tried stimulating her clitoris with his hand "but it just didn't work." She absolutely refused even to try fellatio.

When Lorna saw her, Barbara was upset about her sexual relationship with Tim. A further relevant fact emerged. Barbara had been masturbating since she was four. Her pattern had always been the same. She would lie facedown on the bed with her hand between her thighs, one finger touching her clitoris. She always had an orgasm.

If we step back and analyze Barbara's story, we see that one problem had been her reluctance to say "I like it when you touch me this way," or "Please keep doing what you're doing." Another problem had been her inability to say no when she found she disliked something, particularly fellatio. She had thus built up an aversion to fellatio.

The main goal of therapy with Barbara was to help her identify what, specifically, she did and did not like and to get her to be completely open and honest about her preferences with Tim. In discussing the fellatio experiences she had had with Zachary, it became clear that the real problem had been the fear that he would ejaculate in her mouth. She didn't trust him. When Barbara and Tim talked it over, she realized that she could trust him. She was able to try orally stimulating him—very cautiously at first, and then without reservation. Barbara also identified the type of stimulation she needed. She gave Tim more guidelines and was able to have an orgasm from his manual stimulation.

Finally, Barbara learned that the man-above position she and Tim always used wasn't really the best for her. Through the years of masturbating lying facedown, that position had become eroticized. They found that using a rear-entry position with either one of them touching her clitoris, Barbara could have an orgasm easily.

Barbara's story doesn't cover one final point we want to make about learning to communicate with a partner. We all too often see young women who have not learned to say *stop* even when sex actually hurts. They seem to think that once a man is aroused, they dare not interrupt, so they continue with intercourse in spite of burning and stinging and a total lack of pleasure. If you put up with pain or discomfort once in a rare while, that is probably not so bad. But if you put up with pain all the time or with any regularity, sex becomes paired in your mind with pain. This will almost inevitably lead to serious problems—to involuntary muscle spasms at the vaginal opening (your vagina will say no for you) or to a fear of all sexual interaction.

Young men may be more automatic with regard to orgasm than are young women, but they do have lessons to learn about their own preferences. Often they are so focused on arousing the female, on pushing all the right buttons, that they pay no attention to how they themselves like to be touched. The most typical response made by young men (and older ones, too) to the request,

"Tell me what you'd like me to do" is, "Oh, everything you do feels good." This is usually frustrating to the young woman who is trying to learn about both men in general and this young man in particular, and it doesn't set a good example. She may then find herself too shy to tell him how she would like to be touched.

Some young men have always masturbated in a particular way and have very distinct needs, perhaps for very vigorous stimulation or concentration on one part of the penis such as the frenulum or (less commonly) the base of the shaft. Unless a man can explain his needs or show his partner how to stimulate him, he may lose his erection or be unable to ejaculate. Young women often feel not just shy about stimulating the penis but actually frightened about causing pain or injury. They need to be shown, usually by having the young man's hand over hers, just how firmly the penis can be manipulated.

Some young men who like touching and/or being touched very softly resist their own inclinations because it seems unmanly. We have been struck by the number of athletes who express this conflict. Could it be that behind all the macho rough-and-tumble they have yearnings for tenderness that they have been denying for years?

When it comes to oral sex, both men and women tend to worry that they may be imposing something unpleasant on their partner. Among the students we surveyed, we found that women underestimated the percentage of men who like cunnilingus. Likewise, the male students underestimated the percentage of women who enjoy fellatio. Since oral sex is now so prevalent among young people (among students we studied, 60% of the virgin females had had oral sex experience, and virtually every nonvirgin had), it is particularly important that young couples be able to communicate openly about it.

First Intercourse (A Step? A Hurdle? A Stumbling Block?)

Half of American young women now have intercourse before they graduate from high school. By contrast, in the 1950s, Kinsey found that by age twenty, "only" 23 percent of women had lost their virginity. When we were in college, in the Eisen-

hower–togetherness–gray-flannel-suit 1950s, hardly a female admitted to nonvirgin status, not even to her best friends.

Now not only is a female's first intercourse likely to occur between her sixteenth and nineteenth birthdays, but she is likely to
feel proud about it and to tell her best, and not-so-best, friends.
The cultural script calls for a coolness—a kind of low-key enthusiasm that, unfortunately, is not what many girls who experience
intercourse for the first time actually feel. Almost all studies
agree: The majority have very mixed emotions. A recent study by
David Weis at Rutgers University found that one-third of young
women felt exploited during their first intercourse. Although
about two-thirds of the women said they had experienced sexual
pleasure, half of this group also experienced high levels of guilt
and anxiety. One-third of the total experienced no pleasure at all
but *only* guilt and anxiety.

The rest of the findings in this study sound like what every
mother knows and wishes her daughter knew. If you are older (at
least 17), if you haven't rushed into intercourse but have built up
to it gradually, and if your partner is loving, tender, and considerate, you are more likely to enjoy it and less likely to feel anxious
and guilty.

Conversations with students we teach tend to confirm Weis's
results and add more food for thought. Following are some excerpts from one such conversation with a group of students.

"I was the most uptight girl in my high school. I had hardly
dated because I was known as 'too serious.' When I met Jeff the
summer after my junior year, I was totally naive about sex. No, it
was worse than that—I thought sex was bad and I was scared of
the whole thing, from kissing onward. I don't know how Jeff put
up with me. He was three years older and experienced. The thing
is, I guess, he was experienced enough not to push. But the main
thing that helped me to change was his attitude toward sex. He
was so easy with it. I don't mean casual, just relaxed. In fact, I
would say he's reverential toward sex. He helped me to see that it
could be beautiful. The first time we were naked together, he got
tears in his eyes. When I asked him why, he said, 'Because it's so
lovely and because it shows you trust me.' We knew each other two
years before we had intercourse. The first time I expected problems, but there were none. His penis fit inside easily and it felt
great. I know that if it hadn't happened with someone like Jeff,

who I loved and trusted, I would have been tense and it wouldn't have been a good experience. As it was, well, it was great—really great."

After hearing this story, another woman student said, "I envy you. My first time was lousy. He was seventeen and I was fifteen. We were both virgins and both insecure as hell. He was too short and unathletic and I was too tall and brainy. We did it at his house when his parents were away. We thought we would feel more sure of ourselves afterward. I'd say it was the opposite. I know I felt it was a lousy disappointment. It didn't hurt—not much—but I kept waiting for it to be like in the movies. When I didn't feel anything, I decided I was probably genetically frigid or something. If I could do it over, I'd erase the whole event. As a matter of fact, I've never had sex since that time."

A third woman added this comment: "Neither of you had my problem. One of you was in a steady love relationship, the other didn't want a relationship. My problem was that the guy wasn't in love with me, but I really wanted this relationship to last. We were both eighteen. He wasn't experienced, but he was an athlete and gorgeous so girls were always after him. When he said he wanted to make love, I felt I'd lose him if I didn't. But I was so afraid he'd lose interest in a few months and then I'd be sorry I'd given this special thing to him. I know I sound like my own grandmother, but I think sex is a kind of ultimate gift, but it's not refundable and you can't demand it back.

"So guess what happened? My prediction was right. We slept together and then, about eight months later, he broke it off. The surprise is, I wasn't so upset. I think that's because I gained so much from the experience—not just sexually but . . ." She hesitated.

One of the men students interrupted her. "I know exactly what you mean—at least I think I do. For me, having intercourse the first time was so significant to how I feel about myself. I felt so much more mature, but it was also a kind of loss. The only thing I can compare it to was going from age four to age five. At five, I left home and entered a new world; I joined my brothers' world and my friends' world. You're never quite the same. You know, *You Can't Go Home Again* sort of thing."

A second man added, "You used the word *loss*, and that's what my first time was all about too, but in a different way. I started

going with this girl, Dianne, in my sophomore year. We went out
for a year. Toward the end, we both knew it wasn't going to work
out. We liked each other all right but, you know, it just wasn't *it*,
and we both were sort of restless. Well, we were both virgins, and
one night, just before we broke up, we went ahead and had intercourse. Neither of us expected it to happen and we didn't use any
protection. Her shrink (she was in therapy at the time) told her
maybe we had mixed feelings about the relationship ending. I
think the shrink had a point. It was half a wish to hold onto each
other, and half a way of saying good-bye."

First intercourse is a special emotional event, and it also involves new "technical" steps. Unless pregnancy is desired, it
should involve contraception. It involves the penis entering the
vagina or, preferably (because it tends to work better), the woman
moving her vagina so that it surrounds the penis. Lots of things
can get in the way of insertion: a hymenal strand, a thick hymen
with a small opening (rare), tight vaginal muscles, the wrong angle, not being able to locate the vaginal opening, the man's loss of
erection, or his ejaculating before insertion.

There is the question of position. This seems to be mostly
determined by the culture. We understand that in northern Sweden, 97 percent of couples say they virtually always use the "missionary" position. In Africa and in India, of course, the native
population thought that was a laughable position. We advise the
female-above position for starters because the woman can be in
control of the matter and is therefore less likely to feel frightened.
She should go slowly and give her muscles a chance to relax and
allow the hymen to stretch rather than tear. By the way, the majority of women today report little or no bleeding and little or minimal pain.

Intercourse can be a truly complicated behavior, involving
thoughts and concerns that distract from the pleasure. For the
young man: "Am I hard enough yet? We'd better hurry because
I'm close to coming. Is she ready? Am I hurting her? Can anyone
hear us? If I come, will she know? If she comes, will I know? My
arms are tired (missionary position). It's too dry. It's too slippery.
Maybe she isn't enjoying it."

For the young woman: "How can I tell if he's ready? Am I
lubricated? Who should decide when we actually go ahead and do

it? Can anyone hear us? Will I come? If I don't, will he be upset? How should I move? Should I make noises? What would my mother think?"

Immediately after the very first intercourse experience, people may be surprised by their own feelings, which can range from vague disappointment, shame, and disgust to exaltation, contentment, and overwhelming feelings of love. It isn't unusual to cry—not so much from sadness as from intensity of feeling.

The sessions in which we have discussed first intercourse with students have been searching, revealing, and thought-provoking experiences. These discussions, combined with the histories told to us by individuals, have given us much to think about in trying to understand the potential meaning of first intercourse. It can be a symbol of independence and of assertion, or just the opposite—of dependence and submission. It can be the discovery of a new dimension of shared pleasure and satisfaction or it can be a time of pain and fear and a sense of loneliness. It is a step in the process of separation from mother and father—"like being four and going on five."

We have to conclude that in reality, the experience is rarely all of the positives and none of the negatives. Many of the young people who have told us their story experienced a mixture of feelings. However, it is encouraging to us to see that an increasing number have a positive experience—a step in the right direction for the development of adult sexuality.

Coping with Sexual Dysfunction or "Compulsion"

Some dysfunction is a normal (although not universal) part of sexual unfolding in adolescence. Many young women don't experience orgasm with a partner for months or even years after beginning sexual relations. *Most* young men experience premature ejaculation, and many have transitory problems with erection. A few have trouble having an orgasm.

The impact of a sexual dysfunction on a young person in the midst of sexual unfolding will vary with the person and the situation. Often it passes without any repercussions, but sometimes it can create serious problems.

Penny, a twenty-year-old, talked with us about her lack of social and sexual relationships. For the past year and a half, she had more or less deliberately avoided contact with men, although there were two men she counted among her friends. Penny felt that her unwillingness to date centered on her worry that she was sexually inadequate and always would be. She had had a relationship with a boy when she was seventeen that had included petting but not intercourse. She had enjoyed the relationship and the sex, although she had begun to wonder when the wonderful experience she had heard about—orgasm—would happen to her.

She had no other sexual experiences until she met Dan through her work. He was older and very sexually experienced, and he prided himself on being a good lover. From the beginning of their relationship, he set out to give Penny an orgasm. One of the reasons she decided to say yes to intercourse was her hope that at last she would have an orgasm. Not surprisingly (to us), Penny never could have an orgasm with Dan, no matter what techniques they tried. We say this was not surprising to us because we had heard this kind of story many times before and know that trying so hard to "achieve" orgasm is almost guaranteed to block it.

When the relationship with Dan ended, Penny's self-esteem was badly shaken. She was convinced that if she couldn't respond to Dan's "expert" attempts, she'd never be able to have an orgasm. She thought of herself as sexually abnormal and inhibited. She concentrated on her work, gained fifteen pounds, and withdrew from any relationship that might have involved sex.

If Penny hadn't sought professional help, she might have spent many years, perhaps even her lifetime, with a negative sexual image. In the course of therapy, she was able to come to appreciate herself as a sexual female. This gave her enough self-confidence to risk a relationship with a new young man, and, we are pleased to say, the story had a happy ending.

We are somewhat ambivalent about including "a sex life free of sexual dysfunction" in our list of major steps in sexual unfolding. In fact, as will be seen throughout this book, at every turning point in the life cycle, sexual dysfunction is a possibility and, therefore, it would be inaccurate to assign the resolution of sexual dysfunctioning to the stage of adolescence and young adulthood. This stage, however, constitutes an important testing ground. The issue is not so much whether or not sexual functioning goes smoothly. The issue is learning to deal with one's sexuality, to cope with dysfunction when it occurs, and to avoid getting stuck in one's sexual development because of dysfunction. Unfortunately, this age is a vulnerable one, and we have seen numerous adults "stuck" with a sexual dysfunction that began when they were sexually unfolding and that kept them from continuing the process. For this reason alone, sex counseling for this age group, which helps individuals gain a proper perspective on their experiences, seems to us to be a vital service.

Sexual compulsion is another matter. We use the word *compulsion* in the heading of this section to refer to sexual behavior that is out of control, repetitive, self-destructive, and usually not sexually satisfying. One example would be a young man who had an endless series of one-night-stands that were not pleasurable, although he usually did ejaculate. After intercourse, he was always cold and nasty. Therapy revealed a deep-seated rage against women. He entered psychoanalysis.

Another example would be a young woman whose father deserted the family when she was six to lead a hippie life-style, including drug experimentation. From age fourteen onward, she was attracted to men who were socially inappropriate and sometimes frankly dangerous. Her sexual experiences were never pleasurable, but she couldn't stop the pattern of behavior.

The story of Sarah, who came to us for therapy with her fiancé when she was twenty-four, is an example of compulsive sexual behavior that we will describe in more detail.

Sarah and Jason had been a couple for about a year when they came to us. This was the first time in her life that Sarah was in a close relationship, although she had been having intercourse since age fifteen with many sexual partners. She had never experienced orgasm in any way, and was anxious in all sexual situations. The most significant factor in her life experience was her conflict with her mother, a large, physically powerful woman who had regularly beaten her in order to keep her in line. She was never allowed to express her own feelings or opinions. Self-assertion only led to more beatings. Sarah's father was a kindly, passive man who was never present when his wife administered the beatings. At fifteen, Sarah had intercourse. When her mother found out she said to Sarah, "Well, at least now you know it's not all it's cracked up to be." Sarah tried to persuade her mother that she had enjoyed her sexual experiences, although in fact they were painful, upsetting, and nonpleasurable. Even at fifteen and sixteen, Sarah was aware that she was using sex to get back at her mother and to become independent of her.

At college, her working-class origins made her feel inferior. She rejected the life-style she associated with her mother, her cousins, and her hometown peers: a life of marriage, having children, being "traditional, old-fashioned, and uptight about sex." She felt that being "cool and cosmopolitan" would help her gain the approval of peers at college and help separate her from identification with and dependence upon her mother. She pretended to be casual and flip in talking about sex, although just hearing a sexy joke made her anxious. Her strong career ambitions were another facet of her intense need to break away.

Sarah's feelings about sex were also influenced by three attempted assaults in early adolescence. In all three, she escaped without anything much happening, but she was terrified and felt that her family didn't protect her as well as they might have.

Her sexual pattern was one of inviting males to respond sexually toward her without "knowing" she was doing this, and then feeling trapped into continuing in order to maintain her self-image as someone who enjoyed sex, who was cool and not hung up. She felt unable to assert her own needs or to protect herself. In the guise of meeting the man's needs, she inwardly felt a rage about being used or forced. During these unpleasant sexual encounters, she would often fantasize that the man loved her and imagine being married to him and having children. But she never allowed herself to feel any tender feelings or to admit that she had needs, either emotional or sexual.

The pattern of Sarah's sexual experiences remained essentially unchanged for eight years. During this time, finding a new sense of herself through career goals, making new friends, and gaining some independence from her family, she began to be dissatisfied with her nonrelationships with men. The death of a close relative put her suddenly in touch with her need for love and affirmed the value of family ties and some aspects of tradition. She then had a successful experience in brief individual psychotherapy, in which she focused on her relationships with men and talked about her parents. At this point, she felt ready for a deeper kind of relationship. Soon afterward, she met her fiancé, Jason.

Although she was deeply in love with Jason, she found that she was very anxious during lovemaking and that she felt unaroused and distant. She and Jason were reluctant to get married until they felt there was some hope for a satisfying sex life. Sex therapy was successful, and they did marry.

Compulsion in sexual behavior usually derives from a desperate need to find love and acceptance through any means, and sex is perhaps the easiest way to feel popular and liked and to get some cuddling and touching. When sexual behavior is engaged in for these reasons, the sex itself is usually unsatisfying and often downright unpleasant. The person rarely satisfies the deep need for love and acceptance and comes to associate sex with displeasure. Some people spend years, from their teens into their twenties, in this kind of compulsive sexual behavior. In spite of multiple sexual experiences, they do not mature psychosexually; they do not go through the growing process of sexual unfolding. They usually end up seeking professional help and must, in a sense, go back to work through the stage of sexual development they skipped.

Understanding the Place and Value of Sex in Our Lives

One evening when our daughter was ten or eleven, we were watching a particularly inane situation comedy on network television. We were watching for a special reason. We have a job as consultants to the ABC-TV "censorship" department (Broadcast Standards and Practices), advising them about the presentation of sexual subjects. The program we were watching on this particular night was on a rival network. The story was set in a resort hotel and showed one of the young waiters playing up to a pretty young guest. Toward the end of the program, they were shown going into his room and then reemerging in the morning. After the hotel breakfast, she said good-bye to him; clearly this had been a one-night stand with no follow-up intended.

We asked our daughter if she knew what had happened between the young couple and what she thought about it. She said, "They made love, but they hardly knew each other and then they just said good-bye. I don't know when I'm going to have sex, but I know I wouldn't want it to be like that!"

Our daughter was taking an important step in sexual unfolding by asking, What is right for me? Hopefully she will keep on asking, evaluating, and trying to find answers. If she does, she will be like the majority of young people who are deeply interested in questions of sexual values. They don't want to be told what values they should have, but they are eager to think about values.

In 1970, we helped a group of students make a short documentary-style film about sex on campus. The cameraman walked around the freshman campus on a warm, sunny day in September just before classes had started for the term. Rock music blared from open lead-paned windows, kids milled around in T-shirts and cutoff jeans, playing Frisbee, dancing, talking, laughing. One group had a blanket they used as a tarpaulin, and girls took turns being bounced up and down on it. The air seemed to crackle with unspoken sexuality. Then the camerman began to ask people, "What do you think about sex on campus?" Some people responded with giggles, and there were some jokes. There were also a lot of thoughtful answers. The diversity of attitudes, experience, and maturity was obvious.

One young woman, an Alice-in-Wonderland lookalike, said there were so many marvelous-looking men on campus that it was like being in a pastry shop, not knowing how you were going to choose. After that she blushed and turned away from the camera, saying, "Good-bye. I've got to call my parents."

She and all the other entering students do confront a sexual scene that is diverse and confusing. About three-quarters of the freshmen are virgins. Of those who have had intercourse, about 10 percent have had it only once (usually because it was disappointing). Ten percent of the freshman males have never masturbated. A sizable minority of the fresh-women think they won't have intercourse until they are married.

In that initial year on campus, many students begin to question the values they grew up with. The sheer multiplicity of sexual values they see around them makes moral absolutes seem impossible or irrelevant. It is hard to find any students who are willing to state general principles of sexual morality. They say, for example, "I won't have intercourse until I'm in love and in a really committed relationship, but I don't think it's necessarily wrong to have casual sex."

In the early 1970s, there was one very widely held but unspoken value—to be a virgin was embarrassing and probably meant that you were hung up (heaven forbid). If you were sexually inexperienced, you didn't talk about it, and you hoped to change your status as quickly as possible. Thank goodness, that pressure has eased. Since about the mid-1970s, along with the generally conservative shift on campuses has come a healthier acceptance of diverse sexual values. Some students became outspoken in their support of virginity as an ideal, and people didn't snicker.

What to do about parents and sex is a moral-ethical-emotional dilemma faced by most students. Should I tell them I'm going on the pill? Should I be honest about the fact that we're sharing an apartment next term? What would my father think if he knew I'd gotten her pregnant, just like he did when he was nineteen? Sometimes, at nineteen, it seems morally necessary to be absolutely truthful. Depending on the family and the truth to be shared, this can be fine or it can be a disaster, causing a serious, sometimes permanent rift in the family. It often goes back to a question of the unfolding process—the need to separate emotionally from parents. Some young people need to wrench away; others can make the separation more gently.

It helps to have a person or persons to talk to when you are struggling with questions of sexual values. Peer influence on sexual behavior and judgments is extremely important. In fact, the sociologist Ira Reiss has found that a student's perception of his or her peers' sexual behavior is *the* single most important factor influencing the student's sexual behavior. Notice, we said the student's *perception*—not what the peers are actually doing. The opportunity, then, to receive a more accurate picture of peer sexual behavior is crucial. Virtually all students overestimate the extent of their peers' sexual experience. One student enrolled in a course on human sexual development put it very simply. He said, "The value of this course to me was in learning I'm not the only virgin on campus and not the only one who *wants* to be." Another student summed her experience in the sexuality course and its impact on her values this way: "This course has been an eye-opener. I'm very inexperienced sexually and always thought sex would just happen to me at some point. Now I see that it's complicated and a serious matter—something to think about, not just do. I wonder what would have happened to me if I'd had to learn the lesson the hard way."

Becoming Responsible about Sex

Think back to your adolescence. If you had intercourse during that period of your life, the chances are very great that you frequently used no contraceptive device whatsoever. If you were lucky, you managed to avoid an unwanted pregnancy. You may marvel now at your own lack of forethought and perhaps imagine that today's adolescents would never be so foolish. But statistics show that although there is some improvement in adolescents' use of birth control measures, a majority of sexually active adolescents still have intercourse without protection.

What makes bright, capable young people act so foolishly? A certain percentage are deliberately omitting birth control. They want to become pregnant or at least wouldn't mind if it happened. But most of the time it's a matter of ignorance (everyone knows you can't get pregnant the first time you do it), magical thinking (it can't happen to me), an unconscious desire for pregnancy (for example, a wish to punish Mother or to hold onto a boyfriend), or the failure to accept that you are—you really *are*—having intercourse.

This last point may sound farfetched, but it isn't. It may be one of the most common reasons for failure to use birth control. In 1967, when we were new to the fields of sex education and sex counseling, we saw an eighteen-year-old, who telephoned us late one evening, crying. "I think I may be pregnant, but I don't want to go to the college medical service. I don't trust them. If I'm pregnant, I think they'll tell my parents." We arranged for her to have a pregnancy test, which, to the relief of everyone, was negative. We then talked to her about birth control. She answered, "Oh, I don't need birth control. We're never going to do it again. Besides, both of us are Roman Catholic and don't believe in using contraception." This isn't the end of the story. Several months later, the same girl called and we went through the same sequence, including her statement, "We're never going to do it again." The most remarkable part was her belief that she wouldn't do it again. She was much too guilty about it to admit to herself: "I am having intercourse."

A number of studies have shown that young people who are in conflict about sex—who feel guilty, ashamed, furtive, and fearful—are less likely to use contraception when they have intercourse. Young people who feel comfortable with their own sexuality and right about their behavior are more likely to use contraception. Using birth control requires fairly adult, independent, and assertive action. When a young couple does this together, they are sharing an important responsibility. Each is caring for him or her self, and for the other. The process is fairly intimate. They have to talk to each other about the need for birth control, discuss various methods, and plan an appointment or a purchase.

People are often amazed to learn how many young couples come to see us in our Sex Counseling Service before they ever have intercourse. The numbers keep growing. Maybe sex education is getting a message across.

Intimacy—Combining Love and Sex

The yearning to fall in love is almost universal in our culture. Love is extolled as the greatest human experience. Even if it is unrequited and anguished, we all know it is "Better to have loved and lost, Than never to have loved at all." Freud told us there are only two hallmarks of the healthy, mature person—the capacity to work productively and the capacity to love.

At different periods in history, *love* has been defined differently. The ancient Greeks thought love could only exist between males, since women were not able to experience true love (*agape*). The early Christians separated sex and love. Love was spiritual and holy. Sex was either sinful or just barely acceptable as a means of reproduction within marriage. In the Middle Ages, courtly love became the ideal. The passion of courtly love was fueled by sexual energy, but actual consummation was the enemy of true love. The lady was to be loftily inaccessible. Gradually, over the next few centuries, a new idea of love emerged. Love combined sexual desire, emotional attachment, and intercourse. The Victorians took the concept one step further by idealizing love within marriage.

We are still basically Victorian in our beliefs about love. Although we hear rumblings from time to time of alternative ideals such as open marriage, hardly anyone today questions the assumption that love is some combination of sex and personal intimacy. The definitions of love offered by a group of students confirm this.

You should care deeply about each other as people, respect each other, enjoy being together and be sexually attracted.

Passionate liking.

Love is trust, concern, commitment, and sexual fulfilment.

I don't know yet, but I expect to recognize it by how I feel—yearning to be with him, I guess, and wanting to make love.

I've had some real "crushes" on girls, but I don't think it's real love unless it's mutual. When two people love each other, they naturally want a long-term, exclusive relationship. My image of love is old-fashioned. I want to be a virgin until I marry and hope my wife would also be a virgin. I see marriage as a sacred commitment.

Knowing each other completely—emotionally and physically—without defenses or barriers.

All these definitions assume that love and sex will be inseparable. That's interesting because all of us, including these students, know that love or intimacy can exist without sex and sex can be experienced without any intimacy at all ("By the way, what did you say your name was?"). Intimacy usually evolves over time, although we have heard people describe brief encounters that are intensely close and moving—a moment of mutual openness that is an incapsulated intimacy. We have also heard, sadly, about decades of marriage in which there is no openness or sharing beyond "Where should we go on vacation this year?" and perhaps pro forma sexual intercourse.

Although all humans yearn to connect with others, we don't seem to have an instinct for how to go about doing it. It's something we learn. We learn first of all from being held, cuddled, touched, fed, and loved as infants. Throughout childhood, we learn the "rules" that govern contact between persons. We learn that it's all right to kiss and hug certain people under certain circumstances. If we're lucky, we learn mostly about trust and tenderness. If we're not so lucky, we learn mostly about pain, mistrust, and how to hide and protect ourselves. Boys learn one set of rules; girls learn another. Boys are more likely to learn how to hide their feelings and to make less affectionate physical contact. Girls learn the language of emotional expressiveness, are cuddled more, and may even be accomplished flirts by age three.

A study at the University of Denver showed that by age nine, there were marked differences between boys and girls in their styles of relating. Twenty pairs of boys and twenty pairs of girls were observed, one pair at a time, in a playroom setting. Two children of the same sex were introduced to each other and asked to spend twenty-five minutes "waiting" together. They were told they could play with the toys. Both boy and girl pairs played together, but the nature of the interactions varied. Boys talked *only* about the games and said almost nothing about themselves. By contrast, girls revealed personal information and, to a limited extent, even expressed personal feelings. When these kids were "debriefed" after the experiment, they were asked how well they had liked their partners. The girls were much more likely to express liking than the boys.

When it comes to learning how to integrate love and sex, sociologists tell us that boys and girls once again travel different paths. Boys know about sex but must learn about love from girls, whereas girls know how to love but must learn how to enjoy sex from boys. This was always a rather weak generalization and becomes weaker all the time as the power of the sexual double standard fades. Yet it is consistent with what many people still tell us in their sexual histories.

Males are much more likely than females to describe an early and intense genital focus. Sexual awareness begins with experiences of erection and is tremendously intensified by semenarche (first ejaculation). As we mentioned earlier, in the young boy, the stimulus for genital excitement may be almost anything. Gradually he learns to respond to what the culture tells him is appropriately sexy for a male. For some years, ejaculations are likely to be achieved entirely through masturbation or wet dreams and, for about one third of all boys, in occasional sex play with other boys. The boy's subculture promotes a focus on ejaculation as *the* fact of sex, through jokes and teasing about how many times in a row you can "jerk off," how far you can spurt, and so on. When boys begin to interact with girls, they often have one overriding aim—to see how much they can "get." Girls are experienced primarily as objects of desire, and peer approval is given for "scoring."

The story of John, who came for counseling when he was

twenty because he was sexually inexperienced and wanted to change that but didn't know how, gives an exaggerated picture of the dualism of sex and love that some males tend to experience.

"When I was in the sixth grade, I began having attacks of lust for certain girls in my class, but it wasn't based on their personality, mostly on the fantasy of seeing their tits and touching them. In high school, I had almost a catalog in my mind of various girls' tits—or sometimes legs. I masturbated with these images. Meanwhile, I had some girls who were my friends. I thought it would be dirty to think of them as body parts and so I kept them in a different category—asexual. I've hardly dated, and I've never done more than kiss a girl. I feel as though there are two parallel tracks in my mind: one for sex and that's associated mainly with just bodies, and one for friendship and love. I don't know how to make a bridge between them."

One of John's problems was his idea that in order to be sexually mature and love "properly," he would have to give up his "childish" fantasies and change entirely the things that turned him on. In fact, that isn't necessary or even desirable. Throughout life, many men will continue to be "leg men" or "tit men" or "ass men," without those desires interfering with adult sexuality. It only means that part of male sexuality is made up of these erotic attachments.*

Females tend to describe their experiences differently. Little girls certainly have erotic feelings, and some masturbate with vivid fantasies similar to boys', but the majority—at least as recalled in adulthood—remember romantic fantasies and intense crushes on particular people—boys, men, girls, women. The daydreams are of walking and talking with and pleasing the "loved" one. A little later, the daydreams include a hug or a kiss.

Some women think that they have never had a sexual fantasy because they have never imagined a full-blown erotic scenario with triple-rating. Questioned more closely, they do remember fantasies about a secret meeting with an admired man, a moment of intense eye contact, a kiss. Since women so often take their sexual cues from men, they have tended to dismiss their own

---

*Eroticism in both males and females also includes much earlier and more primitive attachments—fantasies of hurting and being hurt, of urination and defecation, of sucking, biting, swallowing, and merging.

sexuality as "silly girl stuff" and have not recognized that it is just as valid as the male experience.

One woman recalled her earliest adolescent fantasy. "I used to lie on my bed daydreaming that I was a married woman, and a wonderful man, just like my father, was going to be coming home for dinner. It wasn't until much later, maybe at sixteen, when I started masturbating, that I realized that the daydreams used to excite me. How oedipal it was!"

She went on to say, "That warm romantic feeling is how I used to feel when I got a crush on a boy, but even when I felt that way, I didn't like the idea of doing anything sexual. I let one or two boys kiss me, but I didn't respond. When I was fifteen, I just adored a guy who was a senior in my high school, so I let him touch my breasts. I was amazed to find these intense feelings going through me. Then I let him pet me and I touched him. He was wildly excited and at first I was scared, but gradually I got to like it. It was his touching me that gave me the idea to masturbate."

There is another barrier to male-female intimacy that appears in most cultures, including our own; it is the gap between the sexes resulting from a combination of ignorance, superstition, fear, prejudice, and the cultural traditions that separate men and women. In many primitive societies, this barrier is exemplified by a terror of menstruating women, who are kept apart from everyone and whose touch is thought to poison food. The burning of witches is another example.

Today we are more sophisticated: Prejudice between the sexes is more subtle and the ignorance is less profound, but it still exists. When our son was in the ninth grade (fourteen years old), he did a study of his fellow ninth-graders' sexual knowledge as a biology project. He found that both girls and boys were reasonably well informed about their own sex. Girls knew about menstruation and female orgasm. Boys knew about wet dreams, erection, and ejaculation. But both sexes were startlingly ignorant about the other sex.

Most boys and girls put the pieces of the puzzle together during mid- and late adolescence. They talk to friends, read books, see movies, attend a sex education course. They have experiences that teach them not only the facts and the techniques but also the feelings generated by having sex with another person.

One of our culture's injunctions to the male begins to come

into play usually by mid-adolescence: Thou shalt care for the female and be concerned with her pleasure. At age sixteen or seventeen, then, touching a girl's genitals has many levels of meaning. The heart beats faster, the erection becomes harder while he thinks, "Wow, she's letting me do it; wait till I tell Mike and Paul." At the same time, he observes her response. He wants her to like it because he's scared and tentative and he needs her pleasure and reassurance. He may also think that if she's aroused, they could end up having intercourse (often a mistaken assumption). Part of his role as a male in this situation is to give his partner pleasure. If he thinks that she is aroused and enjoying his touches, he is likely to feel good about himself—and about her.

By the college years, there is usually another significant shift for the young man. He is less focused on sex as a means of gaining prestige points with his friends and more concerned about what sex *means* between himself and the young woman. He is more interested in an ongoing relationship and wants to be liked by the person he chooses. If he really cares about her, he will want to do everything he can to keep her attached to him, and good sex (we all seem to know this instinctively) can be a powerful cement. Our culture still gives the male 90 percent of the responsibility for how things go sexually, so he will tend to take the blame if it isn't "good." He can also begin to take very real pleasure in his partner's sexual responses. Now that he feels a bit of security, he notices and feels her arousal; it turns him on. He can enjoy this kind of giving.

Of course, it isn't only sex that promotes male-female intimacy. In fact, sex, in the absence of other forms of contact, can be alienating. The trends toward coeducation, mixed dorms, and male-female equality are vital elements in the story of intimate relations between the sexes today. Boys and girls, young men and young woman are getting to know one another intellectually and socially in informal settings, working together, each respecting the other. Some of the mystique is gone, but in its place there can be— and increasingly there is—real understanding and real caring. Sex, in this context, can be integral to a larger relationship, another way for two people to know one another. Whether you call that intimacy or love, it is one of the best experiences life has to offer.

STAGE *T*WO

Making (or Breaking)

Commitments

1

Young Couples Living

Together

THERE IS an interesting technical problem in writing about living together, and that is the definition of the term. It isn't unusual for us to ask a couple, "Are you living together?" and hear them respond, "Well, sort of." There are shades of gray in the term. They may be living together in a communal house but each has his or her own bedroom. They may both have their own apartment but five nights out of seven they spend the night together at her place. They may even be sharing a bedroom in his or her parents' home, but they don't consider that really living together. In one highly idiosyncratic case, one woman lived with a man every Sunday through Thursday while another woman lived with him on the weekends!

Very often the "almost" living together couple is not quite ready to make the commitment to share an apartment, expenses, and household tasks. They may prefer to drift into increasing levels of interdependence and commitment, or to postpone the decision for a while. And they are right in feeling that full-fledged living together, more or less like becoming a married couple, is a significant step. From the hundreds of young couples we have talked to, it seems clear that living together is often a major turning point.

One reason it is a turning point is that it is a social statement about your sexuality. If it is done openly, it amounts to a public announcement, "we are having sexual intercourse although we are not legally married." There was a time when such an announcement was considered to be an act of social defiance. But in the past two decades, attitudes toward unmarried couples living together have changed dramatically. A recent survey in England found that more than half the people over age sixty-five think there is nothing wrong with living together.

However, there are still some parents who object strongly to their children having sex before marriage. Young people who know that their parents would strongly disapprove of their living together may decide to flout parental judgment, or they may try to deceive the disapproving parents. Jennifer and Dan are an example of a couple who tried deception and paid a heavy price.

Jennifer, a twenty-four-year-old secretary, met Dan, a law student, when she did some free-lancing and typed a paper he'd written. They were very strongly attracted to one another and began a sexual relationship rather quickly. Jennifer said, "I think I had some mixed feelings about actually having intercourse with Dan. I had intercourse once before with a man I thought I would marry. After we broke up—I was twenty-one then—I went back to the idea that virginity was a good thing and I wouldn't actually go all the way with anyone. I know it sounds old-fashioned, but deep down I think I *am* old-fashioned. I grew up in a small midwestern town, and those values are still part of me."

She and Dan started living together, but Jennifer was afraid to tell her family and they kept up a pretense of living separately. When they became officially engaged and set a wedding date to coincide with Dan's graduation, both families were pleased. Jennifer's parents and her maternal grandmother announced a visit to meet Dan and his family.

To make a long story short, her family arrived and discovered the living arrangement. They were clearly upset but didn't want to make a scene. The meeting between the two families was tense. Jennifer's mother was angry that Dan's parents had "allowed" the couple to "live in sin." In the coming months, Jennifer had to cope with her parents' coolness and with Dan's mother's efforts to help plan the wedding.

Dan said, "My mom's intentions were good; she knew Jen was feeling estranged from her folks, and I think she wanted to be motherly, but she ended up being overbearing. I got caught in the middle, trying to referee."

The combination of tension and guilt about their sexual life made Jennifer feel less and less interested in sex. But she didn't feel comfortable just saying no, and she often went ahead when she wasn't really aroused. "After a few months, I noticed that I seemed dry and it hurt when Dan entered me. And then he noticed that I seemed to be flinching when he was ready for intercourse. He tried to discuss it, but I was scared. I think I was frightened of facing my own feelings. And I didn't want to start a big thing two months before our wedding and while Dan was under so much pressure to finish his papers and take exams."

So the wedding plans went forward, and both Dan and Jennifer hoped things would get better once they were past his graduation and the wedding. But when Jennifer flinched involuntarily when Dan reached out to her on the first night of their honeymoon, all of his pent-up frustrations came pouring out. They spent their wedding night fighting and crying.

Six weeks later, when things hadn't improved, they came for sex counseling. It didn't take much help from us—eight weekly therapy hours—for Jennifer and Dan to reestablish a comfortable sexual relationship and begin talking instead of fighting. The most important shift came when Jennifer recognized that she had been blaming Dan for her "losing" her parents. Although she had agreed to having intercourse, she felt that she had succumbed to Dan's intense desires. The counseling helped her see that she hadn't clearly asserted her needs and expressed her feelings. Once she began to do that, she and Dan found that their relationship was actually better than it had ever been.

Could Jennifer and Dan have avoided their problem altogether? Jennifer had deeply ambivalent feelings about living with Dan. She couldn't face her parents, knowing that she was having sex. This is certainly a common dilemma, but one that rarely works out well if a couple tries to hide the fact of living together. It is simply too difficult to conceal.

Jennifer was struggling to separate her values from her parents' values. Rather than deal with it directly, she tried to finesse the issue. When she was found out she felt deeply ashamed. If she had battled it out with her parents, the conflict would have been between Jennifer and her parents, not within Jennifer's psyche. She could probably have avoided the guilt and the shame that caused her to withdraw from sex—but, of course, there is no way of knowing how direct confrontation would have affected her relationship with her parents.

The next story is an example of directly confronting parental values about living together—with an unexpected outcome.

One of the most common areas of tension between parents and their children who live with a lover is whether the children should share a bed when they visit in the parental home. Many parents take a middle position: "We don't care what you do away from here, but this is our house and we're not comfortable with your sharing a bed under this roof when you aren't married."

One young couple made this a cause célèbre. They were morally outraged by what seemed to them to be blatant hypocrisy. "Why," asked Mandy, "if my parents accept our living together, should they object to our being together when we visit them?" She answered her own question: "It's only because they feel embarrassed about their friends and neighbors. They don't lie about the fact that James and I live together, but they certainly don't mention it and they talk about writing to Mandy or calling Mandy—never about calling Mandy and Jim."

After several months of crusading to change her parents' attitude, Mandy succeeded. When Mandy and Jim arrived one weekend, the twin beds in Mandy's old room were made up for them. James and Mandy were delighted. That night, although they were tired after a long trip, they felt almost obliged to consummate their victory by making love. But Mandy couldn't relax. Every squeak of the bed, every rustle of the blankets made her excruciatingly self-conscious. She had to ask James to go back to his bed. As she lay there, in the bed of her childhood, she remembered the times she had heard noises coming from her parents' bedroom. Mandy said, "I wanted my parents to recognize me as a sexual adult but only in the abstract. As for their *really* being aware of it—sensing it directly—I wasn't prepared for that." In fact, it wasn't until after they were married and Mandy was pregnant that she could enjoy sex in her parents' house.

Sharing living space—expenses, cooking and cleaning, waking up together each morning, making the thousand and one decisions of daily life—is certainly different from even the closest relationship in which a couple maintains his and her apartments. Sexually it more closely approximates marriage. Every night you go to bed together, or perhaps at different hours. If bedtimes are going to be an issue, then you confront it. Your diaphragm jelly, your tampons and menstrual flow take on a new reality for him. You experience his morning erections and learn there are times he's more interested in reading or eating than in sex. You have, in short, to blend ordinary life and eroticism.

It's partly the old cliché of fury over her not putting the cap back on the toothpaste or his always talking when the water is running even though you've told him twenty times, "I can't hear you when the water's running." Small irritations like these, and having to cope with each other's "unpleasant" habits, aren't likely to add up to a major problem, sexual or otherwise, but we have heard people comment on such things as *contributing* to a sexual problem.

She wasn't as clean, personally, as I thought she was. Maybe it was my imagination, but after we moved in together I didn't want oral sex because of that.

I can't stand him watching late-night sports on television when we're in bed. He never did that until we'd been living together for a few months. It feels like a sign that all the passion is gone.

When we lived in the big house [a communal living arrangement] it wasn't a problem, I guess because the only telephone was downstairs. But in our place, now, there's a phone next to the bed and if it rings she picks it up and talks, even if we're in the middle of making love. It drives me nuts, but she can't seem to understand how I feel.

Most young people assume that they will be able to handle the nitty-gritty issues of everyday life that are part of living together. We did, however, talk to one young man who was very concerned about it, and we wonder if there aren't many more people who silently share some of his concerns.

Fred, a twenty-four-year-old graduate student, sought help because his girlfriend wanted him to move in with her, but he was very reluctant to do so. He thought that his reluctance was due partly to sexual anxieties, since he was still a virgin. He saw intercourse as a major commitment and had decided that he needed to find out if he could really share with a woman *before* they went ahead and had intercourse. He also thought that the only way he could find out about his capacity to share and be intimate was to live with someone.

Fred explained that he was an only child who had been catered to by his parents. He said, "I'm used to getting things my way, not having to give or even compromise much. Now I've gotten used to living alone. I had my own room in college and my own apartment here. I'm a slob about some things and compulsively neat about others. Just sharing a desk and bookshelves scares me. And usually, when I've spent the night with Annie [his girlfriend], I've ended up sleeping on the floor. I can't adjust to sharing a bed! What scares me, I think, is that I'll have to compromise and change my ways so much that I'll lose my individuality."

Annie and Fred *did* decide to live together, and they were able to make the adjustment. Eventually they did have intercourse. Fred commented, "Having intercourse wasn't the psychological hurdle I originally thought it would be. Once the other things fell into place for us, so did sex."

Living together can be a very significant transitional step—an opportunity to try on intimacy and a sexual relationship in a way that approximates marriage. Many young people imagine that living together will solve all their problems. What it can do is make the issues and the problems very clear. The next story illustrates how one young couple used their living together as a time to learn about themselves sexually and emotionally.

Tammy and Len had been living together for two years, and they were getting along in every area of life except in bed. The problem was that Tammy had never enjoyed sex at all. Len had been willing to put up with her disinterest because he assumed it would gradually change, but now he was worried. He wanted to marry Tammy, but he wanted a wife who responded sexually. Tammy was worried, too. She said, "I'm twenty-six but I feel inside like a little girl and I'm scared I'll never grow up, at least not sexually."

Tammy actually looked about sixteen. She had a very narrow, boyish body, long blond hair in a ponytail down her back, and she wore old jeans and a woolen work shirt. She had a way of moving and sitting so that you hardly noticed she was there.

When we asked Tammy and Len each to draw pictures of a male and a female for us, Tammy drew two people, each with a very big circle for the body and a smaller circle for the head. They looked like snowmen. There was almost no difference between the male and female figures.

We realized that Tammy had some special problems with body

image. For this and several other reasons, it was decided that Lorna would work with Tammy individually for a while.

Lorna learned that Tammy possessed minimal awareness of her body. She never took a bath—only "two-minute showers"— never thought about the feel of clothes or nightgowns when she bought or wore them, never pampered her body in any way. "Unless I'm seriously ill or injured," she said, "I think I more or less ignore my body." Tammy rarely looked in the mirror, since she wore no makeup and could do her ponytail without looking. In fact, Len and Tammy did not own a mirror other than the one on their medicine cabinet.

Tammy's first "homework" assignment was to buy a full-length mirror and to begin looking at herself without clothing on. Other body awareness exercises were suggested, such as baths, applying body lotion, and paying attention to the feel of clothing and textures.

At the same time, we talked, in the therapy hours, about the origins of Tammy's attitude toward her body. Tammy said, "I look like my mother. Both of us are like small birds or maybe young boys, and my father rejected both of us. I often heard him yelling at my mother that she was 'frigid and unfeminine' and, when I was about fifteen, I remember him telling me, 'You're about as sexy as a wet dishrag.' I don't think that did a lot for my self-confidence. My mother didn't help either. I remember her saying, 'We Stuarts—that's her maiden name—may not be voluptuous and sexy, but we're decent and honest.' I assumed it was my fate to be like my mother. My father left the family when I was sixteen. He went to Mexico and lived with a woman whose pictures look like she's a two-hundred-pounder. Speaking of opposites!"

The combination of talking and working on body awareness at home was very helpful for Tammy. Another of her homework assignments was to stand in front of her full-length mirror and purposely exaggerate any faults she saw in her body (an approach recommended by sex therapist Lonnie Barbach) . Tammy hated her small breasts, so Lorna suggested she look at her image with her arms over head, turning to see side views as well as front. She reported that at first she was horrified because she looked like a boy. After a while, she started to laugh, and finally, she said, "When I let my arms down my little breasts looked a lot bigger than they had. I mean there *is* a little something there." She began to feel differently about her body—and about herself. Her appearance changed dramatically. At this point, we began sex therapy with Tammy and Len as a couple.

Phil spent some time getting to know Len. He learned that Len appeared outwardly self-confident but in fact felt anything but self-confident, particularly about sex. Len admitted, "One reason I think I was attracted to Tammy was her innocence. She's the only woman I met who didn't seem to know more about sex than me." Part of Len's sexual insecurity could be traced to a congenital hypospadias. This means that at birth his urethra did not end at the tip of his penis but on the undersurface. When he was three and then again at four he had corrective surgery. He was left with a fairly normal penis but intense anxiety about his genitals. He said that he rarely looked at his own penis, and he and Tammy tended to make love in the dark, neither really looking at the other.

We knew that Tammy and Len would learn a great deal from the shared physical examination that is part of sex therapy, but they were apprehensive about the idea (as are many couples). We explained that the physical examination isn't just for the purpose of ruling out physical causes of sexual problems; it is meant to be educational and reassuring. Tammy would be in the room while Len was examined and vice versa. They agreed it would probably be helpful.

During the examination, Len, in a semisitting position, held a mirror so that he could see his own genitals while Phil explained his anatomy. The facts that Phil described were largely new to Tammy and Len, as they are to most people. In brief, this is what Phil said: In the early weeks of life, all fetuses have sexually undifferentiated genital structures. Unless certain hormones are produced, male fetuses will go on to produce female anatomical structures, such as a clitoris, the small lips at the vaginal opening (the labia minora) and the larger outer folds (the labia majora). With the production of the hormones that determine male genital formation, the following takes place: The gonads, or rudimentary sex organs, descend from inside the space that eventually becomes the abdominal cavity and come to rest in a sac—the scrotum. These become the testicles. (In the female, the gonads remain inside and become the ovaries.) The scrotum results when the cells that had been forming the labia majora fuse in the middle. (It is usually possible to see the fine line on the surface of the scrotum that marks the point where the cells from both sides fused.) The penis is formed from cells on the left and right (the corpora cavernosa) that in females form the labia, and from cells in the middle (the corpus spongiosum) that, in women, become the clitoris. The tip of the penis and its foreskin correspond to the tip of the clitoris and the hood of skin that covers it.

Along the middle of the undersurface of the penis, there is usually a fine brownish line; it marks the place where the cells from the left and right sides fused. These pigmented cells are the male counterpart of the ridge of dark cells that a woman has on the edges of the labia minora. Remembering that the lower part of the vagina is formed basically of skin tissue that grows into the body, one can identify the counterpart in the adult male—the lower part of the scrotum, where the fusion line ends.

The testicles, resting within the scrotal sac, do not hang exactly side by side. One testicle is lower than the other. On each testicle there is a little bump of tissue that can be tender to the touch. The bump is the epididymis—a small organ where sperm cells are stored.

One final point about male anatomy. At the stage of fetal development when the penis and the scrotum are forming, a tube, the urethra, is incorporated between the corpus spongiosum and the corpora cavernosa. The urethra is the tube that carries urine from the bladder out through the penis. When the penile compartments become congested and firm during an erection, the urethral canal is compressed, making urinating almost impossible. When a man awakens from sleep with an erection, he has to wait for some of the penile firmness to lessen before he can urinate. It is also true that it is virtually impossible for a man to release urine when he ejaculates. This is because in addition to being affected by the pressure changes, there is also a small valve that shuts off the tube leading from the bladder during sexual response.

An erection occurs when the corpora cavernosa and the corpus spongiosum become congested with blood. Sometimes one of the corpora cavernosa becomes congested sooner than the other. When this happens, the erection may curve slightly in the direction of the side that is filling more slowly. As the corpus spongiosum (the structure running up the middle of the penis) becomes erect to different degrees, it is common for the penis to become erect at different angles relative to the abdominal wall during a period of sexual response.

When it was Tammy's turn to be examined, she expected to lie flat on her back, the traditional position for gynecological examination, but we prefer to have the woman in a semisitting position so that she feels less vulnerable and can see what is going on. Tammy said she had never really looked at her own genitals before. What she saw first were the structures of the vulva (the external genitals)—the outer, hair-covered lips (labia majora) and the inner, hairless lips (labia minora). The labia join at the top and connect to the clitoris and also form the hood of skin over the clitoris. Most of the clitoris is not visible because it is hidden under skin and fatty tissue, but it extends up to the pubic bone and is about half the length of a pinky finger—much, much larger than most people imagine.

Tammy asked why her inner lips were "so large" and why one side was larger than the other. We explained that this is common. There is a lot of individual variation in the size and shape of labia.

The part of Tammy's examination that was most meaningful to her was the internal. With a plastic speculum in place, it is possible to see inside the vagina. The walls are pink, glistening, slightly "corrugated" tissue. The cervix is pink, smooth, and firm, with a small opening to the uterus.

Tammy was amazed and moved. Afterward she said, "I don't think my vagina had any reality for me; it was some vague space—empty—inside me. I think I thought of it as dark and musty. It's so much more, well, real and even nice." Len added, "Seeing exactly how things look and what's what makes me feel more comfortable—maybe it's more competent."

In fact, Len did begin to feel more and more "comfortable" and "competent." Tammy began to enjoy their touching and began to experience orgasms.

At the end of their therapy, with the sexual problems overcome, we once again asked them each to draw pictures of people. Tammy's drawings showed a transformation. Her female figure was a lovely (willowy rather than voluptuous) nude woman. The lines were faintly drawn—a little tentative—just like Tammy's new sense of herself.

Most couples who live together don't continue living together indefinitely; they either split up or they marry. The couples we have been describing moved toward increasing intimacy and commitment, probably toward marriage. We have tended to present that as if it were the only desirable outcome, the only direction that spells emotional growth. Certainly that isn't so. Living with someone, learning that it doesn't work, and splitting can also be growth. Our bias as therapists makes us add the proviso that you understand *why* the relationship didn't work so you can avoid painful repetition.

A twenty-four-year-old woman told us, "I walked out after a year of pure pain. Greg and I were in a glamorous West Side apartment and I had a job I hated while he was this budding writer, already getting recognition. Sex had been great for us before we lived together, maybe because it was just weekends. But then when we were in New York, he seemed to assume I would be in the mood whenever he was, and it was all on *his* emotional schedule. He was on a high while I was sort of down on myself. It got so I really resented his just assuming I'd want to make love. We struggled and battled over it all year until I left."

A man in his forties told us that he planned to recommend to his children that they live with at least one or two people before they settle down. He had lived with someone when he was young, and he felt it taught him a lot. "To put it crudely, I learned there was more to a relationship than fucking. This girl—or young woman—and I were always at it, day and night. At first I was in paradise with her, but after a while I realized she bored me and I think I irritated her, but our sex life never went below boiling. The night before I moved out, we were still at it."

A woman once sent us a letter asking for advice about birth control pills and included some of her ideas about living together: "I lived with three different men before I decided to get married. I didn't see any reason to marry until I wanted children. Each time I found that the thrill of sex seemed to evaporate. It was still fun and felt good but no big deal. So now I don't expect too much from sex, unlike some of my friends who keep believing it should be rockets going off your whole life long."

Finally, the opinion of a man who never did marry, who would decidedly disagree with the woman just quoted. "I expect to go on having different relationships all my life. I'm a certain kind of romantic, maybe even quixotic, but I expect to be in love and feel my heart pound when I just think of getting near a woman. Marriage, even living together in a permanent way, destroys that after a while, so why shouldn't I have what I want as long as I can find it?"

2

Conflicts over Commitment

THE BEST DEFINITION of *commitment to a relationship* that we have seen is simply "being a little stuck with each other." When you are a little stuck, you don't walk out for good without at least trying to resolve problems. Most people, by their early to mid-twenties, have had several relationships in which they have allowed themselves to be more or less stuck. When we were growing up in the late 1940s and 1950s, the stages of commitment along the road to marriage were codified by names. There was going together; going steady (sometimes called being ringed because the girl wore a boy's high school ring, usually on a chain or string around her neck); being pinned (a girl wearing a boy's fraternity pin); engaged to be engaged (the young woman switched the young man's fraternity pin to the other side of her chest—from left to right); and engaged. Perhaps this way of wading into the waters of formal, socially recognized commitment was helpful. It certainly gave us lots of practice in making decisions about commitment.

Wading deeper into the waters of commitment also used to mean getting progressively deeper into sex—and vice versa. There are still young women who hold back sexually, waiting for a tangible sign of commitment, but now it is more likely to be unconscious holding back; she will have intercourse but will be unable to enjoy it.

For example, a first-year graduate student complained that she never had an orgasm with her lover, although she was able to masturbate to orgasm easily. When I (Lorna) heard that her lover was finishing his doctoral dissertation, I asked what his plans were. She said he didn't know where he wanted to work but had applied for jobs all over the country. She also said that she was in love with him and they would marry.

At the next appointment, she told me about a dream she had had. "I was at a train station with Fred [her lover], and we were saying good-bye. I asked him for his new address, but he wouldn't or couldn't tell me. I felt sad and very frightened. If the train pulled out, I might never see him again." The dream helped her see that she needed a statement from Fred about his future plans before she could allow herself to let go both emotionally and sexually. When he gladly gave her assurance about his love and commitment to their future together, she started to have orgasms with him.

This holding back until commitment is traditionally thought of as a peculiarly female syndrome, but it can affect men, too. A twenty-four-year-old black man, Thomas, was troubled by his inability to ejaculate during intercourse. He had been a very serious college student and was now a very serious executive in training. Thomas had purposely limited his contact with young women because he had the idea that "sex can be a trap. It can lure you away from working toward your goals." He was quoting his mother and also trying not to "end up like some of my high school friends, having to get married or being pressured into supporting a kid. I've seen too many black guys get screwed by sex."

When he did have some sexual experiences, he found them "not intensely exciting, somehow." He did ejaculate on a few occasions but never in a woman's vagina. At the time that he sought counseling, he was in love, but the sexual problem persisted. We will never know if it was the counseling or his decision to get married, but within a week of becoming engaged, he was able to ejaculate during intercourse. He still did need lots of reassurance that there would not be an unwanted pregnancy. His fiancée used a diaphragm with an extra application of contraceptive cream, and he wore a condom!

A wide variety of psychological, interpersonal, sexual, and even cultural issues may make it impossible—or at least extremely difficult—for one person to make a serious, long-term commitment to another. Some feel too emotionally or sexually insecure; others can't risk caring that much; still others don't want to give up the real or imagined benefits of being single. Over the years, we have seen dozens of young men and women whose guilt and/or anxiety about sex makes them fearful of sustained relationships. They may relegate themselves to the category of "unmarriageable." Sometimes a sexual trauma or behavior makes their anxiety clearly understandable—for instance, a man who had nonintercourse sexual relations with his mother for years, or a young woman who was raped at age thirteen and became pregnant from the rape. In these instances, long-term psychotherapy was required. Men who have been voyeurs or exhibitionists sometimes worry about marrying. They can't predict whether their illegal behavior will continue.

In other cases, a person's guilt or anxiety may seem out of proportion to the circumstances. A few men have been so concerned about adolescent homosexual escapades that they thought they should never marry. With these young men, listening to their sexual histories and giving appropriate reassurance and education seemed to be helpful. Similarly, education and reassurance can help those who still carry a burden of intense guilt and shame about masturbation.

It isn't unusual for us to see a young unmarried couple with a sexual problem in which the underlying issue is a conflict about commitment (usually to marriage), but the couple themselves don't recognize that this conflict is causing the sexual symptom. One man of twenty-six wanted help with a problem of losing his erection. He was living with a woman of thirty who had a three-year-old son. She wanted to get married. He didn't. Neither of them related his sexual dysfunction to this issue. After their first interview with us, as they left the office, he stood in the hallway looking first to the right, then to the left. "I don't know which way to turn," he said and stood there as if paralyzed, with a fleeting look of panic. In the next interview, we commented on the moment in the hallway. Our comments helped him recognize that he felt panicky about marriage. His impotence was a way of ending the relationship without having to face his conflicts about getting married.

We probably all know someone who fits into the category of once burned, twice shy—the person who was, as he or she sees it, cruelly abandoned or wronged and for a long time afterward—perhaps forever—is frightened of serious involvement. Women who have been left by a lover often end up feeling wary of sex; at least, we seem to see many women with this story to tell. It's cultural conditioning, fed by rage, that makes an emotionally wounded woman fall back on the cliché, All men want only one thing from a woman. Over and over again, women tell us that sex makes them feel terribly, frighteningly vulnerable. When they have been hurt by one man, the last thing they want to do is become vulnerable to another.

Men sometimes express a similar feeling, but there is a different quality to it—more a fear of sexual failure and humiliation than vulnerability. Is it, perhaps, that women are literally more vulnerable to sex? Sex can make them pregnant, and in ancient days—in fact, throughout history, until very recently—pregnancy threatened a woman's life.

Pamela was a very pretty twenty-five-year-old secretary who wanted very much to meet the right man, marry, and settle down. She frequently met potential Mr. Rights and often fell for them, but she could never get past a certain point in her relationships. She would start out with an initial fear of sex and of involvement. If the man was sensitive enough not to push her, she could very gradually relax and begin to enjoy sex and allow herself to care, but she always stopped short of intercourse and of real commitment. She would either pull back or she would make unreasonable, possessive demands and drive the man away.

Unraveling Pamela's story was like solving a mystery. The origins of the problem were masked by suppressed memories and feelings. When Pamela was fifteen, she and a high school classmate fell in love. After months of petting in cars and on couches, they had intercourse in the backseat of his car. It hurt slightly, but it also felt marvelous to Pamela. The relationship lasted for a year and a half, during which Pamela recalls rapturous sex. She thinks now that he was the most skillful and enthusiastic lover she ever encountered.

When Pamela went to college, they couldn't see each other very often but they were still in love—until Pamela missed her period, went to the health service at her school, and was told she was pregnant. He couldn't handle it. He simply dropped her, wouldn't see or talk to her. She was in a state of emotional shock. Two days later her period started. But there was no way to mend the relationship. She heard through the grapevine that he was already going with another girl.

Pamela became moderately depressed. Her grades suffered. She didn't date at all. She found that she had intense sexual longings, connected with memories of intercourse. She deliberately attempted to blot out her memories and the sexual longings because they were so painful. Seven years after the trauma, Pamela still couldn't have intercourse and was still afraid to care too deeply for a man.

Have you noticed that in the story Pamela's lover has no name? To this day we don't know his name, because Pamela refused to say it. She also refused to remember anything positive about him.

Pamela's reaction to the break with her first lover was unusually strong—although not without cause. This abandonment was a repetition of repeated abandonments by her father. Her father was a flamboyant, romantic, unpredictable character who would periodically disappear to California, South America, and Europe. He would send an occasional postcard and then, as suddenly as he had gone, he would reappear.

Pamela and her family were helped somewhat by a year of family therapy, but Pamela was still wary of men and marriage. During the course of sex counseling, she met a man she liked very much, and cautiously, slowly, over many months, she allowed herself to care for him and to become sexually involved. Meanwhile, in individual therapy sessions (with Lorna), she was letting herself feel her intense sadness and anger over the loss of her first lover—something she had never done.

This story doesn't have a happy ending, at least not yet. Pamela's current lover panicked at their closeness and broke off the relationship. Considering her history, Pamela handled it fairly well. What will happen in the future remains to be seen.

So far we have been describing people in whom panic about marital commitment manifests itself as sexual dysfunction. In others, the panic leads to a crisis over sexual fidelity, usually an eleventh-hour affair.

Marriage implies sexual fidelity. Most of us still believe in fidelity as a moral value, even if we don't always act in accordance with the belief. Even those who have had intercourse with several partners before marriage tend to assume that once they are married, they will be monogamous. But some people approach marriage and the idea of lifelong fidelity with more than a bit of ambivalence, and sometimes with total dread. In the movie *A Mid-Summer Night's Sex Comedy*, Woody Allen's script has a recurrent line: "Marriage is the death of hope." The characters are frantic for one last fling on the eve of legal commitment.

Clinging desperately to bachelor freedom can be a cultural tradition, as it is, for example, in Ireland, where many men postpone marriage until they are in their thirties or older. We recall one young man who had been living with the same woman, Katie, for four years, struggling to accept the image of himself as a married man at the age of twenty-five or twenty-six. "My father tells me," he said, "that no male in our family ever married younger than thirty-five, and he can't understand my rush to be tied down." When he had been sexually faithful to Katie for one entire year, he decided he was ready for commitment and bought Katie an engagement ring. Two weeks later, he began an affair with his best friend's girlfriend. He and Katie struggled together for two more years until they finally married.

One needs the wisdom of a Solomon and the insight of a Freud to know how to interpret an eleventh-hour affair. Is it just one last wild oat, a foolish but fairly meaningless act, or is it, perhaps, a portent of something chronic? Could it be a sign, a "reason why these two should not be joined in holy matrimony?"

Not long ago, a young woman came to see one of us (Lorna) in a state of paralyzed indecision. While her financée was away for a month, she had begun a sexual relationship with a man who had been until then a close platonic friend. She now felt that affairs were something she would forever find hard to resist, indeed, wouldn't want to resist. Her fiancée, she said, was more conservative in his views about sex and would never agree to an "open marriage" contract. She didn't want to marry him under false pretenses, but she was terrified that he would leave her if she told him what she really felt. In the end, they did talk with complete honesty. She was right about one thing; he insisted that their marriage be monogamous. She promised to try.

3

Abortion

THE PROFESSIONAL LITERATURE states that abortion does not carry a high risk of adverse psychological reaction, yet the decision to terminate a pregnancy by abortion is rarely taken lightly in our society. For some women or couples, it poses a tremendous moral and emotional conflict. Many of the people we have counseled before, during, and after an abortion have been deeply troubled by the experience. Not a few have had sexual problems. Of course, we see a biased sample. Many are young and unmarried, and by the nature of our role, we are sought by those with problems.

Becoming pregnant when you don't mean to or want to—at least not consciously—is a trauma in itself. Once it has happened, there may be no way out that won't exact a heavy toll. Now that abortion is legal, some of the terror and stigma are gone. Many people choose abortion because no other alternative seems viable. There can be an apparent lack of conflict that lulls the woman and man, as well as professionals who see them, into assuming that there is not much emotional stress. Sometimes, of course, there isn't, but often the stress is there, below the surface.

The abortion procedure itself, while it is not medically serious, can be frightening to some women. There can be—and often are—several minutes of sometimes intense pain. This has tended to be traumatic for women who didn't expect it. They can panic when they feel this pain, their anxiety adding to the subjective pain of the experience. When there has been a preexisting fear of medical procedures or of vaginal penetration, some women have subsequently developed vaginismus (involuntary tensing of the muscles surrounding the vagina).

Sometimes the pain has symbolic meaning. One woman de-

74

scribed her reaction in this way: "The memory of the pain stayed with me for months. I've wondered why. I mean it hurt, but not as much as when I broke my leg. I've decided the pain seemed like a kind of punishment for not using my diaphragm. After the abortion, I had a dream that may be a memory, I don't know. My grandmother slapped me on the face because I'd eaten some food I wasn't supposed to. When I woke up, I remembered that my mother slapped me, as a kind of Jewish ritual thing, when I got my first period. It's all tied up together in some way—punishment for being naughty, for being sexual."

If women can have adverse psychological reactions to the procedure, men can react to *not* having a procedure. Fred and Alexis, a couple in their mid-twenties, had been living together for only two months when she learned she was pregnant. They both had tremendous conflicts over having an abortion, but they felt they simply couldn't have a baby before they knew whether their relationship would last. Fred told us a few months after the abortion, when he had lost interest in sex, "I just can't get it out of my mind, the fact of the abortion. Alexis had the procedure done on her body and I envy her because it's a kind of release I never had. I mean, one morning she was carrying this baby growing inside her, and by noon there was nothing. I had come to terms with the pregnancy. That was real to me. I think the end of it never became real for me." Fred was moderately depressed and was referred for psychotherapy.

Other men have reacted to the atmosphere in the place where the procedure was done. In many abortion centers, there is a palpable antimale bias, understandable, perhaps, but not ultimately helpful. Men may feel left out, put down, or attacked.

A day or two after an abortion, some women have a brief (one- to two-day) depressive reaction, which is almost certainly related to the sharp drop in hormone levels when the pregnancy is terminated. This reaction is more common when the woman has been further along in her pregnancy. While hormone levels usually return to normal within four to six weeks, it can take longer. Menstruation may not resume for as long as three months. Cervicitis and vaginitis appear to be prevalent during this phase, possibly due to temporarily low estrogen levels.

In the weeks and months following the abortion, feelings tend to become less intense. Most women say they feel fine. Interestingly, almost every woman with whom we have spoken during this period can recall at least one dream in which the theme of the loss of a baby is apparent. Some dream about it recurrently for months. Men, too, may have similar dreams.

If there are long-term, negative side effects for a woman's—or a couple's—sexual relationship, these usually involve fear of another unwanted pregnancy. When trusted contraception failed, it may be hard to trust that method, or any method, at least for a while. While anxiety about pregnancy is running high, a man may temporarily have problems with erection, or a woman may lose her sexual interest or develop vaginismus.

Occasionally a traumatic abortion experience lies dormant, only to resurface years later. We saw one couple in their mid-twenties whose sexual problem was at least in part traceable to the woman's abortion five years earlier.

Vanessa had been a sexually naive twenty-year-old in a new relationship with a man of almost thirty. They had had intercourse a few times without contraception before he started using condoms. She became pregnant and he walked out of her life, refusing even to give her the fifty dollars she needed toward the cost of the abortion. Vanessa went to the cheapest clinic she could find. "The place was horrible," she remembered, "not really even clean, and patients in and out one, two, three. No compassion. I was alone and very scared. The pain was bad. So was the bleeding afterward. I think I never felt so alone and helpless in my life."

Vanessa stayed away from men for almost a year. When she started dating again, she went on the pill but, in three years, she only had sex with one man. "When I met Ed, I was extremely attracted to him, and we very quickly had a wonderful sex life. We fell in love, very passionately. I think I was completely happy. We lived together for a while and it was clear in my mind that I wanted to marry him, but then we hit a snag."

Ed was assigned to a job in Central America for two months. Ed later told us, "The week or so before I left, we made love all the time. It was heaven, but I'm afraid it was the beginning of the problem." On the day Ed left, Vanessa discovered that there was blood in her urine, urination was painful, and she had a fever. She had a severe case of cystitis, almost certainly brought on by the week of endless lovemaking (and probably aggravated by the fact that she was taking a very low estrogen birth control pill, which can affect the bladder and urethra).

Unfortunately, she had a resistant case and had to have repeated examinations using a cystoscope. At the time, she didn't associate any of this with her abortion, but later, when Vanessa and Ed were in sex counseling, she realized that the events had seemed connected in her mind. "The sense of aloneness was the same. Ed hadn't dumped me like the other guy when I got pregnant, but he wasn't there. He wasn't there to hold my hand when the cystoscopies were done or when I was worried about the blood. And the same damn position—legs apart and draped and some damn doctor ramming me and hurting me. Shit, look at what sex gets me into. Who needs it?"

Vanessa and Ed probably would have been okay but, after Ed returned from Central America and they resumed having sex, she developed cystitis twice in three months. The combined effects of the recurrent cystitis, repeated medical procedures, and the old psychic wounds of the abortion led to a severe case of vaginismus and a complete loss of interest in sex.

Fortunately, a combination of hormonal treatment and sex counseling proved helpful for Vanessa and Ed. When they could finally enjoy sex again, Vanessa told us, "I do think I had to recognize how, in a way, I was taking out my feelings about my abortion on Ed. It scares me to think that my rage at Kevin [the man who had gotten her pregnant and then left] could have ruined my relationship with Ed."

Sometimes an unwanted pregnancy can actually be a positive sexual turning point. A twenty-three-year-old graduate student told us that her pregnancy and abortion changed her sexual pattern completely. "I was too casual about the whole thing—about sex, birth control, and my body. This has made me grow up fast. I've finally started taking myself seriously." Not uncommonly, women who have never been pregnant before feel reassured about their own fertility, and this reinforces their self-confidence as women.

STAGE THREE

Marriage—

for Better or Worse

(in Bed)

4

"Our Sex Life Was Fine until

We Got Married"

AMONG our friends aged forty-five to sixty or so, a surprising number have no married children. Some of the children are entering their thirties and now, just recently, one or two have begun to talk about marriage. We asked one of our friends' daughters about her not marrying. She said, "I've lived with four different men and never thought of marriage, really. Frankly, it seemed too unimportant to bother about; almost trivial. I'm thinking about marriage now because I want kids, but the marriage part still seems unimportant to my relationship with Chad. I can't imagine it will change anything—although having kids will be a change." Oddly enough, her brother, two years older, had once said to us, "I don't know if I will ever get married. It seems much too big a decision to ever be able to know, one way or the other."

Today's youth are understandably confused. There are many factors that appear to make marriage seem trivial and rob it of the real and symbolic importance it has had for centuries. If you started having intercourse at fifteen, have had sexual relations with eight different men, lived with two men, are economically self-sufficient, live two thousand miles from any relatives, and think you may not want children—then getting married will seem very different to you than it did to your mother and grandmother. It will be a more personal and private act, probably less formal, involving less of a change in life-style.

Why, then, do we all hear about couples who have lived together for twelve years splitting up six months after they get married? Why do we two, and others who do counseling, see so many individuals and couples agonizing over whether to marry? Why do we so often hear people say, "We had a great sex life—until we got married"?

The reason is, we believe, because marriage is *still* a monumental step. Even shorn of the trappings of a rite of passage, even when it outwardly changes nothing except legal status, marriage is still a turning point. Even sexually, although virgin brides and grooms are a small minority, marriage is a sexual turning point.

Let us examine some of the reasons marriage is a sexual turning point. What happens psychologically and sexually as young people move toward marriage for the first time? We have found that fear of sexual inadequacy prevents some from making the commitment to marriage, while others, seemingly ready to walk down the aisle, suddenly develop sexual problems. Getting married actually involves major psychological shifts. For most people, it is the final shift away from the primary tie to parents. The wedding and the honeymoon can be wonderful, but they are also stressful, and for some, more sexual pressure than they can handle. Setting up house together for real means making hundreds of nitty-gritty decisions. Suddenly differences between his and her cultural, religious, and sex-role expectations crop up. Not surprisingly, these issues sometimes invade the marital bed. Finally, there are some special issues facing many young couples today, such as dual careers and prolonged geographical separation, which put extra stress on marriage in its early years (and beyond). All these factors combine to make today's young marriages a challenge.

Deciding to get married—and adjusting to being married— obviously have an impact outside the sexual sphere: on work, leisure, social relations—on personality in general. Sex is only one barometer, but it is a sensitive one.

Experience with couples has helped us understand why getting married can be a sexual turning point—and a stumbling block—even for a couple who previously had a fulfilling sexual relationship. Marriage, in our society, symbolizes the shift from the "family of origin" (sociological term for the family in which you were brought up) to the "family of procreation" (the family in which you would have and rear children). Unlike many primitive societies and our own agricultural society of the past, newly marrieds today are expected to be financially and emotionally independent. Often the young couple live far from both sets of parents. Although many people, by the time they marry, have worked through the complex and difficult emotional process of separating from their parents, many others are still tied in ways they themselves don't recognize. Marriage suddenly confronts them with separation and loss.

This was true of Anna, who married when she was twenty, interrupting college and moving away from home for the first time to live with her husband, Michael, in France. Anna had never considered sex a problem. She had petted with one boyfriend in high school and had enjoyed it. When she and Michael became engaged, they had intercourse. Sex with Michael had been "blissful," although they saw each other only on weekends because of geographic distance.

They were completely unprepared, then, for Anna's reaction, which set in not during their honeymoon in Vermont but as soon as they reached France. Michael was immediately involved in his work as a sculptor. Anna was studying French and trying to set up her workshop for making jewelry. Suddenly she lost all sexual and romantic feelings for Michael and began to daydream about other men. "Although I felt frightened, lost, and lonely, I didn't reach out to anyone. I didn't even write or call home. My parents could have been on the moon, I felt so far from them. When they called me or wrote and gave advice of any kind—even if it was good advice—I found myself getting furious at their invasion of my privacy. One night I remember ranting about it to Michael. I said, "They're trying to keep me their little girl and tell me what to do even though I'm thousands of miles away. I don't know how Michael saw through me, but he did. He said, 'You really miss them, don't you?' I just started to cry so hard I thought I'd never stop. Michael held me like a baby.

"That was some kind of breakthrough. It's as if I recognized how dependent I did feel, especially on my father, I think. And I could let Michael cuddle me like my father used to, yet I knew he was still Michael—my husband. After that, my fantasies about other men decreased a lot and my pleasure in touching with Michael grew more and more."

Anna had made the necessary emotional transition from being a daughter to being a wife. She acknowledged the pain of "losing" her parents, particularly her father, and transferred many of the positive feelings she had had toward him to her new husband. She described an important symbolic moment when she recognized this shift. She said, "I *really* got married the night I called my parents from Paris and told them how lonely and depressed I had been. They started to get upset but I told them not to, because I knew I'd turned a corner, and Michael and I would make it."

Another psychological hurdle that can come with marriage is the pressure it seems to create to become *wife* and *husband*. And where did we all learn our most unforgettable lessons about how to be *wife* and *husband*? From our parents, of course.

Cheryl, a woman who married in her early thirties, had consciously and systematically worked at being different from her mother. Her career, her adventurousness, her amiability all set her apart from her mother. She told us, "For me, I think the problem started with the housekeeping and the joint bank account. Suddenly Peter and I were doing things that reminded me of my parents, like sitting down together with the checkbook or planning who to invite for dinner. My parents always argued a lot, and I prided myself on *not* arguing. Suddenly I found myself sounding like my mother. I actually used some of her phrases, like, 'You never listen to me.' It felt like overnight we'd become the old married couple, bickering and yelling. Peter lost all sexual interest in me, and who could blame him?" Peter felt the same way. He said, "It almost feels like we're acting out some sort of script for married couples, and for me that means failure, since my parents divorced when I was five and my mother's second marriage also broke up."

Peter represents an increasingly common problem. As more and more children live through divorce, marriage may become something associated with fighting, crying, pain, and breakup. There may have been many happy moments in Peter's parents' marriage, but he remembers the traumatic ones.

There is also a psychoanalytic explanation for the decline of erotic feelings when we shift from being lovers or fiancées to being wife and husband. The incest taboo makes us feel that it is wrong to have sexual feelings for our parents. When Cheryl started to see Peter as *husband*, a role she associated with her father, a kind of incest barrier arose between them, cutting off her sexual feelings. Therapy for Cheryl, therefore, had to include help in differentiating Peter as a unique person—a person different from her father, for whom it was safe to have sexual feelings.

Sometimes the struggle to separate from parental ties is not *just* psychological. It can also become a problem as a newly married couple struggles to establish themselves as a separate twosome while one or both sets of parents are hovering in the wings—sometimes even in the same house. The physical proximity of parents can feel comfortable and nurturing, but it is usually a mixed blessing—mixed with resentment over "intrusion." An emotional tug-of-war sometimes develops—between loyalty to parents versus loyalty to spouse—which can result in a kind of sexual self-consciousness.

Sue and Tony are a good example of a couple whose close-knit family ties nearly wrecked their sex life—and their marriage. Their traditional, large Italian wedding, on a sunny Saturday in May, was exactly what they had dreamed of. But the bride and groom were both tense about what would happen that night.

Sue was tense for two reasons. She was a virgin and was worried that the first time might be difficult. But her older sister and her doctor had reassured her on that count. What really worried Sue was Tony—not the fact that he was also a virgin (she respected him for that), but the awkwardness and hesitancy he displayed when they kissed and touched. Although they had been naked together and had caressed each other, he had never ejaculated and, in fact, seemed less eager for sex than Sue. She believed—at least she hoped—that getting married would solve everything.

But Tony was no more sexually confident on their four-day honeymoon than he had been before. They "sort of" had intercourse a few times. Sue felt intensely disappointed and confused. She had never discussed the details of sex with anyone. Neither had Tony. They couldn't even begin to talk about their problem.

After the honeymoon, they settled into the life they had anticipated. Tony worked with his two older brothers in their father's garage. Sue stayed at home. They lived in a "cottage" (a converted garage) behind Sue's parents' house. Most nights Tony played poker with his brothers and their friends. When Sue complained that she and Tony spent no time together, he became furious. He was only doing what all the men in his circle did. Sue and Tony had almost no sexual contact. When they did, it was hurried and clumsy and Tony often lost his erection.

Sue began to feel that her parents "knew" something wasn't right in her sex life. Actually, after only three months, her mother seemed to expect Sue to become pregnant. Meanwhile, Tony had to endure his brothers' jokes about all the great sex a new groom is supposed to be having.

One night the pressure became too much for Tony. He drank almost a case of beer, and then he and Sue had a loud fight. Her parents burst in. Without thinking, Sue blurted out, "He's not a real husband to me. He's a mama's boy." Tony punched her and ran out.

When they came to see us several weeks later to try to resolve their sexual problem and hold their marriage together, it was clear that they would have to begin by setting some clear boundaries between themselves and their parents. They needed psychic space and privacy in order to develop some genuine intimacy. Tony told us that he had a deep, dark secret he had never been able to share with anyone. He and a cousin had had a homosexual relationship for a year or more when they were about fifteen. Ever since then, Tony had been terrified of sex and women, sure that he was homosexual and would "fail" heterosexually. This paralyzing fear made it inevitable that he *would* fail.

His conviction that he was sexually inadequate had bound him more closely to his family. He hadn't dated until Sue came along and asked him out. He hadn't really imagined himself as an independent, married adult. His not-quite-conscious self-image was that of a dependent, almost handicapped young man who would stay close to home, because, as he put it, "Only your parents just accept you and love you, no questions asked, no demands."

Although Sue appeared to be more comfortable with sex and was the initiator, she had problems of her own. She viewed sex as a normal part of marriage but primarily for having children. She felt an obligation to her own parents to have intercourse so that there would be grandchildren. But Sue knew that her own mother had never really enjoyed sex, and she had very mixed feelings about experiencing sexual pleasure. She had only had an orgasm with Tony once, and she remembered wondering whether her mother would somehow know this too about her sex life.

After much soul-searching, Tony decided to tell Sue his secret. This was the first real sharing they had ever done. With our help, they were able to discuss more of their feelings and to talk about sex. Although it was a financial hardship and Sue's parents were hurt, they moved to their own apartment in another town. They were beginning to be a married couple.

Tony's fears about sexual performance on his honeymoon were unusually severe because of his concern about homosexuality, but performance expectations can plague any man, particularly on the "command performance" of a honeymoon, which may be especially anxiety provoking for a man who has had no previous experience to reassure him. High tension and arousal can trigger premature ejaculation. Or there can be problems with either erection or ejaculation.

One couple was so upset by the fact that the husband couldn't sustain an erection on their wedding night and consummate the relationship that they called us the next day and asked to see us as an emergency. It wasn't difficult to figure out that tension, champagne, and awkwardness in using a condom for the first time were all significant factors. We recommended that the wife use a chemical spermicide temporarily instead of the condom, that they have no more than one alcoholic drink, and that they take the pressure off the need to have intercourse. They left for their honeymoon right from our office and called two weeks later to say all was well.

Performance pressures can be intensified by getting married, because married couples are expected to have sex with some kind of "normal" regularity. The idea that sex is now an obligation can affect the level of sex drive. "Sex used to be optional. Now I feel it's expected two or three times a week—the national average—or there's something wrong. I never reacted well to *having* to do something. I tell myself this is all crazy thinking, but I can't stop feeling it's this *obligation* I want to get out of."

Or just the opposite: "If I'm really truthful about it, I think I used to push myself, you know, to give her lots of sex, because I knew she liked it and I wanted to marry this woman—more than anything in the world, I wanted *her*. Now that she's mine, I feel happy, relieved, lucky—but I know I'm not pushing myself the way I used to, to get in the mood for sex. I think I'm a low-drive person, basically, and I'm letting my true nature show itself."

The couples we have been describing have had trouble with the psychosocial changes that marriage demands. A turning point such as marriage can be a hurdle that trips us up. But turning points can also be opportunities for growth. For most people, marriage ushers in a phase of sexual discovery, relaxed pleasure, and unique intimacy. The separation from parents and the attachment to a spouse can be exhilarating. Many women find that the security of marriage frees their sexuality and they can be more abandoned, more responsive than ever before.

Those for whom marriage is a sacred religious vow often feel a new spiritual dimension in their lovemaking. Two national surveys on sexuality have found that devoutly religious women reported *more* sexual satisfaction than other women. Other women, not necessarily religious, find that marriage adds an important sense of "rightness" to sex. As one newly married young woman told us, "For me, getting married made a huge difference in how I felt about sex. We'd been having intercourse for more than a year before the wedding. It was a joint decision and we felt okay about it—at least I thought so at the time. Now I see it differently. I don't think the option of *not* having intercourse was there, because of social pressures. Absolutely everyone I knew was not a virgin. Being in love and engaged and *still* not having intercourse would have felt almost freaky in my peer group.

"It wasn't till after the wedding that I realized how much guilt and mixed feelings I had had about it, because being married felt like such a relief. Sex seemed, I don't know, more right or more comfortable. There was no more slightly furtive staying at his place or mine. We had *our* place and we had secure privacy. I wish now that I'd had the courage of my convictions. No, that's not it exactly, because I didn't even know my own convictions at the time. I guess I'm just a bit sad that sex couldn't have started out with me feeling a hundred percent good about it."

When the bride and/or groom are still virgins (somewhere between 5% and 30% of brides and grooms are), first intercourse is obviously an important symbolic event. Intercourse is still a kind of initiation rite. Men and women alike tend to feel that vaginal penetration by the penis means "Now I'm really a sexual adult." Hopefully, that has positive connotations.

One woman described her feelings in words we have never forgotten. She said, "On our wedding night, I lost my virginity. It wasn't blissful sexually but it was one of the strongest emotional experiences of my life. I woke up a few hours later. It was still dark. A feeling came over me that I had never had before—a sense of connection with all the women who had ever lived on earth. We all had this in common. I knew then that I was a *woman* —and I loved it."

5

Wrestling with Sex Roles

MARRIAGES, like other partnerships, need to function smoothly in day-to-day operations. In business partnerships, we usually have job descriptions. In marriage, we used to have traditional sex roles. They greased the wheels of household management, kept husbands and wives off each other's turf, and lent an aura of mystery to their separate domains. When he couldn't boil water, her soufflé was a minor miracle. When she couldn't balance a checkbook, he resembled a bank president every time he paid the bills. And everyone knew that sex was something a man "did" to a woman.

One result of the recent shifts in ideas about sex roles is an inevitable increase in friction between women and men, wives and husbands. The grease of established, unspoken custom is gone, or at least thinned out. Almost every couple we have seen in sex therapy over the past dozen years has been struggling with sex-role issues. A surprising number of sex-role conflicts between husbands and wives center around apparent trivialities, such as the dishes or the laundry. Perhaps they are not really about dishes or laundry but about fairness, sexual politics, and power. Such conflicts often carry over into the bedroom.

In the struggle for liberation, many woman find themselves angry at men in general and their husbands (if they have one) in particular. A woman's anger can destroy a marriage or turn it into a perpetual battleground. Anger can also be a constructive force for change within a marriage. A wife's newfound self-assertion can liberate her husband from his stereotyped role as decision maker and protector, sometimes with negative results, as was the case with Helen, who described herself as becoming "mysteriously turned off." She and Tim had been married for three years. In their first year of marriage, they were at school in different cities and saw each other only on weekends. Since Helen was under pressure to finish her dissertation in mathematics, they usually ate in restaurants. Tim took care of his own laundry, weekday meals, housecleaning, even sewing and "decorating." There were no sexual problems.

Helen's decreased sexual drive seemed to begin about six months after they moved in together. At first, Tim continued to do the household tasks he had always done, but gradually he left more and more of them to Helen. When she complained about the division of labor, he seemed to agree with her but then he would "forget" to do his jobs and she would finally do them.

Tim had always tended to ejaculate rapidly, but Helen usually had an orgasm before him or else after him from manual stimulation. Now she found that she rarely had an orgasm before Tim, and she became more reticent about asking him to stimulate her to a climax. She began to feel resentful of Tim's "selfishness" (her word) in bed. She thought he could delay his ejaculation if he really wanted to and believed he should offer to stimulate her. "He just isn't aware of my needs," she said.

Of course she was speaking of more than her sexual needs. She simply hadn't understood the depth of her anger over what she called silly nonsense—housekeeping tasks. With a little encouragement, the anger surfaced. She realized she had been feeling that Tim didn't take her academic career seriously and that he *really* wanted an old-fashioned wife and mother. Part of her wanted to meet his needs; part of her fought against him and, as Helen put it, "the whole weight of Western civilization."

The breakthrough for Helen came when she recognized that the conflict was not only between herself and Tim. It was a conflict within herself—the warring halves of her identity. "I think I almost wanted to let him take over as the Man—with a capital *M*— and I'd be his adoring slave. I know some of that comes from my being really scared of academic competition. I could have copped out and blamed him."

Tim was able to be honest about his own mixed feelings. He told us, "If I'm honest about it, I have to admit that part of me would rather have Helen do the cooking and the laundry and all the stupid errands, but now that she's made me face the facts, it's obviously got to change. And I can even see that in the long run, I don't want Helen to be like my mother, because I don't want responsibility for both of us. I think I'd rather have her be strong and independent if that means I wash some shirts."

There is a kind of heroism about the struggle Helen and Tim are waging. They are, in their small and private way, forging new territory. They seem to represent the best ideals of women's liberation. Others, by contrast, use the concept of women's liberation in the service of psychopathology. Two examples follow.

Mrs. and Mr. A. sought our help for a problem of inhibited ejaculation. Mr. A. very rarely ejaculated during intercourse, although he could ejaculate regularly during masturbation. The only reason the A.s sought help was that they wanted a second child. Their role reversal was striking because they hadn't so much done away with role stereotypes as exchanged them. Mrs. A. was a busy lawyer. Mr. A. stayed home, shopped, cooked, and watched soap operas. He had completely given up his career as an accountant. This might have been a satisfactory arrangement, but Mr. A.'s passivity was pathological. He was unable to assert himself, even to the extent of returning an obviously spoiled chicken to the market. He never initiated anything, including sex. They rationalized their life-style with the rhetoric of liberation, but neither felt free. Each felt trapped and helpless. We suggested referral for individual psychotherapy for both, which they accepted.

Mr. and Mrs. B.'s concern was that Mrs. B. had never had an orgasm. They had been married for eleven years and come for help only when Mr. B. had had a few episodes of erectile failure. Mrs. B.'s sexual problem was part of a larger picture of a woman so intent on what she called independence that she never allowed herself to be given to, never accepted a suggestion, never let down her guard. Mrs. B. owned a shop that was open seven days a week and several evenings. She didn't believe in depending on employees, so she was always there. Mrs. B.'s mother, who lived nearby, looked after the children. Mrs. B., like Mr. A., couched her philosophy in terms of women's liberation. She said that women had to be strong or they would be totally dominated by men and lose their identity. Mrs. B. wasn't very eager for therapy but thought her husband might leave her if she didn't at least try it. She also believed that sexual satisfaction was a woman's right.

About midway through the therapy, Mrs. B. experienced an orgasm when her husband was fondling her genitals. Far from being pleased, she felt repulsed and humiliated. She hated the sense of losing control in her husband's presence. She decided to stop the therapy, and Mr. B. acquiesced.

In the section on Sexual Unfolding, we mentioned the shifts in role behavior among adolescents—the increased willingness of young women to acknowledge sexual interest and the decrease in young men's high-pressure tactics. Among college students, sexual relationships are usually perceived as being between sexual equals, not between a horny male and a reluctant, chaste female. About fifteen years ago, at the end of a lecture we gave for several hundred college students, a young woman raised her hand and asked, "Can a female ever feel horny?" The students all looked at us with expectant curiosity. And we (we blush to tell) hesitated, started to say no, then reluctantly halfway reversed ourselves. Today it seems inconceivable that anyone would even ask such a question, and we hope our "Yes, of course" response would be without hesitation.

This illustrates the point that social conditioning influences what all of us—including professionals in the field—"know" about sex. At any given point, our vision is myopic. Sex-role norms can be so deeply ingrained that we see as "natural" or "normal" what is simply the *cultural* norm.

What is "natural" sexual behavior for the male vis-à-vis the female? We won't venture into those waters. But we would like to illustrate how one can never know what may develop between male and female. The range of sexual roles may be infinite.

At a meeting of sex researchers in November 1981, one presenter told this story about observations made at the Yerkes Center for Primatology Research in Atlanta. The orangutan colony at the center was in trouble because the pregnancy rate among the females was very low in spite of the fact that there was a high rate of sexual intercourse. For every hundred matings, there were only three pregnancies.

It was thought that the nature of the sexual interaction between males and females might be part of the problem. The unvarying pattern was this: male "decides" he wants to copulate, he violently and suddenly attacks the female, climbs on top, thrusts rapidly to apparent point of climax and dismounts. It always happened so rapidly that no one ever saw the male's erect penis. During intercourse, the female seemed perturbed and made sounds of complaint. Females did not show any signs of sexual arousal, pleasure, or climax.

To see if this pattern could be altered, one female was placed in a cage by herself with a male in an adjacent cage. A steel barrier was placed over the usual opening between the cages, just large enough to permit the female to enter the male's side but too small to allow him access to her. At first he was enraged and continually tried to tear down the barrier.

After several days of this, he seemed to give up and was observed exhibiting a new behavior. He lay on his back quite passively, and an erection developed. The female seemed curious. After watching him in this posture for some time, she entered his cage, walked around him, staring, and then returned to her side.

The next day the male was seen in the same passive posture, again with an erection. This time the female did more than look. She sat down near his feet and touched his penis in a kind of exploratory, playful way. He just lay there.

The next day she repeated this and then mounted him and began thrusting. She seemed to be enjoying it, and he wasn't complaining. He didn't show any of the usual roughness. Observers thought the female had an orgasm.

Subsequently, using this "female privilege" cage, four out of five female orangutans became pregnant within a short time.

Many people think that this is an interesting story about orangutans but they don't see its relevance for humans. As sex therapists, the human implications were immediately clear to us. We know how often, in cases of low female sexual interest or general dislike of sex, our main task has been to stop the male from following his usual male role as *the* sexual initiator, *the* sexually needy one. Given some breathing space, given an opportunity to ask herself what she wants, quite apart from his insistent needs, a woman often discovers her own curiosity, interests, and desires.

Let's return, for a moment, to the story of Helen and Tim described at the beginning of this chapter. Helen had lost all interest in sex after she and Tim began living together, and he gradually stopped doing any housekeeping tasks. Helen had started to feel that sex was a duty, something she did to satisfy Tim's male needs. She stopped initiating sex and often found excuses when Tim showed sexual interest. She began to think of Tim as over-sexed, while he viewed her as undersexed. As part of the sex therapy, we told Tim and Helen that they must take turns with initiation. This automatically put a lid on Tim's "constant" sexual overtures. When days went by without Tim making advances, Helen began to feel her own sexual interest reawaken. It was crucial that Tim not "pounce" on Helen as soon as she showed any sexual interest. If she wanted to touch for a while and then stop, he had to be willing to stop. Tim, like other men, discovered that he didn't always need to ejaculate. He could play and stop. Just like the female orangutan, when the male remained passive, the female became more exploratory and sexually active.

We are not saying that the answer to human sexual rela-tionships is a role reversal in which the male is always passive, the female always active. We are suggesting that the traditional pat-tern of the sexually dominant and aggressive male may not be the most satisfying sexual pattern for the female *or* the male. There *are* alternatives, and our society seems to be in the process of exploring and testing these alternatives.

Now we would like to explore one of these alternatives, a kind of relationship that has become more prevalent as a result of women's increased sexual freedom.

Once upon a time, young American men had much more sex-ual experience than their female age mates. The double standard of sexual morality meant it was permissible, even desirable, for young men to be initiated into sex in their teens or early twenties. Fathers often took their sons to benevolent prostitutes who would be patient teachers. In the 1950s, at least 25 percent of college men had sex with a prostitute. Now it is the rare male under-graduate who has—perhaps 1 or 2 percent. Since the demise of the double standard and the fading of the good-girl/bad-girl dis-tinction, young men have sex with young women like them-selves—dates, girlfriends, young women they meet at "mixers."

The number of young men who remain virginal past their early twenties hasn't changed very much, even though the nature of the sexual experience has. The big change has been among young women. The age of first intercourse has been falling stead-ily, while the average number of premarital partners has risen. On

college campuses now, about one in five young women who graduate are still virgins, and many of these have intercourse in the year
or so after graduation. About the same percentage of men leave
college still virginal. Among those who go on to professional education, the proportion who are sexually inexperienced is higher
still. At one medical school, approximately 25 percent of the entering males were virgins. Of course, each one thinks he is the
only virgin in his class.

What this change has meant to marrying couples is the
emergence of a new kind of pair. Some of these sexually inexperienced men meet and marry sexually experienced women.
Such pairs have always occurred, but never in such numbers.

We have coined a not terribly original but apt phrase to describe men who have postponed sex until they are older (some
well into their thirties, a few beyond that). We call them late bloom-
ers. The late bloomer has usually been intensely focused on
school, grades, competition, learning, and getting ahead in a career. He hasn't had the time, energy, or motivation to deal with
women and sex. Just below the surface is often a fear of sex.
Whatever his adolescent anxieties may have been, now that all his
peers have left him in the dust, he feels hopelessly inadequate and
doesn't dare admit his ignorance or his fear to anyone.

When he finally looks up from his books or test tubes and
meets a woman he loves, he faces a dilemma. If she is sexually
sophisticated, it is a double-edged sword. He may feel both terrified of her supposed sexual superiority and grateful for it, since
she can teach him. If they agree to acknowledge her as the
teacher, they may both accept this reversal of traditional roles with
grace or, alternatively, one or both of them may harbor any
number of misgivings.

Judd and Carla presented a classic example of a late bloomer
marrying a modern woman. She had enjoyably had sex with about
ten men. He had been studying for the priesthood until he decided instead to become a psychologist. When they met, he was
twenty-nine and she was twenty-four, but so far as sexual knowledge, confidence, and experience were concerned, he was sixteen,
she thirty. He hadn't even masturbated until he was twenty-seven.

Judd had dated a few women but had never gone beyond
kissing and some breast fondling. When he and Carla met and
started to care for one another, he was honest about his lack of

experience. She was also truthful about the extent of hers. During the courtship phase, they gradually moved toward and then did have intercourse. He was always eager and tender but tentative. She had to take the lead at every step. Sometimes he lost his erection. Frequently he ejaculated a few seconds after vaginal penetration. But they did love each other, and sex was very emotionally satisfying. Carla assumed things would improve with practice. They married.

Three years later, things had gotten worse rather than better. Judd came alone to see us and was surprised that we wanted to talk to Carla also. He thought he would be given instruction in the how-to's of sex and that would solve it all. He was eager to learn, but also very deeply ashamed of what he felt was his unacceptable ignorance. Later on in therapy, we learned that he had another reason for coming alone; he felt ashamed of Carla's sexual history. He had always pretended to himself and to Carla that he had no feelings about her past, but in fact the priest in him judged her behavior as sinful and the frightened boy in him felt defeated by the image of the "great lovers" who had preceded him.

After Judd acknowledged his own conflicts about sex and about Carla, he became very anxious. We thought he might need to spend some time in a psychiatric hospital. He chose to go on a week-long religious retreat. When he returned, he felt much less anxious. He said, "One thing I recognized during this week away from Carla is that *I am* a sexual person. I'm not just responding to 'Carla the temptress.' I think I still have lots of hang-ups about sex, and I was blaming Carla for my having sexual feelings."

During sex therapy, Judd's sexual self-confidence increased. He learned that even if his erection went away, it could return if he didn't panic. He was able to tell Carla that if she used oral stimulation (fellatio) after he lost his erection, he felt under pressure to become instantly hard again. She had never known that he felt that way. Like many women, she had assumed that oral stimulation would always be helpful for a man to get an erection.

Carla told Judd that she would like to make love about three or four times a week. Judd said he didn't think he could live up to that. Carla explained that for her, lovemaking didn't always have to include intercourse. After a while, Judd began to believe her, and then he found that they could "just fool around" and it was nice for both of them.

Near the end of their time in sex therapy, Carla said, "When we started this therapy, I thought you were going to tell me I would have to squelch my sexuality a lot if I wanted Judd to function sexually. I was sure the problem was my being too sexually demanding. What amazes me is now I think I'm being *more* openly sexual with Judd, but he's not feeling it as a pressure (or a sin) so now it's okay; in fact it's good."

We'd like to think that there is a lesson to be learned from Carla's statement. Contrary to myth, most men will *not* lose their potency and flee from sexually assertive partners if there is effective, clear, and open communication between the man and woman. The men who are intimidated by a woman's sexuality are the men who subscribe to the macho ethic, the men who can't ever say, "I'm uncomfortable" or "No thanks, I'm not up to a second time." He—no different from she—must be able to express feelings, including anxieties. Then the couple is likely to discover, as Carla and Judd discovered, that sex can be relaxed and satisfying for both partners.

6

Dual Careers

As more and more women plan not only to work but to have a career, we see many young couples on the threshold of commitment, trying to cope with prolonged separations. There are certain sexual issues that tend to arise for these people. On the simplest level, separation and passionate reunion can easily trigger premature ejaculation. One couple found that their weekends together every six weeks took on a predictable sexual pattern. On Friday nights, he would ejaculate even before entering her vagina. On Saturdays, two minutes afterward. Sunday nights he left. She had stopped experiencing orgasm. He was feeling guilty and sexually inadequate.

It was easy to help this couple. Telling them that abstinence normally leads to faster ejaculation relieved some of his anxiety. We helped them to think about other ways in which she could climax—using manual or oral stimulation—and that took a lot of the pressure off. We tried to make them less goal oriented, to focus their attention on shared sensuous pleasure rather than an end point. We instructed the couple in some simple techniques to delay rapid ejaculation, which they found worked well.

Other couples complain that the very idea of a passionate reunion creates problems. As one young woman put it, "I get off the train. He hasn't seen me in months and right away he wants to make love. I feel like it's his penis greeting my vagina, not him greeting me. I need to ease back into closeness, to talk and just be together before I get sexy. But he says I'm cold and rejecting him."

Passionate reunions can also feel like a demand to perform sexually. After a lecture we gave to a group of doctors, one of them came to talk to Phil. He said, "I think your lecture really helped me to understand a sex problem I've been having. My fiancée has been working in Boston for the past six months now, and we only see each other about every three weeks. We've never been apart and never even wrote each other any letters before. Well, she started writing these, well, hot letters, about how horny she was. I liked it and the letters got even more explicit, telling me her fantasies about just what we'd do together. We both found the letters—oh, and telephone calls, too—very erotic. The weird thing is, I've been having trouble getting erections when we finally do get together. It made no sense to me, because I was really eager for sex. When you talked about performance pressures in your lecture, I suddenly realized that the letters make me feel she's so horny I just have to be fantastic for her or she'll be disappointed. It's as if she's written a script and now I'm supposed to step in and play the part. I mean, I'd like to play the part; I want to play the part. But my body says different."

This doctor and his fiancée solved their own problem. No, they didn't stop their sexy correspondence. He just talked to her about his feelings. She was relieved because she had started to imagine he was in love with another woman.

Different people react in different ways to separation, and these reactions can be very intense. Separation from those we love is universal in childhood, but each of us has experienced it in our own unique way. The child whose mother died when he or she was small or whose father deserted the family may feel "irrationally" distraught and angry at even minor separations. One recently married couple who consulted us about a sexual problem dated the onset of their problem to a time about two years before their marriage, when he moved five hundred miles away to study architecture. June, the wife, said, "I felt so alone. A lot of my friends had graduated [from her college], and now Nick was gone too. I handled it by throwing myself into work, but underneath I was miserable and even angry at Nick for deserting me." June's use of the word *deserting* led to her seeing a link between Nick's leaving her and the feelings she had at age thirteen when her parents divorced. At that time, too, she had thrown herself into school-work to avoid painful feelings. She had never forgiven her father for "deserting us."

June added, "I might have handled the separation from Nick reasonably well, but then Nick decided to spend his Christmas holiday on a trip to Europe with a few friends. I understand why—a last fling, and he got to see so much great architecture. But, emotionally, I think it was the coup de grace. It did me in. If I'd been able to express my anger more, maybe it would have helped. Instead I just withdrew from Nick while at the same time clinging to him and pressuring him to marry me. After that Christmas, I had no sexual feelings whatsoever."

June's feelings about her parents' divorce were very strong, and her tendency to transfer her feelings from her father to Nick kept getting in the way of their relationship. On the verge of divorce, June decided to try individual psychotherapy. Meanwhile, they remain married and essentially celibate.

In the cases we have been describing, the stumbling block for the couples has been the *emotional* distance generated by geographic distance. Jules Pfeiffer, the cartoonist, tells a story about himself that illustrates the meaning of distance. He used to travel on the lecture circuit and would be gone on lecture tours for weeks at a time. He was, naturally, the center of attention, being interviewed constantly, his every word a valued object. When a tour ended, he would rejoin his girlfriend and his daughter (this refers to a time after he and his wife were divorced). *They* were not interviewing him, not hanging on every word. They had been living their own lives, doing things that they wanted to talk about. Pfeiffer found that he had a hard time reconnecting with them. He was somehow disappointed—even angry. His solution was to give up the lecture circuit.

When the separation isn't optional, the only thing a couple can do is try to keep in touch emotionally. Letters, telephone calls, cassette tapes, and visits all help—if both people can communicate their feelings, and that is a big *if*. Some couples have been very creative in their communications. One woman kept a diary with her most of the time. She made short entries at odd moments. She would then photocopy her diary pages instead of writing long letters. Another couple used videotapes.

One vital issue about which geographically separated couples should communicate clearly is sexual exclusivity. Do they expect to avoid all sexual interaction with others? Or would some strictly recreational sex be all right? Do they plan to tell each other about any and all sexual involvements? Close friendships and attractions? If so, in how much detail? Can they anticipate, from past experience, whether they are likely to suffer from jealous feelings? If a couple's life-style is likely to include periods of separation after marriage, resolving these issues, or at least keeping the lines of communication open, is vital.

In addition to all the usual marital issues, a dual-career couple often has special problems, including the need to integrate two work lives, chronic fatigue, distraction, and a tendency to feel guilty about sex as a time-wasting indulgence.

Workaholism—à Deux

We see a great many couples who are ambitious and hard-working to a degree that verges on workaholism. We see biologists, physicists, and doctors who never leave their labs until nine o'clock at night, often stay until the early morning hours, *and* work most weekends. We see lawyers who are at the office until seven or eight o'clock and then bring home several hours of paperwork. We see adademics whose every spare moment is occupied with writing papers and books. We also see couples for whom the issue is less ambition than survival or maintaining a reasonable life-style, with both husband and wife having two jobs and never taking a vacation.

The workaholics are usually very happy in their work. The problem is that when career demands take up so much time and energy, there are only worn-out bits of leftover time for fun, talking, or sex. The relationship, like a plant that gets too little water and light, gradually weakens and droops and is in danger of dying.

The literature on workaholism suggests that to most work-aholics, work is like a lover—an exciting, stimulating, ego-boosting, satisfying extramarital affair. How can an ongoing relationship and an ongoing "affair" thrive together? Some couples seem to manage with apparent ease. One contributing factor to this is likely to be a comfortable, problem-free sex life that serves as a source of emotional nourishment and relaxation. Couples run into difficulties when a sexual problem makes sex unsatisfying or a source of anxiety. Then the energy required for sex seems to increase exponentially. The idea of going to bed to make love feels like one more piece of work at the end of a day and evening already filled with work. Sexual desire seems to evaporate, and some couples stop having sex altogether.

Carolyn and Ted are an example of a couple who were handling dual careers and marriage happily until they encountered a minor problem in their sex life that promptly escalated into a major problem and threatened their relationship. Ted described the problem this way: "We were married about a year when Carolyn got cystitis [inflammation of the bladder]. She felt pretty rotten with it and lost a few days at work. Then, over the next year or so, she got cystitis two—or was it three—more times, and once they thought it might be a kidney infection. She kept losing time from work, and the whole thing made her very anxious. But I shouldn't be talking for her, should I? Why don't you tell how you felt, Carolyn?"

"I think I overreacted to the cystitis because of what Ted was implying—the time I lost from my job. I'm a computer engineer, the only woman in my department apart from the secretary and one of the few women in the whole company at a high-level job. It's a job I started when we got married, and it's taken a big toll. I feel as if I have to outwork and outproduce the men just to earn a place of respect. Anything that sets me back at all in my work puts me in a tailspin. And I knew the cystitis was brought on by intercourse. In fact, it seemed to me that it was the times when intercourse was most pleasurable and I got into it most that the cystitis would develop afterward. So I started avoiding sex, making up excuses. We haven't made love once in three months! I can hardly believe it's happened, but I still feel no desire. Ted and I are fighting a lot now. We never did before. Some kind of balance or smoothness we had between us is gone, and I'm scared we'll end up splitting."

We helped Carolyn and Ted in two ways. One was to help them identify that they had been having intercourse in a way that probably contributed to Carolyn's cystitis. Sometimes, when Carolyn was particularly aroused and in the female-above position, she would press down extremely hard on Ted's penis. The very rigorous rubbing was pleasurable for her and might continue for five minutes or longer. This certainly could have tended to cause trauma to her urethra (the tube leading to the bladder) and could lead to cystitis. Carolyn and Ted were able to find other positions and ways of moving during intercourse that both liked, and when no cystitis followed over a period of time, Carolyn's interest in sex began to return.

We also helped Carolyn and Ted with the issue of ordering priorities. Carolyn decided that the pressure placed on herself to outwork her male colleagues was not worth it. Of course, this was after she had been with her company for a while and had already won respect and a sense of security.

Toward the end of their therapy with us, we suggested some basic guidelines to Ted and Carolyn that help couples with busy lives stay in touch with one another. This is what we told them:

Never let more than twenty-four hours go by without a chance for some time alone when you can talk not about trivia but about something personally meaningful—a worry, a hope, a feeling about the other, an idea. Don't let small hurts build into an emotional wall. Talk about them. And touch. Touch a lot. Touch at *least* every forty-eight hours. That doesn't necessarily mean sex; just real body contact. Talk and touch are the water and light a relationship needs.

Sometimes dual careers in very different fields present the added problem that wife and husband live in vastly different worlds, with different sets of friends and different subcultures, each with its own values, social norms, and "in" language.

A couple in their early thirties sought our help because of the wife's increasing aversion to sex. They had met and lived together when she was an art-history student and he an artist. After their marriage, she made a dramatic career shift and went to a prestigious business school with the goal of becoming a corporate executive. Suddenly her unconventional artist husband began to look different to her. His long hair and dirty fingernails were socially embarrassing to her now; before they had seemed charmingly unconventional. She wanted to learn disco dancing and play tennis, in part because she believed this would be expected of her in the corporate world. He loathed dancing and tennis. Her resentment found expression in a particular complaint. She said he was always dirty and emitted an odor she couldn't stand. In the early years of their relationship, it hadn't bothered her. He admitted he didn't bathe very often but felt her demands for cleanliness to be part of a scheme to clean him up for the role of executive husband. So he refused to change his habits. Eventually, with therapy focused on talking out their feelings, they were able to compromise and, at least temporarily, reestablish a satisfying sex life.

Yet another issue that can rear its destructive head for dual-career couples is competition. There is probably a degree of competitiveness between all spouses, but it is accentuated in ambitious, aggressive people who have always competed at school and probably will always compete at work. Competition becomes a way of life, something you don't even notice.

For a man reared in a male-dominated society, it is hard to accept that your wife may outrank and outearn you. Statistics show that the divorce rate goes up for every $10,000 of the wife's income. There are many reasons for this, but one of them is the husband's gut reaction to the situation. He may be intellectually pleased, happy about the money itself, even proud of his wife, but at another level, he feels cheated, somehow, of his role as protector, breadwinner, and kingpin. Sometimes these feelings, which he would find very hard to articulate, lead to a loss of sexual desire or problems with erection.

The theme of competition between spouses can be elusive, as it was in the case of Peggy and Stan M. They came to us with the following story: Peggy was a minister, a pioneer in her denomination. Stan was a tax attorney in a large, successful firm. Their sex life, during the first few years of marriage, had been satisfying for both of them. They struggled to keep their relationship as a high priority and spent time alone together and with friends. Their sex problem puzzled them. Over the last few years, they had had sex less and less often. Stan seemed embarrassed when he told us they hadn't made love in the past two months.

A careful delineation of the history of sex between them showed that a few years before, Peggy had begun to say no to Stan's sexual advances more often than not. She also found that when she agreed to make love in spite of some hesitancy, she often didn't enjoy it. Peggy wasn't sure what had caused the change in her.

We got an important clue when we learned that Peggy and Stan spent an hour or more every evening playing chess, Scrabble, or Go (a very challenging oriental game). When we asked them to tell us about the way they approached games, we discovered an unusually intense competitiveness. Both were "sore losers," sometimes becoming angry or sulky when they lost. They had a kind of understanding that Stan was better at Scrabble, Peggy at chess. If he lost at Scrabble or she at chess, the loser would feel particularly annoyed and even anxious.

Once the theme of competition and envy emerged, it was possible to see how these feelings had been involved in precipitating the sexual problem. Peggy and Stan hadn't thought to mention a "small" change in their lives that had come about a few years before. Stan had been invited to give a sermon to a small "radical" congregation in their neighborhood because he had a special interest in one area of Bible history. The sermon was well received. Stan joined this congregation and started giving regular sermons.

As they told us this story, Peggy's face became tight and she turned away from Stan. A few minutes later, she started to cry as she told us, "I was so angry at him, but I never said anything. How could I, when what he was doing was everything I believed in? I remember he used to get so high when he worked on those sermons. Afterward he'd often want to make love. I just couldn't. And then it seemed to me he'd often want to make love when I was in the middle of preparing one of *my* sermons. I felt he was dismissing my work, putting it down—like oh, of course she can just drop her work anytime because it's so easy. After a while, I got almost paranoid. I thought he was purposely interrupting my writing so my sermons wouldn't be as good as his. That's when I really turned off sexually." Peggy cried.

Stan looked astonished but sympathetic. He reached out, touched her knee, and said, "Why didn't you talk to me about it? If I had known how important it was to you, I'd have given up the sermons." Peggy said, "No, that wouldn't be the answer. We've got to deal with these feelings of competition and turf or they'll destroy us."

Stan added, "In retrospect, I think I sort of sensed Peggy's anger at me. I know I felt sexually rejected and put down. My ego was boosted by doing the sermons, but it was destroyed by feeling a sexual failure with Peggy. So after a while, I think I stopped initiating sex to avoid the blow to my ego if she said no or didn't respond."

As with some other couples we see, sex therapy with Peggy and Stan focused largely on couples' psychotherapy. They stayed in therapy for five months, addressing mainly nonsexual issues. At the end of that time, they felt more loving, less competitive, and a lot sexier.

More than half of American wives now hold jobs outside the home. Futurists predict that unless there is a prolonged, severe recession, this figure will continue to rise. This is simply one part of a larger picture of changing marital patterns. Keeping intimacy and a satisfying sex life alive in the face of frequent separations, competing demands for both spouses' time and emotions, and ever-changing priorities requires hard work and frequent recommitment to the relationship. It isn't easy. But it certainly isn't boring.

7

Sexual Disenchantment

IN our sex therapy work, we see a great many young couples, married anywhere from one to ten years, who complain that the excitement and passion have gone out of their marriage, that sex has lost its magic and is rather boring. Sometimes both partners feel this way, sometimes only one, but it is always deeply disturbing.

The survey we conducted in 1980 on sex and intimacy confirmed our clinical impression. The first year of an ongoing relationship was the year in which most people found sex most satisfying. After that, for women, there was a slow but steady decline in sexual satisfaction. For men, there was a sharp decrease in sexual satisfaction in the seventh through the tenth years. The survey showed that the average percentage of men who rated their sexual relationships as no better than fair during the first six years (14%) more than doubles (30.9%) for those in relationships that have lasted seven to ten years.

In asking ourselves what explanations can be offered for these findings, we have identified four factors we think help explain sexual disenchantment. They are (1) the long-term effect of stressful situations; (2) falling out of love; (3) habituation; and (4) pregnancy and parenthood.

Stress

Marriages don't exist apart from the rest of life. The quality of give-and-take and of sex between husband and wife are influenced by a thousand and one factors, from the economy to the weather. Certain stresses are likely to exist by about the seventh year of marriage: the initial stress of getting married and setting up one's own household, having one or two small children, the illness or death of a parent, early career pressures and beginning advancements, moving to a new apartment or buying a house, perhaps moving to a new community. Stress leads to anxiety, irritability, fatigue, physical symptoms, and distraction. Often we take our frustrations out on our spouse at the end of a tense day—a perfect antiaphrodisiac.

It often surprises us that couples who come to see us about a sex problem are not consciously aware of the impact life stresses have had on their sexual relationship. This seems to be particularly true of young couples. Perhaps they expect that they should be able to roll with the punches, and so they don't allow themselves to acknowledge disappointment, loss, or fear. Often we can be helpful simply by pointing out the significance of stress.

For example, a couple in their late twenties who were married for six years were puzzled by her loss of sexual interest and response in the last three years. As we always do, we encouraged them to tell us about what had been going on in their lives—not just to focus narrowly on the sexual problem. The wife, Sally, said, "Three years ago, my mother died of cancer after a long, painful illness. I was pregnant at the time. I wanted my mother to live to see her first grandchild, but she died when I was in my sixth month. I don't know if it was the stress, but anyway I gave birth prematurely to our twins—identical girls. Both babies were in intensive care for a few weeks."

We asked what had happened after the twins' birth. The husband, Greg, answered. "I think it was a terrible time for Sally. She'd always had a fantasy of her mother's living with us for a while after she had a baby, and she couldn't face the idea of replacing her mother with a hired nurse so she tried to manage on her own. Eventually she realized she couldn't handle it; who could?"

Sally talked about her feelings during these months. "I felt angry all the time. I was angry at Greg because he could escape to work every day and spent two nights a week playing squash. It wasn't fair to blame him. He was helping out a lot and begging me to get baby-sitters but somehow I couldn't. I felt trapped and helpless." What Sally couldn't acknowledge was all the anger she felt at being "abandoned" by her mother and at the twins for being two sick babies rather than one healthy one.

Meanwhile, Greg was under pressure on his job but didn't dare tell his wife, who, he said, already had enough to handle. When Greg felt anxious, he tended to want physical comforting and so reached out to his wife even more than before. She, unfortunately, tended to think that any touching was a request for intercourse and started to feel put upon by his "demands." Much of the therapy work with Sally and Greg revolved around helping them cope more effectively with the stresses in their lives, individually and as a couple. One of the most important lessons they had to learn was how to stay emotionally united in the face of stress—how not to let stress pull them apart when they most needed each other.

Sally had to learn that Greg's need for physical closeness wasn't always sexual. We asked them to touch and snuggle frequently, and to touch each other without clothes on but with boundaries— no genital touching and no intercourse. Sally was amazed to see that Greg could have an erection for a long time and still not feel he had to ejaculate.

At the end of the therapy, Greg said something that we believe to be true: "I don't think a marriage can survive unless you learn how to comfort each other when things get rough. But it's not easy to do. It's a matter of being able to say what you need, like, 'Hey, I need a back rub or I need to cry or maybe go out to the movies by myself.' But we don't want to be selfish so we try to tough it out. I see now that doesn't work. The trick is staying in touch—in every way."

Falling Out of Love

We all know about the realities of life, and we all know, intellectually at least, that marriage won't be perpetual bliss. But at another level of wish and fantasy and hope, we can't quite accept what we know. The ideal of the happy marriage is, after all, one of the central myths of our culture. Each generation embroiders the myth with special details, but "they lived happily ever after" has been with us for centuries. Problems arise because of our confusion about the word *happy*. Too often we think that being happily married means being in love the way we were once upon a time.

Experts are now telling us what wise people have always known intuitively—that the state of being in love is *always* temporary, lasting anywhere from six months to two years. When we are in love, we are in an abnormal state—obsessed by the one we adore, euphoric, in an almost constant state of sexual awareness, desire, and arousal. Lovemaking is marvelous even if it is awkward or downright inept. When this phase passes, many people panic. They think that they no longer have a happy marriage or any chance for one with this mate.

In Proust's novel *Swann's Way*, being in love ends in a single moment, as if a glass had shattered. But for most couples, it happens, mercifully, as a barely perceptible series of changes. The extraordinary becomes the ordinary; sexual awareness is less constant, less intense; and lovemaking loses some of its magic.

When this happens, something else must come in to fill the void or the marriage will be empty. The things that can and often do fill it are friendship and a calmer love, satisfying talk, humor, shared fun, children, friends, possessions, plans for a shared future, pride in each other as people, and, after a while, pride in the relationship and its history—and last but not least, fairly constant and enjoyable, if not ecstatic, sex.

If that sounds boring, it isn't. Or at least it doesn't have to be. Friends of ours who have been married for thirty-nine years tell us there are two secrets. One is really to enjoy the small pleasures of married intimacy, such as taking showers together, making out during commercial breaks in a late-night TV movie, having the fun of a "quickie" in the morning. The other secret is more elusive. It's managing somehow to have some magical moments when passion is just as intense, maybe more so, than in the earlier in-love stage. These moments usually happen after an intense emotional experience which can't be planned, but a bit of stage management can sometimes work. Our friends say they both remember a night when they were supposed to go out to a party but it started to snow and they decided to stay home instead. They cooked an omelet of leftovers and opened a bottle of wine they had been saving for ten years. Then they gathered all the blankets from their bed and put them in front of the fire, where they made love while the snow piled up outside.

Habituation

The husband and wife whose desire for each other decreases over time are demonstrating what seems to be a rule of mammalian nature. It is called *habituation.* In both rats and primates, when a male and female are together in a cage for a while, their rate of sexual intercourse declines until it reaches a plateau. When an unfamiliar female is placed in the cage instead of the familiar one, the *novelty effect* can be observed: The rate of intercourse soars, but only temporarily. Gradually habituation sets in and the frequency declines again.

Studies of the sexual behavior of married couples indicate a decline in frequency of intercourse over time. A recent study by Dr. Bill James at University College, London, showed that there is quite a marked decline in frequency of intercourse after the first year of marriage. Then there is a more gradual decline in the following decades. At age twenty-six to thirty, the frequency is about two or three times a week. At age thirty-one to forty, it is once or twice a week. By forty-one to fifty, it is twice in ten days, and past age fifty, once a week. Remarriage causes a temporary increase in frequency.

One of the recurrent issues in sex counseling is the difference between partners' desire for sexual activity once habituation sets in. In one survey, frequency of sexual activity was the subject couples talked about most if and when they did talk about sex. For thousands of respondents, it was the only subject.

For both men and women, sex serves more than one function. Yes, it is a behavior that reinforces closeness and trust and offers an opportunity to be open and spontaneous. It is also, quite simply, a release of tension. When a pattern is established that doesn't allow for sufficient release of tension, alternatives must be found. Easiest, of course, would be masturbation. And yet, surprisingly, countless millions of married couples look upon this option as inferior or taboo or as a sign of inadequacy in the marriage. As a result, sex between the couple has to carry the burden of being the way to resolve sexual tension while at the same time serving to promote intimacy.

The kind of problem that can develop is illustrated by Mr. and Mrs. E. Mrs. E. is four years older than Mr. E. Married when he was thirty and she was thirty-four, they were very sexually compatible at first. Mrs. E. was more experienced. She was fully aware of the satisfactions she derived from sex and played the initiator's role most of the time. Mr. E. was quick to learn. Gradually sexual intercourse became their only mode of sexual expression. Mr. E.

had been accustomed to masturbating two or three times a week, but in the six years of their marriage, he had not masturbated once.

Starting in the first year of their marriage, there were occasional times when Mrs. E. just wasn't interested in sex. At times, she would go ahead anyway. At other times, she simply said, "Not tonight." Mr. E. reacted by withdrawing. He had felt tense and was frustrated because he felt there was no outlet for the tension; so he turned inward. For a day at a time, he would not speak to his wife. Needless to say, Mrs. E. felt abandoned and very upset by his reaction. Still in the early years of marriage, the reaction could be accepted. However, by the time we saw Mr. and Mrs. E., the reaction had become exaggerated. Mr. E. would withdraw for as long as three days at a time. Mrs. E. became more frustrated, angry, and depressed and eventually developed the problem of loss of sexual desire.

Recognizing the need for various means of releasing sexual tension, the E.'s accepted the idea of engaging in other sexual behavior—including masturbation—which helped deal with the "sexual" aspects of sex without placing demands on the relationship. In only three weeks, Mrs. E. experienced a return of sexual feelings and began once again to share an initiating role. For the first time in their lives, the E.s talked about masturbation. Mrs. E. said she hadn't masturbated since she was sixteen and didn't want to, but she accepted the idea of her husband masturbating. She asked if she could be with him sometimes. At first he was self-conscious, but as he overcame his reluctance, he found it exciting. To her surprise, Mrs. E. found that watching him aroused her. Within a month, Mrs. E.'s level of sexual interest was, according to her, higher than ever and the E.s' sexual problems were solved.

Pregnancy and Parenthood

Most married couples want to have children. They look forward to it and think of being a family as one of the most important reasons for marriage. Ironically, becoming parents turns out to be one of the greatest stresses on the husband-wife bond. We discuss the sexual turning points of pregnancy and parenthood in the next section. We will just mention some of the factors here.

The physiological and psychological changes of pregnancy cause many women to feel decreased sexual interest, sometimes throughout pregnancy. The postpartum period has its own difficulties: decreased estrogen production may lead to vaginal dryness and slowness of sexual response; vaginitis is common; the wife is now very much *mother*, perhaps a less erotic figure. She is psychologically focused on the baby, and everyone is adjusting to the new family structure.

A study done in California in 1970 found that couples raising children were much more likely to be dissatisfied with their marriages than couples without children. The number of children didn't matter; it was the fact of parenthood itself that made the difference.

A survey we did also demonstrated what we call the Dennis the Menace effect—people with children at home rated their sexual satisfaction lower than others.

It is important to remember that we are only pointing out a statistical trend. Not all couples find the parenting years to be a sexual low point. Some couples have told us that their children added an important dimension to their sex life. One couple described the excitement of "hiding" from the kids the way they used to hide from parents when they were eighteen. Another couple felt that playing with their three small children had reminded them how nice it was to play, and they began to enjoy playful sex together—sex in a bubble bath, or her chasing him, or tickling each other. And certainly some women say that after they have given birth, they seem to enjoy sex more. Perhaps researchers should devote more time to studying the happy exceptions to life's problems!

8

Sexual Hurdles

IN approximately half of all marriages, there will be a serious sexual problem at some time. It is possible for a marriage to go on indefinitely, even happily, despite a sexual problem. A woman of about sixty-five once asked us, "What is an orgasm like?" When she heard the description, she thought for a moment and then said, "I don't think I've ever experienced that, but [winking at her husband] we've had a great sex life for forty-five years, so I guess we're doing *something* right and I don't care what it's called." We have even seen couples who had what is technically called an un-consummated marriage—they've *never* been able to have inter-course—but other than that, they are very sexually satisfied and regularly make love in other ways.

For other couples, a sexual problem can be a major turning point in the marriage. If it is not dealt with, the problem often becomes worse, compounded by guilt, anger, mutual accusations, and lowered self-esteem. A man's problem can trigger a problem in his wife and vice versa. The inability to talk about what is going on sexually can cast a pall over the entire relationship.

Of course, a sexual problem is often not the initiating distress but can be the end result of relationship problems, stress, illness, loss, or other upheavals. Here, however, we want to examine the effect of the sexual problem itself. Interestingly, the effect is not necessarily negative—at least not in the long run. Like any other life crisis or turning point, it is a hurdle; jumping it successfully can start couples down a new and better path.

Premature Ejaculation

Kinsey believed that ejaculating rapidly was biologically normal. He may have been right, but couples aren't looking at this question as biologists. What people are concerned with is their own satisfaction and their partner's. Premature ejaculation is only a problem if it interferes with your pleasure. Sometimes a man tends to ejaculate within ten seconds after entering the vagina but his partner doesn't care; either she comes as quickly as he does, or she doesn't care if she has her orgasm when he's inside her—in fact, intercourse itself isn't so important to either of them. So why call that *premature* ejaculation? It isn't too premature for mutual pleasure; therefore it isn't premature.

But what if a woman wants an hour of vigorous thrusting to feel satisfied and her partner can "only" last forty minutes; is that premature ejaculation? It seems unreasonable to give it that label. We actually worked with a couple who had this complaint. You may not be surprised to learn that their underlying problem wasn't sexual at all—at least not in the sense of "in-bed" sexual; it was a power struggle. Once she gave up the idea that he owed her an hour of thrusting to make up for certain grievances, she found that she really didn't need such a long time. She had to learn to ask him to meet her emotional needs, and he had to stop withholding approval and affection.

There are two kinds of premature ejaculation in which there can be no doubt about the problem. The first is when the man ejaculates before there is vaginal penetration. We once worked with a man who found his fiancée's voice so arousing that he occasionally ejaculated while talking to her on the telephone— with no other physical stimulus. Men may come from kissing, rubbing against a woman, receiving the slightest manual stimulation, or from pressing against the vaginal opening. If it happens once in a while, it's not a problem, but if it is a pattern that makes intercourse impossible, it is.

The other form of premature ejaculation that can be labeled with certainty is less common, and most people have never heard of it; it is ejaculation that takes place without an erection having formed. Ejaculation is a reflex reaction, and erection is not necessary. Men who ejaculate without erection have often been conditioned to react that way by early experiences, for example, learning to masturbate by pressing against a bed.

The complicating factor in diagnosing premature ejaculation is the fact that there may be no overt sign of a problem. A couple may kiss, fondle, have intercourse for five minutes, and both have an orgasm. The hidden problem lies in his head and maybe also in hers. He is nervous even before they kiss because he is already planning how he will manage not to come too quickly. He maneuvers his body so that she doesn't touch his penis very much because he wants to avoid "too much" stimulation. He has already told her, ages ago, that he doesn't like her to stimulate his penis with her mouth, so she never does. Actually that is his favorite fantasy, but he's terrified he would lose all control and come in her mouth, and he is convinced that a good lover should hold back so that he can satisfy his partner during intercourse. During much of the kissing and fondling, he does not allow himself to have very stimulating fantasies, and once intercourse has begun, he actually distracts himself by thinking of nonarousing situations or tasks. He can only allow part of his attention to be directed toward his wife. He has to monitor her responses and stimulate her expertly. When she has her orgasm, he allows himself to let go, and then he ejaculates.

She may know nothing of this, although she may complain that technically he's a good lover but "there's something missing." Or she may be aware of his concern about coming too quickly and may do her own private mental gymnastics to try to be sure it all works out.

They have a problem with premature ejaculation.

What can be done about premature ejaculation? There are a few simple principles and suggestions.

- Abstinence usually predisposes a man toward ejaculating more rapidly. If a man is accustomed to ejaculating every day, then even three days' abstinence may lead to a faster-than-usual ejaculation.
- Some couples find that increasing the frequency of lovemaking helps too-rapid ejaculation.
- Some couples have adapted to premature ejaculation by allowing the man to ejaculate quickly and then resuming stimulation and intercourse. Some men will then go on to have a second

orgasm. This adaptation tends to be easier for the younger man, who is more likely to regain full erection soon after he has ejaculated.

- There is a procedure, called the valsalva maneuver, which can help delay ejaculation. When he feels close to coming (but not on the very brink), he should hold his breath and bear down as if he were going to move his bowels. It is best if partners have discussed using this procedure before he tries it.
- There are two techniques commonly used in sex therapy that can be tried by a couple. One is called the squeeze technique. This involves the woman squeezing the penis firmly around the ridge near the tip of the penis and pressing on the underside where a small strand of tissue from the shaft joins the tip (the glans). The squeeze is applied when the man feels he is close to ejaculation. The other technique, called the start-stop, is described in detail in a later sex therapy case.

Ejaculatory Inhibition

Women are not the only ones to have trouble reaching an orgasm; some men have the same difficulty. The married couples who have sought our help with this problem have often been more concerned about infertility than sexual pleasure, particularly if the husband can manage to ejaculate by way of manual stimulation but is unable to ejaculate in his wife's vagina. Ironically, the husband's inability to climax during intercourse is not uncommonly due to (unconscious) fears of pregnancy. Other specific fears or past traumas may also be involved. In one of Masters and Johnson's more dramatic cases, the ejaculatory inhibition began when the husband walked in on his wife and her lover just as the lover was ejaculating inside his wife. Generally speaking, this is a problem that requires professional help.

A less severe form of ejaculatory inhibition is seen in the man who requires very prolonged stimulation before he can ejaculate. One woman described a situation in which she stimulated her husband's penis with her hand for up to an hour and a half. She said, "He's very particular about how it's done, and if I move or do anything that is not what he is used to, it throws him off and just ruins the whole thing." Obviously sex for them had become an arduous, tense task—both of them focusing anxiously on making him come, and worrying every moment that something might go wrong.

We know that sexual arousal and the release of orgasm has an enormous psychic component. This couple seemed to have forgotten that. They were acting as though sex equaled friction. We helped them become less focused on forcing his orgasm. He needed to feel that she was enjoying touching his penis. In fact, that was a new idea to her. Once she gave up "working" on him, she did begin to find his erection more of a turn-on. He also had to give up his goal-oriented approach. It wasn't easy for this man, since his personality was geared toward compulsive hard work. He had to practice being hedonistic and relinquishing control over his body, but eventually he was able to ejaculate more spontaneously.

Perhaps most common among men who have difficulty ejaculating are unexpressed feelings of hurt, rejection, and anger. The men are often unaware that they are suppressing their reactions to feeling hurt or put down. An accumulation of these hurts can cause a sexual problem in a man who may appear cheerful but whose every smile masks underlying anger. Most sex therapists would therefore agree that getting couples to share their hurt and angry feelings is an integral part of sex therapy. It is akin to getting the poison out of the system, for unexpressed feelings lead to psychological distancing, which in turn only serves to deepen a couple's problems. Men with ejaculatory inhibition who learn to deal with their hurt and angry feelings often find that their sexual problem disappears.

Problems with Erection

No sexual difficulty creates half so much anxiety as the failure to get or keep an erection, and yet, at some time or other, virtually every man has this experience. It is generally not considered to be a significant problem unless it happens more than a quarter of the times a couple wants to make love.

Until very recently, professionals believed that almost all chronic erectile difficulties were caused by psychological factors, but now a variety of physical factors have been identified and it is quite likely that there are still more as yet undiscovered physical factors. We know now that some medications (e.g., some antihypertensive drugs), illness (e.g., diabetes), and blood-flow irregularities in the penis can contribute to erectile difficulties. It appears that any medical condition or medication that affects the ability to receive sensory stimulation or that interferes with the normal flow of blood or the ability of muscles to become tense can interfere with sexual response. Psychological disorders such as depression and some psychiatric drugs can also be implicated. For these reasons, careful evaluation should *always* include a medical history and physical examination.

In the course of a marriage, there are moments when some problems with erection which, if not to be expected, then at least need not come as a complete surprise. These moments include some of the turning points we have already discussed: getting married, deciding to have a baby, and so on. Others may include a husband losing his job or receiving some other blow to his self-esteem, such as discovering a wife's secret affair, or his being involved in extramarital sex that causes him conflict. There are also recurrent factors that can cause a single episode of loss of erection: fatigue, alcohol, unexpressed anger, reaction to a wife's lack of lubrication. Male anxiety about possibly hurting a female during sex is one of the more common factors in erectile difficulty that many people—including professionals—fail to recognize.

Sex therapists are aware that when the occasional problem with erection starts to become chronic (and if there are no biological causes), *spectatoring* is surely involved. Spectatoring is when the man and his wife are both anxiously focusing on his erection. Is he getting hard? Will it last? What on earth will we do if he loses it? Should we hurry on to intercourse while he's still hard? Often the husband is sure his wife will be angry or despise him if he can't "perform." Occasionally he is right, and she *is* angry. She believes that he can control his erection and that if he were attracted to her, then of course he would get an erection.

Men cannot will themselves to become erect, and if a man thinks his wife is demanding an erection, he is much more likely to have problems. We did hear one story, perhaps apocryphal, about a wife who used to snap her fingers at her husband and say, "Okay, get it up now!"

Many wives, in an effort to be helpful, will use oral stimulation of the penis, assuming that this will produce an erection. In fact, if it is used when there is no erection, fellatio can feel like a demand to produce an erection. "After all," he thinks, "if she's giving me the *ultimate* stimulation, I've just *got* to respond."

When a husband and wife are focused on "Will he or won't

he?" and he does, but then loses it, they often panic or give up in despair. In fact, erections grow and subside somewhat as a natural part of the so-called excitement phase, and even a complete loss of erection doesn't have to mean the end of everything. Given *relaxed* and arousing sex play, it is likely to return. And even if it doesn't, sex play without an erection can be marvelous.

One of the destructive offshoots of a chronic problem with erection is the breakdown in communication between husband and wife. As one woman sardonically stated, "Instead of his penis, it was a wall that got erected between us." She went on to say, "At first, I didn't talk about it because I didn't want to make a big deal over the fact. Then, as time went on and it happened more often, I had all these feelings. One minute I felt angry, the next I felt sad and sorry for him. I wanted to say something—*anything*. I couldn't find the right words. I thought he'd think I was disappointed, which I sort of was, but I know a wife's not supposed to pressure. Then one night when it didn't work, I started to cry, really out of control. It startled my husband and got him very upset.

"The next day I decided to take the plunge and so I said something like, 'We have to talk about our sex problem.' I said 'our,' not 'your' but he still reacted badly. He said, very loud and defensive, 'What do you mean, *problem*? I think we do okay.' After that, I tried a few more times to talk, and he always said he didn't want to discuss it. He told me talking would only make it worse. Then one night, out of the blue, he came home and said he was ready to talk about it. I guess he just needed some time to think about it, but I wonder what would've happened if he never decided to talk."

This couple came for sex therapy, but some couples try to solve the problem on their own. There are no statistics on the effectiveness of self-help, so we're not sure whether it is or is not advisable. As therapists, we tend to see the couples for whom reading and self-help approaches have not been successful.

The Issue of Sexual Desire

The commonest sexual issue between married couples is a perceived or real difference between their levels of sex "drive." We put the word *drive* in quotation marks because it implies a biological energy source with a fixed intensity. Sexual interest is really much more complex than that. Yes, there are inborn differences between people, and yes, biological variables do matter. But sexual interest is also influenced by love, anger, fatigue, the setting, extraneous worries and distractions, one's sense of the importance of sex, and a thousand and one nuances in a couple's relationship. It is very easy for myths to replace reality—the myth that he is oversexed, that she is insatiable, or that either he or she is a "low-drive" person.

When there appears to be a marked difference in the level of sexual interest between a husband and wife, the difference can become exaggerated over time because a kind of scarcity-economy psychology can take over; sex is "hoarded." The more interested spouse tries to take advantage of any favorable moment. In fact, the less interested spouse often does the same thing. For example, a woman who feels that she seldom wants sex while her husband "always" wants it will think to herself, "This would be a good night for me to initiate something because I'm not feeling too negative about it and I don't have to get up early tomorrow and besides, maybe that will keep him satisfied for a while and he won't bother me over the weekend."

Sometimes exactly the opposite happens. Instead of seeking every possible opportune moment, the couple gives up. Each feels so battered and bruised by the emotional battles over sex that they do nothing rather than risk another battle. For example, Susan, a twenty-seven-year-old, told us, "I was the one who got things going between us ninety percent of the time. It was all right with me at first, but over the past two years, Bill's lack of enthusiasm started to get to me. Every time he said no, it hurt more and more. It hurt most when I sensed he was trying subterfuges to avoid the issue, like pretending to be asleep when I came out of the bathroom or complaining about a stomachache at ten P.M. so I'd keep away at eleven P.M. So I just gave up. I decided I'd wait for him to get interested. The result is, we have sex maybe once every three weeks."

Clearly one of the central problems in Susan and Bill's case was absence of communication. Sometimes the failure to communicate comes about very slowly, simply by allowing "little" things to go by.

Not long ago, a couple came to us in a state of rage after he had called her frigid and she had screamed back that he was "sick and oversexed and should see a shrink." As the story unfolded it became clear that this couple loved each other and had no tangible sexual problem. They just didn't understand what the other was all about sexually.

Beth and Gary had lived together for two years and been married for four. Their sex life had been great at first, then slackened off but was still satisfying until Beth went off birth control pills and got a diaphragm. Gary hated the smell and taste of the contraceptive jelly but didn't want to complain because he felt it was Beth's "right" to go off pills, and he knew he didn't want to use a condom. He didn't say anything, but gradually his stimulating her orally, which had been a fairly regular practice, became less and less frequent until he stopped it altogether. Beth felt hurt, deprived, and angry but didn't say anything. She assumed he had never really liked cunnilingus anyway. In a kind of retaliation, she stopped stimulating him orally and he made the same mistaken assumption—that she had always done it as a kind of duty to please him. In time, Gary began to feel that the zest had gone out of their sex life. His mother had always made it clear that sex was a woman's burden, so he was predisposed to seeing women this way. He began to think that Beth was simply putting up with sex, although she in fact enjoyed it. He bought some sex how-to books and some soft-porn magazines and left them around, trying to communicate his need for variety and excitement. Beth, unfortunately, reacted defensively ("Does he think there's something wrong with me?") and decided Gary was obsessed with "dirty" sex. An argument over something trivial triggered the name calling. When Beth and Gary were able to hear one another's stories, they were amazed. They had constructed a wall between them. Each brick in the wall was an issue that had gone undiscussed, a wrong guess about the other's motives, an unearned label, or an unexpressed feeling. In just over an hour of honest communication, most of that wall had come down.

There are some common misconceptions, which tend to aggravate the problem of a discrepancy in sexual desire between spouses. One is the assumption that each and every sexual interaction should be a totally shared experience in which both partners are aroused, active, and (usually) have his-and-her orgasms. This is the way sex is invariably portrayed in novels and films. It is a very unrealistic picture. We don't expect always to be equally hungry or to feel the same amount of enthusiasm for every party we ever attend, so why should we expect uniform reactions about sex?

Once we give up the notion of the absolutely equal sexual experience, we are much freer to explore options. One option, which Masters and Johnson call "be my guest," involves the less aroused partner providing stimulation for the more aroused. As long as a woman is lubricated, she can go ahead and have intercourse even if she feels only the mildest responses herself. It can be very nice—a chance to give, to watch his pleasure without trying to will yourself to respond or summon energy when you'd rather be passive.

While husbands can't as easily have intercourse unless they are aroused, it can be done. Erection happens early in the sexual response cycle—as early as lubrication in the woman—so a man can have intercourse without being *very* turned on and without even approaching a climax.

Alternatively, of course, there are hands, mouths, and shared masturbation. None of these options need be thought of as second best or a sign of failure in the sexual relationship. They are a way of matching sexual behavior to the complex rhythms of two people with individual needs and moods that can be very liberating.

The other misconception that tends to aggravate desire problems is the idea that desire is like a purple kangaroo; you are sure to notice it and recognize it when you see it. In fact, desire can be terribly elusive. We can be turned on, as measured by our physiological responses, and still be absolutely certain that we are feeling nothing erotic at all. Ask yourself if you have ever had this experience. You have not had sex for a week; neither have you masturbated. You aren't even thinking about it. If someone asked if you were feeling horny you would say no or "I'm not sure." And then your partner begins to touch you and two minutes later you recognize that you are a mass of urgent sexual needs.

This phenomenon is so common, particularly among women, that Kinsey came to the (false) conclusion that women don't have premonitory desires at all. He said that women must be physically stimulated before they can feel sexual desires.

Sex therapists sometimes recommend keeping a desire diary. That consists of randomly stopping what you are doing about half a dozen times a day and asking yourself, "On a scale of one to ten, how interested in sex am I at this very moment?" This can help you tune in to your body's more subtle messages. It also helps the so-called oversexed partner recognize that there are plenty of times when he or she has absolutely no interest in sex.

Sexual Aversion

At the extreme end of the spectrum of desire problems, there are some people who are very fearful of sex—usually of any kind of sexual interaction, not just intercourse. Aversion is more likely to occur in women, but men can also be aversive. Aversion can be confusing because once the fear is past, on a given occasion, it is possible to be responsive, enjoy sex, and have an orgasm. Yet the fear recurs virtually every time.

One young woman who had been married for three years found that she could usually get past her vague sense of dread when her husband began to touch her by concentrating on a sensuous fantasy of floating on a rubber raft in the sunshine. Gradually, however, her fantasy stopped working, and she began trying to avoid sex altogether. Her fears had started when she was sixteen and was almost raped by three boys. They had been touching and undressing her, shouting humiliating taunts and threats. An adult chanced to come on the scene and prevented the rape, but from then on, sexual "preliminaries" were anxiety-filled moments. She had never told her husband about the near-rape because, like so many victims, she had always felt that she was in some way to blame. Telling him was taking the first step toward overcoming her fears.

Aversion is not always traceable to so dramatic a trauma. Its origins are sometimes rather obscure, and self-help is often insufficient. When it is a man who is aversive, there is the additional problem that intense sexual anxiety is so completely at variance with an idealized male image. One man told us that he thought he would have been less ashamed to have leprosy than to be fearful of sex. He also expressed a feeling commonly stated by people with this problem. "One thing that bothers me a lot is how unfair it is to Janet [his wife]," he said. "She's not the cause of it. *She* doesn't intimidate me. If anything, she's supergentle and accepting. So why do I feel like this with her?"

It is the apparent irrationality of the feeling—its inappropriateness here and now, with this man or with this woman whom I love and trust—that can cause the greatest emotional pain of sexual aversion.

Sex therapy and/or psychotherapy are often helpful *if* the problem is diagnosed correctly. The partner plays a very crucial role. Like Janet, the wife just mentioned, the spouse must be patient, accepting, not pushy and yet not a self-effacing doormat. Unresolved sexual aversion is very stressful for a relationship, but couples who manage to work it through together are some of the closest couples we've ever seen.

Female Orgasm and Its Problems

Female orgasm is one of the most controversial subjects in all of sexology. Everyone has had something to say about it, sometimes influenced more by a theoretical or even political viewpoint than by observations or research. When Freud and, later, neo-Freudians were considered the reigning experts on female orgasm, we were told:

• *Sigmund Freud:* "The sexual function of many women is crippled by their obstinately clinging to this clitoris excitability."
• *Marie Bonaparte:* "Vaginal sensitivity in coitus . . . is largely based . . . on the child's immense masochistic beating fantasies. In coitus the woman, in effect, is subjected to a sort of beating by the man's penis. This sensitivity must be deep and truly vaginal."
• *Helene Deutsch:* Intercourse must be experienced "in a feminine dynamic way—not transformed into an act of erotic play or sexual equality." She described two kinds of orgasm, "malicious" and "benevolent." If there was erotic play including the clitoris, the orgasm was "malicious."

Then along came Masters and Johnson's research. They didn't rule out the pleasures of intercourse for women; they simply emphasized the importance of the clitoris. The publication of their findings happened to coincide with the rise of the women's movement in the early seventies. Some feminists incorrectly read their discoveries as saying that the clitoris is everything. For example, Mette Eiljerson wrote that intercourse "is completely devoid of sensation for the woman."

Now there is new information about vaginal sensitivity with the discovery of the famous "G spot." The finding was reported almost simultaneously by an Israeli gynecologist and by a team of sex researchers in the United States. They both describe an area of great erotic sensitivity about an inch or two inside the vagina on the anterior wall (the upper wall, when you lie on your back. When this bean-size spot is stroked firmly, with pressure, it enlarges. At first, many women report a vaguely uncomfortable sensation, but then the feeling changes to intense sexual sensations. In many intercourse positions, the penis rubs against this spot, apparently accounting for some of the pleasurable feelings during intercourse.

We need to be wary of experts who state that you *should* feel this way or that way or else you aren't normal. Women's sexual responses are complex, individual, and will vary, in the same woman, over time. The range of physiological reactions, feelings, and attitudes is very great. Ignorance and anxiety about being "normal" create problems when no problems need exist.

The whole debate about clitoral versus vaginal orgasm will probably die a natural death, done in by its own irrelevance. Hopefully, we are already past the era in which women of intelligence stayed in psychoanalysis for ten years, searching for the "right" kind of orgasm. Many women still do worry about their need for clitoral stimulation. Here, for example, is a letter we received not long ago, typical of *hundreds* of such letters we have received on the subject.

I was a virgin and very sexually inexperienced when I got married two years ago. Our sex life wasn't bad but I didn't have any orgasms. Then, a few months ago, my husband said he read somewhere that he should touch my clitoris while we're having intercourse. It does seem to help although I have only had a few orgasms and sometimes I'm sore afterward. What I would like you to tell me is this: is it a normal practice, and can it hurt me in any way? Also, how can we improve on the results?

This was our response:

Studies suggest that at least half of all women need to have some direct stimulation of the clitoral area in order to climax. This stimulation might come from a hand (yours or his), the man's leg or pelvis, or even a vibrator. There is nothing abnormal or unusual in such practices.

The fact that you are sore afterward suggests that your husband may be rubbing or pressing too hard. Perhaps he thinks this is the right way to stimulate the clitoris. Actually there is no one right way. Different women enjoy different kinds of touching of the clitoris. You could experiment with a variety of touches. You may find that light pressure feels just as nice or even nicer than firm pressure.

Many people are confused about just where to touch. The clitoris is mostly covered by a hood of skin. (If you don't know what we're describing, look at your genitals in a mirror and become familiar with the anatomy.) The tip of the clitoris peeps out from under the hood. Many women say that direct touching on the tip of the clitoris is not arousing because it is almost uncomfortably sensitive. Usually the most pleasurable sensations come from stroking the hood over or alongside the body of the clitoris with one or two fingers, but some women prefer more generalized pressure on the area with, for example, the heel of the hand.

Preferences in clitoral stimulation can be highly idiosyncratic. Some women say they only get feeling from rubbing one side of the clitoris, not the other side. Other women find that only a circular motion is arousing.

It is also important to know that the clitoris undergoes changes as you respond sexually. When you become aroused, and particularly if there is stimulation to the clitoral area, the clitoris enlarges and stiffens (although in some women this is barely noticeable). Then, as you become more aroused, the clitoris retracts up underneath the hood and its tip is no longer visible. You may find that the kind of stimulation you prefer will vary depending on your stage of arousal.

We often recommend that women experiment with touching themselves as a way of learning their particular pattern and as a way of pleasuring themselves. Self-touching can also be carried into lovemaking. Once a woman learns how to stimulate her own clitoris, she is often much better at it than her partner. During intercourse, it is often more effective for the woman to touch her own clitoris. Some people say they don't like this idea because they believe the partner should provide all the stimulation. Some women worry that their partners will feel put down or useless. You could talk this idea over with your partner. You may well find that he not only accepts the idea but welcomes it and may find it is sexually stimulating for him.

Once you have a better idea of how to stimulate yourself, you can try guiding your partner's hand with yours. Some guidance from you can become part of your pattern of lovemaking, since it is virtually impossible for your partner to know exactly how to stimulate you from moment to moment.

Some women worry whether it is normal to have an orgasm "only" from oral stimulation. It is certainly a common enough pattern. If it feels nice and is satisfying, why label it a problem?

Another fairly fruitless quest has been for the simultaneous orgasm as the "proper" way for a couple to climax. Along with vaginal orgasms, this commandment from on high (actually a favorite idea of one man who wrote a popular marriage manual of the 1920s and 1930s, Theodor H. Van De Velde), is losing its influence. Yes, it can be nice for a man and woman to reach orgasm at the same instant, but it can be at least as nice for them to watch and share in one another's orgasms at separate moments.

The majority of women do not have an orgasm every time they have the opportunity. Masters and Johnson somewhat arbitrarily mark the "normal" cutoff point at between 50 percent and 70 percent of opportunities. One of the variables in female sexual response is the menstrual cycle. Hormones do influence responsiveness, but researchers disagree about exactly how this operates. Some studies have shown that orgasm is most likely to occur at mid-cycle; others indicate that heightened responsiveness occurs the week before menstruation. Some women are sure that their peak time is *during* menstruation.

Men sometimes expect their partners to have an orgasm every time they make love. They may see a woman's orgasm as a measure of their prowess, or they simply want sex to be "fair." When men pressure women to have an orgasm, it usually has the opposite effect. She becomes anxious about producing an orgasm, and the anxiety can interfere with her ability to abandon herself to her sexual feelings.

Then there is the question of multiple orgasms. Now that we know it is possible, we could get hung up on this as a performance demand. If my friend Stephanie can have ten orgasms in a row, shouldn't I be able to have at *least* five? But not all women have multiple orgasms. Some have one, feel satisfied, and find it a chore to keep going. Why *should* they keep going?

Apart from how our bodies react or don't react, many of us worry about what goes on in our heads. If we don't have sexual fantasies, we wonder why not. Actually, we all probably do have sexual fantasies, but they may not resemble the ones you read about in magazines, novels, or books that compile fantasies. Not all sexual fantasies are stories. They aren't even necessarily visual. We asked a woman who said she never had a sexual fantasy to tell us what went on in her mind during lovemaking. She had to concentrate to capture it, but then she responded, "I'm very intensely aware of what my husband is doing to me. Like, if his hand is on my breast, I think I'm sort of *in* my breast. Or when we have intercourse, I feel as if I *am* my vagina, feeling him move in and out." She added, "Oh, I guess you could call that a fantasy, couldn't you?"

The content of their sexual fantasies, or having an orgasm stimulated by a magazine or an X-rated film, makes some women nervous. Many women are concerned because they find it exciting to look at the pictures in their husband's *Playboy*. This letter is an example.

I never had an orgasm with my husband until we went to an X-rated movie together. That night I had an orgasm, and since then I've been able to have an orgasm only if I think about scenes from that movie. The orgasms are getting better, but the guilt and shame of the way I have them are increasing and I'm getting very reluctant to make love. I want to be excited by my husband and the way he makes me feel, and I try to have an orgasm the natural way, but I can't get excited enough. My mind wanders on to problems—anything—even though I try to concentrate on what's going on. I feel I'm betraying my husband. Please help me.

We replied to this woman in this way:

A study by Barbara Hariton and Jerome Singer demonstrated that women experienced sexual fantasies during intercourse, that such fantasies increased sexual desire and pleasure and were *not* related to neurotic daydreams and problems of relationship, competence, or enjoyment of sexual activities. So the fact that you conjure up a sexual fantasy when you make love is not abnormal, although it is something you obviously feel upset about.

The sources of the imagery women conjure up during sex are quite varied—memory, invented scenarios, scenes from books or movies. The fantasies' themes are also varied—from "romantic" scenes to intercourse with their regular partner to the most far-out situations involving acts or people that may be strictly off limits for actual behavior.

The fact that sexual fantasies often include forbidden acts can make them a source of anxiety. Women who are aroused by the fantasy of being forced into sex or by imagining two women making love may wonder if they unconsciously wish to be raped or are homosexual. Fantasies are usually *not* a guide to what people want to do; they are mental games, a source of erotic arousal, a way of experiencing the forbidden, and—last but not least—they are a way of concentrating on something, which helps many people get turned on or have orgasms.

This last point is particularly relevant to your situation. You say that you were not having orgasms with your husband for a while, but that since seeing the X-rated film, you have been able to achieve orgasm regularly. The night you saw the film, its imagery stayed with you, and you probably imagined a scene in the film rather spontaneously during lovemaking. It had the effect of heightening your arousal, and perhaps most important, it kept your mind off the question, "Will I have an orgasm this time?"

As sex therapists, we know that nervously watching for an orgasm is almost sure to block it. We often recommend that a woman try to have some kind of fantasy, either sexual or sensual—like swimming or lying in the sun—when she feels close to orgasm. If you are picturing yourself luxuriating in soft sand or imagining something supremely sexy, you won't have time to worry about orgasm—it will just happen.

You say that you want to have an orgasm the "natural" way. There is no one way that is natural for everyone. What turns a person on or helps trigger orgasm is highly individual and will even vary somewhat in the same person on different occasions. Sexual response is always a complex blend of feelings, touch, imagery, the setting, and so on. What matters is your being comfortable with your individual self rather than trying to fit some imagined norm of how one ought to feel.

You seem to have an idea that you should be responding solely to your husband's lovemaking, that your fantasies are a betrayal of him. This amount of guilt is obviously harmful. You already find that you are withdrawing from sex. That certainly won't help! Many people have found that they can tell their partner about the kind of sexual fantasies they are having. The partner is often relieved and responds by sharing some of his or her own fantasies. This can promote a special, trusting intimacy.

Somewhere between 7 and 10 percent of American women never have an orgasm. The percentage may well be decreasing now with all the self-help books, groups for women, and couples' sex therapy that is available.

Why should a woman never, ever have an orgasm? The reasons are remarkably varied and individual. There can be deep-seated psychological blocks: all sex is sex with my father, therefore I can't enjoy it; orgasm is equated with death; I can't have a pleasure my mother never had; orgasm equals loss of control over rage and aggression. More commonly it is a combination of relatively minor factors: fear of the unknown, trying too hard so that sex is always tense, not knowing how to go about it, fear of looking or acting foolish.

A woman may never have had an orgasm because she has never tried to masturbate and her sexual partner(s) haven't been very adept or considerate, or perhaps they have had a sexual dysfunction. The most common male dysfunction accompanying lack of orgasm in the woman is premature ejaculation. Sometimes it's simply a matter of the woman and/or her partner trying too hard to "achieve" her orgasm and, instead, creating anxiety. Sometimes it's simply a lack of learning, skill, and experience.

There are several books on the market that help women learn to have orgasms, first through masturbation, then with a partner. An excellent one is Lonnie Barbach's *For Yourself*. There are so-called preorgasmic groups for women in many communities now, which also approach learning to have an orgasm through masturbation. Led by skilled and experienced people, the success rate for these groups is about 80 to 90 percent. Couples' sex therapy can also be effective. Some women find it easier to let go sexually with their husbands than in masturbation. The couple approach would probably be preferable for them.

There are women who can have an orgasm during masturbation but not with their husbands. Sometimes this is a question of technique. For example, a woman may come to orgasm through very precise and delicate touching on one side of her clitoris. It may be almost impossible for her husband to duplicate this stimulation and she may have difficulty learning a new pattern of response that will bring her to orgasm. If it is acceptable to the couple, there really isn't any reason they shouldn't just enjoy lovemaking and let her touch her own clitoris, perhaps during intercourse or before or after—or all three!

People can also learn new patterns of response by very gradually varying the pattern each time.

We have already alluded to one aspect of the man's role in all this. It is counterproductive if he is overly eager; if the woman feels him as observer, teacher, or policeman. He must give her room and time, get out of her way and let her experience what she can. His most valuable gift would be his own sexual pleasure and excitement. We tend to mirror one another.

Pain with Sex

We'd all like lovemaking to be joyful and pleasurable—but that's not always the case. Almost all of us, it seems, have some pain with sex now and then. Some of the causes may be technical: For example, penetration may be uncomfortable simply because the angle of entry is wrong, or because there hasn't been enough foreplay for a woman to become lubricated. Pain also may occur at certain times of the month. Around the time of ovulation, a woman's ovary or the area around it may be quite sensitive and tender, making intercourse uncomfortable for a day or two.

None of these types of occasional pain with sex is reason to worry. It's important, though, to discuss any discomfort with your partner. If one person tries to hide pain or discomfort, the other usually senses that something is wrong and becomes vaguely anxious. Also, keeping such a secret gradually breeds resentment in the partner who feels the pain and eventually creates an emotional distance in the relationship. By talking to one another, you'll be able to work things out together when either of you feels discomfort.

On the other hand, it is not normal to have pain with sex time after time (and by *sex* we mean all forms of sexual stimulation, as well as intercourse). If you regularly have painful sex, it's likely that there's a medical reason for your discomfort, and we urge you to visit a professional. In almost every case, such pain can be eliminated. Here are the common medical causes of painful sex—all of which are treatable.

VAGINISMUS

Vaginismus is the involuntary tensing of the muscles at the vaginal opening. It makes penetration uncomfortable and difficult or, in some instances, impossible. It is a very widespread problem that often goes undiagnosed even when a gynecological examination is done.

It is characteristic of mild vaginismus that the pain usually subsides once the penis has penetrated. The sensation is often described as an uncomfortable burning sensation.

What causes vaginismus? Essentially it is a response to the fear of penetration. This fear is usually the fear of pain. When a woman has had experiences of painful penetration (from tampons, medical examinations and procedures, or intercourse), she comes to expect that penetration will hurt. The vaginismus is rather like a flinch when someone goes to touch an injured part of your body. It is an involuntary, self-protection reaction. Psychological factors may also be involved, such as reluctance to have intercourse, fear of pregnancy, or anger at one's partner.

Vaginismus is 99 percent curable, but the ease of treatment varies. Some women develop vaginismus after many years of comfortable penetration. Perhaps a series of painful pelvic examinations or an untreated vaginitis has disrupted their pattern. Usually such women can overcome their muscle spasms easily. Other women who have been severely traumatized (rape victims, for example) or who have never experienced comfortable penetration will usually find they need professional help.

Whether on her own or with the guidance of a professional, the fundamentals and the procedures are the same. The basic idea is for the woman to teach herself that vaginal penetration can be comfortable. In order to do this, she must abstain from intercourse while she takes the first steps. She begins by practicing inserting something that is totally comfortable (a lubricated finger or small dilator) and slowly, over the course of days or weeks, builds up to the point where she can insert something about the width of an erect penis without any discomfort. Then she is ready to move on to intercourse, preferably in a female-above position. She must guide the penis, going slowly, *not doing anything that hurts*. If need be, she will stop. Knowing that she is in control of what will happen is half the battle. Her partner's patience and cooperation is the other half.

We mention a dilator because many physicians and sex therapists have a standard set of dilators in graduated sizes that are used to treat vaginismus. The woman takes the dilators home and uses them daily. We must emphasize that the use of the dilator is to have the experience of vaginal penetration both without pain and with a sense of self-control.

Vaginismus has been and will continue to be mentioned frequently in this book because it is so very common and so often goes undiagnosed. The education of doctors and nurses has lagged in the area of sexual problems in general but more particularly with vaginismus. There are two reasons for this. The first is that until very recently, vaginismus was defined as muscle spasm that made entry of the penis *impossible*. Such extreme vaginismus is relatively rare, and therefore attention was hardly ever directed toward it.

The second reason for underdiagnosis is simply the ease with which it can be overlooked. When a doctor performs an internal vaginal examination, he or she can usually manage to insert a speculum or two fingers even if the vaginal muscles are in spasm.

Many women don't complain about the discomfort because they assume it is a normal part of being examined. It isn't—or at least it shouldn't be. If the doctor does become aware of the woman's discomfort, it is often dismissed as tension due to the examination, which it may be. However, the woman whose muscles tense strongly during a pelvic examination often has the same reaction to her partner's penis. Ideally, the doctor who notices the tension should ask the woman about her experience with intercourse.

Until education catches up with medical professionals, women may have to diagnose themselves or at least ask a doctor whether they might have vaginismus and not wait for the doctor to notice the symptom.

MONILIA

Monilia (also called yeast) is the most common infection in the female genitals. Although a monilial infection is not dangerous, it can cause irritation of the tissues of the vulva (the external lips and the clitoris) and of the vagina. The vulva naturally swells during sexual arousal, and when the tissues are irritated by infection, there can be a burning sensation. A monilial infection also tends to make intercourse uncomfortable, producing a dry, rubbing sensation.

Some women who have severe moniliasis say that ejaculation in the vagina causes intense burning; this is the result of further irritation of the vaginal walls by the alkaline seminal fluid. Some women have resistant monilial infections that tend to recur, but perseverance usually leads to its cure and then, it is hoped, to its prevention.

Because vaginitis is so common and is not medically dangerous, its impact on a couple's sex life can easily be underestimated by both the couple and their doctor. For example, Mr. and Mrs. L., a couple in their forties, came to see us because their sex life had deteriorated drastically over the last four years, since Mrs. L.'s surgery. She had had surgery to correct a problem of leakage of urine. Following the surgery, her doctor instructed her to have intercourse regularly in order to maintain vaginal responsiveness. But Mrs. L. and the doctor didn't realize that the antibiotics she had taken had led to a severe monilial vaginitis. Mrs. L. didn't complain about the pain she felt during intercourse because she assumed it was a postsurgical reaction that she would get over through "practice."

Mr. L. was upset by the doctor's recommendation, and by the pain his wife experienced when they had intercourse. He was a gentle man whose life was geared to helping other people and alleviating their distress. He tried to talk about his feelings with the doctor, but on every occasion the doctor found no time to see him.

In describing to us what sex had been like in the last year, Mr. L. broke down and wept. It was obvious that he had experienced as much pain emotionally as his wife had experienced physically. He had recently been losing his erection when they had attempted to have intercourse.

Mrs. L. had been feeling guilty about not being an "adequate" sex partner. In the past, lovemaking had been important and satisfying for both of them, but now she was completely unresponsive. She had been willing to put up with pain to "satisfy" her husband.

Mr. L. blanched when she said this. He felt that she had demeaned him by thinking of him as a penis that needed to ejaculate. Thinking that she was meeting his sexual needs, she put him in an impossible bind. He, on the other hand, had never managed to convey to her the depths of his despair over inflicting pain with his penis.

We asked if they would like Mr. L. to be included in Mrs. L.'s gynecologic examination. Both accepted the idea. She was given the option of holding a mirror along the inside of one thigh to watch her examination. She was a little afraid of what she might see after surgery and so much pain, but she decided to risk looking. She was relieved that she looked okay "down there." Both were able to see the signs of irritation from the vaginitis, and Mr. L. even looked at the monilia organisms under the microscope. He felt that for the first time, he understood something of what was going on inside his wife's body. Her medical condition and her experience with the doctor were no longer a mystery. This was just the beginning of a therapy process for the L.s, but the realization of what her pain had meant to Mr. L. was an important first step for Mrs. L.

PELVIC INFLAMMATORY DISEASE

Pelvic inflammatory disease, or P.I.D., can be either a sudden or a chronic infection of the internal genital organs (uterus, fallopian tubes, and ovaries), and it is usually due to gonorrhea or other bacterial infections. If an infection has left scar tissue around the uterus and tubes, the normal movement of the uterus during sexual response can be painful. And when P.I.D. is active, it causes abdominal pain that is intensified by sexual arousal and intercourse. P.I.D. is treated with antibiotics; surgery is sometimes necessary if pain becomes chronic.

HERPES

Herpes sores on the external lips of the genitals can be extremely tender and painful. To avoid further irritation—and certainly to avoid contagion—there should be no contact with the affected genital area.

OTHER ORGANISMS

Organisms other than yeast, such as trichomonads and chlamydia, can cause vaginitis. These organisms can cause pain similar to that caused by monilia. All these infections are easily treated, but they do require medical attention.

CYSTITIS

Cystitis is an infection of the bladder. Because the bladder and the urethra rest directly on top of the vagina, prolonged or vigorous intercourse can be a factor in causing cystitis or urethritis (infection in the urethra). Women who have repeated bouts of cystitis should try to avoid prolonged intercourse and should ask their doctor about various positions for intercourse that will result in less pressure on the urethra and the bladder. Another factor in chronic cystitis that is often overlooked is low levels of the hormone estrogen (see p. 263).

Preventive measures that seem to have worked for some of the patients we've seen include changing the diaphragm to a smaller size, urinating soon after intercourse, and drinking extra fluids.

When cystitis recurs frequently urologists may treat the condition by urethral dilation. This procedure, which involves stretching of the urethra can be experienced as a quite painful penetration. The woman who has such treatments over a period of time may come to associate this pain with vaginal penetration and may then develop vaginismus. Recently, a female urologist has shown that recurrent cystitis can be caused by a too-large diaphragm. We hope this new finding will lead to more careful evaluations of diaphragm size and eliminate one of the main causes of cystitis.

ENDOMETRIOSIS

Endometriosis is a condition in which tissues that normally line the uterus begin to grow outside the womb, in such places as the fallopian tubes, the ovaries, or the lining of the abdominal cavity; swelling and scarring occur in these areas. During sexual arousal, the uterus swells and lifts slightly, causing pulling or pushing on these tender areas, and pressure from intercourse causes deep pain, often described as going to the back. Medical evaluation is needed to make the diagnosis. Treatment involves the use of hormones and/or surgery.

INADEQUATE ESTROGEN

Normal amounts of estrogen are usually necessary for normal vaginal lubrication. When lubrication is minimal or absent, penetration is usually painful and difficult, and movement of the penis in the vagina leads to further discomfort. A woman may have too little estrogen if she is breast-feeding, if she is taking birth-control pills that are low in estrogen, if her ovaries have been surgically removed or have stopped functioning (which happens to only a small percentage of young women), or if she has reached menopause.

Women whose ovaries are not producing sufficient estrogen and who have symptoms should discuss hormone replacement with their doctor. There are now safe approaches to hormone-replacement therapy. Breast-feeding women should not take hormones, however, because the hormones enter the breast milk. Instead, lubricants are available that counteract vaginal dryness. (Lubrication such as body lotions or petroleum jelly are not recommended.) Women taking low-dose birth control pills who have vaginal dryness should discuss the problem with their doctor. Sometimes a higher-dose pill is recommended, or perhaps an estrogen supplement to the birth-control pills. Of course, any woman may choose to treat vaginal dryness with a lubricant and avoid hormones altogether.

SENSITIVITY REACTIONS

Some women react with allergic irritation to some contraceptive chemicals, douches, deodorant sprays, or even soaps. When the vulva and/or the vagina are irritated and swollen, any sexual response or touching of the genitals can be unpleasant. Trial and error will usually make clear what substances, if any, a woman is reacting to.

ANATOMICAL CONDITIONS

A small minority of women have a hymen that will make initial penetration painful and, perhaps, impossible. We think all women should have a vaginal examination before they have intercourse for the first time. Then, should they have a problem, the entrance to the vagina can be gradually dilated or, in rare instances, enlarged with surgery. If the hymenal opening is partially blocked by a strand of tissue the strand can be removed by a simple office procedure.

After an episiotomy during childbirth, a distended vein or scar tissue may become sensitive during intercourse. This can be corrected surgically or through the use of vaginal dilators.

After gynecologic surgery or radiation therapy in the pelvic region, the vagina may be shortened or the vaginal opening narrowed, causing pain during penetration. In this case, too, treatment with vaginal dilators can be effective.

MISCELLANEOUS CAUSES

A variety of other conditions sometimes cause pain during sexual response and/or intercourse. These include ovarian cysts or tumors; fibroid tumors of the uterus; a tear in the ligaments of the uterus, which can occur after a traumatic childbirth; prolapse of the uterus (often called a dropped uterus), or an intrauterine device (IUD) that is incorrectly positioned, causing pain when the uterus contracts around it during sexual response. In rare instances, blockage of a duct leading from one of the Bartholin's glands (two small glands, one on each side of the vaginal opening, that produce mucus during sexual response) may cause a sharp, knifelike pain on one side of the vulva when a woman becomes sexually aroused. Painful uterine contractions at the time of orgasm can occur in postmenopausal women.

A sexual problem can arise at any time in a marriage. None of us is immune to loss of desire, painful sex, or a dysfunction. We can try to avoid problems by keeping the lines of communication open, being alert to warning signs, staying as healthy as possible, and understanding sexual function. If a problem should arise, it is crucial for husband and wife to confront it and work it out together as soon as possible. The natural history of sexual problems tends to be toward deterioration in the sexual relationship and, eventually, the entire relationship.

A sexual problem does present a hurdle, one that often seems impossibly high. The hurdle looks particularly high to couples who have never or only rarely communicated clearly about sex. Like other sexual turning points, a sex problem can actually be an opportunity to deepen and strengthen a marriage if a couple can face up to it. The next chapter, about a couple who came to us for sex therapy, illustrates how resolving a sexual problem can be a step rather than a hurdle that trips you up.

9

An Intimate Look at
Sex Therapy

MORE THAN A DECADE after the publication of Dr. William H. Masters and Virginia E. Johnson's book *Human Sexual Inadequacy*, which described the authors' clinical work with men and women having sexual problems, and despite countless articles and numerous television interviews, most people still have only a vague notion about what they would experience during the course of sex therapy. They envision doctors in white coats watching them make love or assigning them surrogate sex partners. Or they imagine having to try sexual practices they think may be all right for others but not for them.

That isn't what goes on at all. And we think the best way to explain what *does* happen is to present one actual case in detail from start to finish; it is based on two people we treated a few years ago. This case, like every other, is unique, but our basic approach, the therapeutic philosophy, and the principles presented here are the same in all cases of sex therapy as we have practiced it for more than ten years.

The Initial Visit

Tom and Laurie Parker (not their real names) had been married for five years when they came to see us. Tom was thirty, very tall and muscular, with craggy features that on first meeting made him look slightly menacing. Sitting with his shoulders hunched in his leather jacket, eyes downcast, he looked somewhat angry or scared; it was hard to say which.

Laurie was a striking contrast; she was short and round, and had an amiable face and a sweet manner. In this initial meeting, she did almost all the talking, frequently interrupting Tom. It was Laurie who articulated their problem.

"I'm having trouble getting satisfied," she explained, "because . . . well . . . Tom ejaculates a few seconds after he enters me." Glancing at Tom, who was looking intently at his boots, Laurie continued, "We don't make love very often, and somehow it isn't as much fun as it used to be. Before we were married and during our first years together, Tom took more time with me—you know, more foreplay—and I had orgasms more frequently. Now I almost never do."

After we had asked them about other aspects of their relationship, it seemed clear that Tom and Laurie loved each other very much. They would stay together, they said, even if their sexual problem couldn't be resolved. When Tom talked about their overall relationship and their future, he was finally able to look directly at us. With obvious pride, he said, "I've finally settled into a construction job I like and we've saved some money."

We told Tom and Laurie that we believed sex therapy could be helpful to them because their relationship appeared sound and the sexual problems they described—premature ejaculation for Tom and some lessened interest and arousal for Laurie—were problems with which we can usually be helpful. We explained that they would have to make a serious commitment of time, money, and emotional energy for about two months.

"Maybe this is a dumb question," Tom said apologetically, "but will we have to . . . well . . . will you want us to do things in the office?"

We assured Tom and Laurie that there would be no sexual activity in the office. All touching was to be strictly private, at home. Commitments to work, friends, and relatives would have to be minimal, with no overnight guests, so they could spend time together spontaneously, not just to touch or make love but also to play, talk, and relax together. We also said they would have to limit alcohol intake to two drinks a day.

We asked them to go home and think about it. Tom and Laurie seemed ready to plunge ahead, but we feel that all couples should have a chance to discuss alone the decision to enter therapy. We told them that before setting up a therapy schedule, we would need a written "autobiography," about three to ten pages long, from each of them that summarized what they felt had been the most important life experiences in the development of their sexuality.

The Autobiographies

The Parkers did decide to enter sex therapy, and a few days after our meeting, their autobiographies arrived. Laurie's began, "My father died shortly after I was born." She was raised by her mother and grandparents until she was twelve, she wrote, when her mother remarried. "My mother never talked about sex, and my stepfather has some pretty sick views on it. When I was nineteen, I fell in love with a young man who died in an accident, and later I was almost engaged to someone else, but I broke it off when I met Tom."

Laurie continued, "I feel that sex should be free and open. I want to be able to express myself with Tom, but the way things are, it's difficult." She said she hoped to regain the sexual drive that she'd "just about lost in the last few years."

Tom wrote, "My parents are old-school Catholic. They never talked about sex—not even about what not to do. Before I met Laurie, I was married to someone else. I was just nineteen, and we both were virgins on our wedding night. It was nothing to write home about, with my ejaculating fast and not being able to penetrate her hymen. Our sex life was never good. In fact, we rarely had intercourse. She was involved in her work, and she traveled a lot. We drifted apart, and she eventually asked for a divorce."

Describing his relationship with Laurie, Tom wrote, "She is probably the best friend I have. But our sexual relationship has fallen off. I have a hard time getting her to come and I come too soon. Intercourse isn't very often." He concluded, "I am sorry for my poor handwriting and spelling."

The First Session: Establishing Trust

Several weeks later, the therapy began with a two-hour session devoted to history taking. For that session, Phil met with Tom, Lorna with Laurie. In this way, Laurie had a female on her side,

Tom a male to turn to. (Not all sex therapists use this team approach, but it is the one we prefer.)

We wanted to explore with each of them the development of their sexual attitudes, to hear about their experiences in greater detail, and to learn about their current sexual life in order to identify patterns that had been working against sexual pleasure and spontaneity. But, most important, we wanted to establish good rapport with them—not only as a couple, but also as individuals. Tom and Laurie had to trust us; otherwise they might not share important feelings or facts.

LORNA'S NOTES

I began by asking Laurie to talk about her childhood. She zeroed in on her relationship with her stepfather. "He was so strange—cold and nasty. I don't know why my mother married him. He used to say awful things—kind of indirect insults to her and to me—about how ugly the female body is or how women are right to be frigid because sex is for animals." Laurie actually shuddered as she talked about this man.

And yet her feelings about men in general were rather positive. She said she thought that must be due to her relationship with her grandfather, whom she described as "a big, warm teddy bear." He had doted on her. "We were very close until his death, two years ago," Laurie said, and her eyes filled with tears.

"You must miss him?" I asked.

"You know, I do, and yet I never really cried when he died. I wonder why."

Laurie and I then discussed her early experiences with sex. She recalled playing doctor with friends when she was about six. "When I was nine or ten, I started touching myself . . . down there." Laurie paused, embarrassed. "Is there some better way to say that?"

"You could say, 'I started masturbating or touching my genitals or my vulva—the outside parts of the genitals—or my vagina.'" Laurie said she liked the word *genitals*.

Laurie had had some experiences with petting during high school, but it was with Charlie—her first "real love"—that she "came alive sexually." Laurie described Charlie as "a real take-charge guy." She said, "He prided himself on his sexual prowess and focused a lot of energy on pleasing me. I started having orgasms both before and during intercourse."

They became engaged, but less than a year later, Charlie was killed in a plane crash. Laurie was terribly upset, but, as she put it, "I didn't let myself brood."

"I was almost engaged to another guy when I met Tom. I really fell for Tom fast—I just knew it was right. During the first years of our marriage, the sex was fun. He didn't last very long during intercourse, but somehow I'd manage to have an orgasm anyway lots of times. Sometimes I didn't, and that was okay. I'd say things started to go downhill maybe two years ago. We just got off the track. There was less and less foreplay. It seems like as soon as he gets near me, he gets erect and moist at the tip of his penis and he wants to get inside right away. I'm scared to touch his penis for fear of bringing on his climax even sooner. His body, his actions all seem to be saying, Hurry up! Hurry up! Often he enters me so soon that I'm dry, and it hurts. All the horsing around we used to do is gone. It's tense and—well—there's nothing in it for me. I've let myself gain weight over the last two years, but he still wants me. The funny thing is, the fatness really affects me. I feel like the Goodyear blimp—asexual. I haven't touched myself in over a year. The sexual part of me has evaporated. I used to like sex with Tom. I'd initiate it oftener than he did, but now I never do."

I asked Laurie if she ever said no when Tom initiated sex. "No, I never do. Not because he's pushy—he's not. The thing that I can't handle is his apologizing all the time that he's not a good lover. I hate to see him so down and defeated. He's the same way about money. I think he's just beginning to believe me when I say I'm satisfied with what we have. What can you do with a guy who won't believe you?"

I asked how Tom's apologetic style had affected her. "Oh, I've learned to be careful about what I say. I'm scared to hurt him. But then sometimes I'll get tired of walking on eggs and blurt out something—complain or criticize. And what does he do then? He just looks sheepish and says, 'Yup, you're right!'" Laurie added, "I wish he'd fight back, but he gets all tongue-tied and mixed up."

As she left, Laurie commented, "It's been a relief to tell you all this. I think Tom and I may be able to work things out."

PHIL'S NOTES

In the two hours Tom spent talking with me, he frequently apologized for not remembering facts or for being "bad with words." In fact, I thought he had a quick mind and managed to express himself well, and about an hour into the interview, I told him so. He smiled, sighed, relaxed more in his chair and from then on didn't apologize for himself. I really liked and respected this man, and I think he could tell.

The fact that Tom felt comfortable with me was crucial, because he had always resented people in positions of authority. "My father was like Attila the Hun. He beat us kids at the drop of a hat. Once when I was eleven, he smashed me with a two-by-four and gave me a concussion. I could never talk back, so I rebelled. I was in fights a lot, but I was clumsy, so I usually lost. And anyone who was a teacher or a boss—boy, I automatically had a chip on my shoulder; but I couldn't tell them no if they wanted me to do something."

Of his early sexual experiences, Tom said, "I never was aggressive with girls, so I never had much experience. With my first wife, it's almost like we didn't have sex. What I remember is that it was a chore for her and it always hurt. So we just didn't do it. I masturbated instead. At least with masturbation, I wasn't hassling or hurting anyone.

"What was so nice with Laurie was that she enjoyed sex a lot. I never felt like it was me pushing her into it. It was mutual. But I think that was the stage when everything was new and almost automatically exciting. After a while, when the enthusiasm fell off a little, I started to have that old feeling that I was a lousy lover and couldn't please her."

I asked Tom if he and Laurie had tried to improve their sexual relationship. "I remember one time," he said, "she read a book and decided to give me some lessons in sex. I admit I don't take very well to the idea of learning what to do."

I asked Tom if he knew where that feeling came from. "Maybe I think I'll do it wrong anyway because I'm so clumsy. Come to think of it, I don't like to try anything unless I think I can do it well."

Second Session: General Goals

When Tom and Laurie visited us the next day, Lorna met with Tom, Phil with Laurie. Each was asked to talk about the other—not about himself or herself—for about forty-five minutes. During this meeting, we asked what we call the magic-wand question: "If you had a magic wand and could change one thing about your spouse, what would it be?"

Tom said he'd like to see Laurie be healthier. In the sexual sphere, he wished she'd stop wearing great big granny nightgowns to bed to hide her body. "She may be a bit heavy, but I like her body just fine."

Laurie responded by saying she'd like Tom to be a good dancer. Asked what that would mean to her, she said, "I guess I'm really saying I'd like him to loosen up and be himself. He seems to control himself so much, it makes him clumsy and awkward. I think if he'd relax, he'd find he wasn't a klutz." In her own way, Laurie had summarized what this sex therapy was going to be about for Tom.

The Physical Examination

We give a physical examination to all couples with a sexual problem to diagnose medical factors that may be involved and to teach people about their own bodies as well as their partners'. We described the procedure to Tom and Laurie, asking each if he or she would be comfortable having the other present during the examination.

"Well, that's a new wrinkle," Laurie said, "but I guess it's okay with me."

Tom said, "Sure, fine, anything you say."

Laurie chose to be examined first. With Tom standing near the foot of the examining table alongside Phil, Laurie assumed a semi-sitting position, holding a small mirror so she also could watch as we explained the parts of her genital anatomy. Phil pointed out the large lips, the small inner lips, the way the small lips joined in the hood of skin over the clitoris, the clitoris itself, the urethral opening, and the vaginal opening.

Tom was surprised to learn that the pea-size part of the clitoris that peeks from beneath the hood is only a fraction of the clitoris, which is actually about half the length of a pinky finger. He was also surprised to hear that most women don't like stimulation directly on the exposed part of the clitoris. We reassured him that many men—and women—find this confusing.

With a speculum inserted into the vagina, both Laurie and Tom were able to see the walls of the vagina and the cervix at the back. They were fascinated. Tom said, "It's bigger inside than I thought."

During Tom's examination, Laurie seemed very interested when Phil explained how male genital anatomy evolves from female structures in the fetus. She asked if the lumps she sometimes noticed on Tom's testicles were normal, and Phil explained these were part of the epididymis, a small organ where sperm are stored, and were entirely normal.

Before they left that day, Tom commented, "Frankly, when you told us about it, I thought this examination was a kooky idea. But it was really good. I learned a lot."

The Case Review

The diagnosis phase of the therapy was now complete. We knew Tom and Laurie fairly well and thought we understood most of the factors that had caused their sex life to deteriorate. From this point on, we met as a foursome. We summarized our view of the situation for them.

Although the Parkers appeared to have a strong, loving relationship, there were many ways in which they were not in touch with each other's feelings. Because he was so down on himself, Tom often assumed that Laurie was fed up or angry when she wasn't. And she in turn tiptoed around for fear of making him depressed, holding back and exploding later—often about something minor. They would have to learn to be more direct and open in their day-to-day interaction and effect a change in their communication patterns that would have to carry over into sex.

In reviewing some of the factors from Tom's background, we emphasized that his extremely critical family had undermined his self-confidence early. His low self-esteem was further undermined during adolescence, when his lack of coordination and his shyness made him feel that all the other guys were more sexually knowledgeable and experienced than he was. Tom's one serious relationship before meeting Laurie—his first marriage—had reinforced his sense of inadequacy.

With Laurie, Tom was always evaluating his performance— usually negatively—and even when they were playful and spontaneous, he was thinking, "I'll probably come too fast and disappoint her." We know that worrying about sexual performance interferes with normal functioning and can perpetuate the problem of premature ejaculation. And viewing sex as a test you expect to fail certainly takes the fun out of it!

With Laurie, we stressed her unrealistic expectation that a man would magically know how to pleasure her. Her sexual relationship with Charlie could be said to have spoiled Laurie. She expected men to "give" her orgasms without her saying what she liked. Men, she thought, should be experienced and confident and just *know* what to do. Because of this attitude, she tended to be impatient with Tom's sexual technique and to criticize him. Although Laurie did this fairly gently, Tom's poor self-image made it impossible for him to use criticism—or even suggestions—constructively. He would immediately despair and simply give up.

Tom also worried about hurting Laurie. He was so big, she so small. Like many big, strong men, he had always been concerned about getting carried away and hurting a woman. We quote his own words: "I seem to like intercourse more when Laurie's on top. When we're in the—you know—missionary position, I'm such a klutz; I get an elbow in her eye or I lean too hard. I can't even relax because I'm being careful every minute."

We also spoke of Laurie's unresolved losses—her grandfather and her fiancé. We urged her to share her feelings about these two men with Tom, something she had never done before. Laurie's eyes filled with tears. She said, "He's been so down about so many things, I didn't want to talk about my sad stories." Turning to Tom, she said, "Besides, wouldn't it hurt you to have me talk about Charlie?"

Tom took her hand and, half-serious, half-joking, said, "Hey, I can take anything you can dish out."

Laurie smiled. "That goes for me too."

Tom and Laurie had already begun the real work of sex therapy; they were trying to open themselves up to each other, to share their feelings. But openness and effective communication don't happen easily. For many couples, this emotional risk taking is extremely difficult, because they are afraid of being hurt, of trusting, or of getting too close. Some learn to handle it, some cannot. Looking at the Parkers, we wondered, Are they going to be all right?

Here is what happened in the rest of their meetings with us.

March 15

Today we focused on communication skills, providing Tom and Laurie with some simple but important guidelines. To begin with, they would have to accept the idea that feelings are facts. In other words, there are no right or wrong feelings—no room for thinking, I shouldn't feel this way, or, You shouldn't feel that way. Tom and Laurie would have to listen to and accept each other's feelings no matter how different they were from their own.

"For example," Phil explained, "when you leave this room, you may be experiencing a lot of mixed emotions. Ask yourselves what they are and then talk about them. But there are some rules about talking that are important."

Lorna continued, "Start your sentences with the word *I* instead of *you*. Remember, we want you to focus on *self*-expression. Don't say, 'You never' or 'You always.' Talk about your own feelings."

We also asked Tom and Laurie to have two touching experiences before we had our next meeting. In sex-therapy jargon, we call this touching *sensate focus*. It has a definite structure: no intercourse, no touching of breasts or genitals. Each takes a turn touching the other—not to turn on or even to please the other, just to do what he or she wants. There are no goals, no ways to fail. The person being touched just experiences the touching, except that he or she must, if something is uncomfortable emotionally or physically, say so and the other person must stop. Although it is extremely simple, sensate focus incorporates the building blocks for a satisfying sexual relationship: self-assertion (doing what you want) and self-protection (saying *ouch*).

During the next few days, Tom was to decide when he wanted to try sensate focus, and he was to say, "I want to touch now," not, "Would you like to touch?" or, "We're supposed to," or, "Let's touch"—but "I would like to." Laurie was to say yes if she felt neutral or positive. She was to say no if she didn't want to—and no explanations were required.

Phil reminded Tom that he was to be honest about his feelings. "If Laurie says no and you feel hurt, say so. We're sure you two can handle that together. And if things don't go perfectly, don't worry about it."

March 18

The few days following our meeting were intense ones for Tom and Laurie, as they explained when they returned to see us. "I was sort of weepy for a day or two," Laurie began. "Just hearing you summarize our problems and our lives made me think a lot about the past, about how I never knew my biological father and how sad I was that my grandfather died. Tom didn't know what to make of all my crying. I think I finally got through to him that it was *good* crying."

Tom told us, "At first Laurie's crying put me off. I was sure she wouldn't be in the mood to touch."

But the day before their visit, Tom did say to Laurie, "I'd like to touch now." He began by stroking her hair and her back and then her legs. "I really liked it," he told us, "but I kept wondering if she was enjoying it—if I was too rough or anything."

"I'll let you know if you're too rough," Laurie chimed in. "I'll sing out loud and clear."

Laurie described how she felt when they touched. "I was surprised how shy I felt with Tom at first—as if we'd never been naked together. I was being a little silly, drawing pictures on his back and tickling him. Maybe I was tense, so I got silly. I know that the second touching session, I was tenderer. Both were nice."

We asked the Parkers to continue following the same communication and touching guidelines with one new addition. They were to try touching with body lotion or oil. If either one disliked the lotion or oil, he or she could stop using it.

March 23

The Parkers' mood was definitely lighter today. They joked and chatted as they walked down the hall toward our office. Tom spoke to us first, saying these had been a good few days except that one day on his way to work, he had seen a large dog killed by a car.

"When Tom walked into the house that night, I knew he was upset," Laurie told us. "I think in the past he might have brooded and not said what was on his mind, but he did tell me and we talked a lot about it."

"It really helped to talk," Tom added.

Later that evening, Laurie told Tom she wanted to touch and he agreed. "I began touching with lotion, the way you suggested, but I didn't like it. I use lubricating oil on my job, and the lotion reminds me of work," Laurie went on to explain. "I like the natural feeling of his skin and his body hair, and his hair gets all matted down with lotion, so I switched to baby powder. I had a good time. I remembered what you said about touching any way I wanted to, without worrying if Tom was okay. Actually he seemed to be having a grand time."

Tom agreed. "I liked the lotion and the powder. I think I just liked her touching me—any way at all. When I touched Laurie I did it very lightly, not like any way I ever touched before. I was afraid it might be too ticklish but she didn't complain."

The Parkers told us about a second time of sensate focus the following day, which had been extremely postitive for both of them. "Tom seemed to get more sexually excited than the other three times," Laurie said. "I was pretty excited too. Not being allowed by the rules to go further is a real turn-on, but I was worried that it might be frustrating for Tom even though he said it wasn't."

Phil explained to the Parkers that it's all right for a man to be sexually aroused and not ejaculate. In fact, it's normal for an erection to subside and return several times during the first stage of sexual excitement. Some fluid usually comes out of the penis during the so-called *plateau phase*, just before orgasm, and after ejaculation, a man can still experience arousal and attain a full erection.

"What about Laurie?" Tom asked. "Isn't it frustrating for her when we play around and she doesn't have an orgasm?"

Lorna answered Tom's question by explaining that many women who regularly experience orgasm don't always climax when they make love. They may want further stimulation, or they may feel entirely satisfied without an orgasm. She also explained that vaginal lubrication is the physiological counterpart of erection and occurs just as quickly—within ten to thirty seconds of stimulation—but because it takes place inside the vagina, a woman and her partner may not always know right away whether she has lubricated.

After answering some additional questions from the Parkers

about sexual response, we explained that we wanted them to add something more to their touching. Phil said, "Tom, after touching Laurie for a while just as you have been doing, if you want to go on to touch her breasts and genitals, get into a sitting position, leaning back against the headboard of your bed, using pillows. Laurie should sit in front of you, between your legs, so that you're both facing the foot of the bed." Lorna added that although Tom would be touching as he liked, Laurie should from time to time guide his hands to show him what felt best for her.

"Laurie, when it's your turn to touch," Lorna explained, "begin touching as you have been. If and when you want to include touching Tom's genitals, use the following position. You sit up, your back against the headboard, legs wide apart. Tom should lie with his head near the foot of the bed, his hips up close to you with his legs spread out over your legs.

"Tom," Phil added, "you can guide Laurie's hand from time to time."

We then taught Laurie a technique for reversing Tom's pattern of premature ejaculation. She was to stimulate him to a point close to orgasm. When Tom signaled that he was close to coming, Laurie would stop briefly and then resume. After three "start-stops," she was to stimulate him until he ejaculated.

Laurie and Tom had no qualms about following these instructions. They left with the understanding that Laurie was to initiate the first time, Tom the second.

March 25

Some couples are almost shy about reporting breakthroughs, but Laurie could hardly wait. With a cat-who-ate-the-canary grin, she announced, "We had a fabulous time—like the best of our good old times, but in some ways even better. I touched Tom first, and after a while we got in the position you suggested and I must say, what a bird's-eye view! I never looked at him that way. It was sort of neat. We did the starting-stopping thing and it went okay. I was really sort of curious to watch it all happening."

Before we could ask more about that part of the touching, Laurie rushed on. "And then when he was touching me, I had an orgasm." Suddenly Laurie stopped, looking triumphant, but also embarrassed.

Lorna asked, "How did you feel about what happened?"

"Great," she replied, "but I suppose I feel funny telling you about it. You see, when Tom was touching me, I guided his hand the way you suggested, but I also touched myself some. At the time it felt very natural and nice, but afterward I wondered if that was okay with Tom."

"I liked it," Tom said without hesitation. "Seeing your pleasure turned me on."

Laurie looked very relieved, and Tom seemed to be feeling very positive, so we asked them to continue the same "homework" until we met again. It would be up to Tom to initiate first.

March 29

At this point in sex therapy, we always change the format of our meeting. For the first twenty minutes, Phil met alone with Tom while Lorna talked with Laurie. We wanted to be certain they weren't withholding feelings in order to protect one another.

Phil learned from Tom that they had not touched at all during the past few days. "Laurie has a cold," Tom explained, "and also she fell at work and got bruised all over. She was in no shape for touching."

Phil asked, "Was there any time you might have liked to touch?" Tom nodded. "So you were guessing what her response would be?" Tom nodded again. "Could you, in the future, risk saying what you want without being sure you'll get a yes response from Laurie?"

"Yeah, I could do that now," Tom replies. "I turned her down and we survived. I think we've both been oversensitive."

Meanwhile, in another room, Laurie was describing a very different view of events. She had been extremely upset about Tom's not inviting her to touch. "I think maybe he interpreted my cold and my bruises as a down mood. He can't seem to handle it when I'm depressed, so I've grown to feel I have to hide my sad moods. I think this is a big barrier between us."

When we were all together again for the last part of the visit, Lorna encouraged Laurie to tell Tom what she'd been feeling. "I kept expecting you to say you wanted to touch. Once—now that I think of it, it was kind of funny—I was going out and you said, 'When you get back would you like to . . .' and I was sure you were going to say 'touch,' but you said 'make popcorn'!"

Lorna asked, "Laurie, is it hard for you to tell Tom when you feel disappointed or sad?" She answered, "Yes, it's hard because he reacts as if it were his fault and he gets so down I can't stand it. Like when I was falling apart after my grandfather died—not crying, but just being real down—Tom felt there was nothing he could do to help."

"Well, there *wasn't* anything I could do," Tom interrupted, "and I can't stand not knowing what to do."

Laurie reached out to touch Tom and, with tears in her eyes, said, "Can't you believe that your just being there is a help?"

There was a long pause. Tom was clearly very moved as he said, "Yeah, I guess I can believe that."

Phil used this opportunity to help Tom identify other feelings. "Does that sense of helplessness or confusion sometimes occur during sex?" Tom thought a bit and then said, "Yes—when I think I'm doing the wrong thing, not pleasing Laurie. I hate to make mistakes."

Lorna noticed that when Tom said, "I hate to make mistakes," Laurie turned her body away from him and placed her pocket-book on the seat, forming a kind of wall between them. Realizing this was an important issue, she said, "We were talking about Laurie's feelings of sadness that Tom can't fix."

Suddenly Laurie burst out talking with intense feeling, leaning forward in her chair. "He's such a perfectionist! And when he can't do something at work or at home, he gets in such a bad mood. I don't even want to live with him sometimes!"

Lorna said to Laurie, "You have a lot of very strong feelings about this. Has this issue come up at all in your touching since the start of therapy?"

"Yes," Laurie replied. "Once Tom thought he wasn't touching me right and he stopped cold and said, 'I'm being such a klutz.' I had had it. I started crying."

Just then Laurie's mood changed; the anger and sadness were replaced by a small smile. "Remember what I said then?" she asked, turning to Tom. "I said, 'The next time you say you're a klutz, I'm gonna hit you on the head—hard!' " At this point, Tom and Laurie were laughing and smiling at each other. There was no need for us to say anything; they were working something out.

They left with the same instructions—although it would first be up to Laurie to invite Tom to touch.

April 5

Tom and Laurie had had only one time of touching since their last session, but according to Laurie it had been "nice, comfortable—beautiful."

"We've been asking each other all kinds of questions," Laurie explained. "I asked Tom if he liked touching me after he had his orgasm and—oh, lots of things. I think we've spent hours talking about this stuff."

We felt the Parkers were ready to move on to intercourse, which in therapy we call *vaginal containment of the penis*. We use that awkward phrase to counter the common notion that the penis is the only active organ during intercourse. The vagina is in its own way just as active. We also want intercourse to be a new experience, not a repetition of hundreds of past experiences, and a new experience seems to call for a new name.

We told Laurie that after she and Tom had been touching for a while, she could get on top, kneeling above and straddling Tom, and slowly guide his penis into her vagina. (We believe that the woman should always guide the insertion process because she can sense the proper angle more easily than the man.) After insertion, Laurie was to stay still briefly and then begin to explore movement gently, without getting into a thrusting position. We told Tom that if he came close to orgasm, he should signal Laurie to remain still until the feeling subsided. They should stop in this way three times, and then Laurie should continue moving until Tom had an orgasm.

We told Laurie not to focus on the goal of orgasm for herself during intercourse. It might happen and that would be fine, but we wanted her to concentrate simply on identifying sensations and movements that were comfortable and pleasurable.

April 12, 19, 26

The three weeks following our last meeting were positive ones for the Parkers. "Intercourse—I mean vaginal containment—was easy and nice," Tom told us.

"Vaginal containment did seem different from intercourse," Laurie added. "It was more relaxed, and with all the starting and stopping, it took a good long time. I liked that. And there was a lot of talking. Tom told me that for about half a minute after he comes, he feels supersensitive and just wants me to stay still. I never knew that. I'm glad he told me."

Our instructions to the Parkers were to continue exploring vaginal containment. Either one could invite first.

At the end of their April twenty-sixth visit, we taught the Parkers an intercourse position called the *lateral* position. Like vaginal containment, it begins with the woman on top of the man. They then make several shifts. The man turns his body slightly so he is lying almost on his left side, and he slides his left leg up, bending his knee. His leg is flat on the bed. As the man does this, the woman leans forward—as if she were going to lie down—and moves her right leg so it is between his legs. She then shifts her upper body slightly toward the right. She may want to rest her head on a separate pillow, placing her right arm underneath it.

This position has a number of advantages: Either partner can move; it is comfortable and can be maintained for a long period of time; men with a tendency to ejaculate prematurely find they do not come as rapidly; and some women find that they can experience orgasm more easily in this position.

May 3

It was remarkable how the theme of mortality wove itself into the Parkers' therapy. During this visit, they told us about witnessing a traffic fatality that had been very upsetting, but they had been able to talk about their feelings. It seemed that the two taboo topics between them—sex and death—were now able to be discussed.

Their first touching session had been very pleasurable, but they hadn't tried the lateral position. They had, in fact, stopped before Tom had an orgasm. "I was really tired," Tom explained, "and I realized I was pushing it. So I told Laurie I'd like to stop, and when she said it was okay with her, it was really sort of liberating."

Two nights later, Tom had said to Laurie, "I'm really feeling that I need you sexually," and they had then gone on to touch and to try the lateral position, which they enjoyed. Afterward they spent some time discussing their need for sex. No matter how frequently or infrequently they had intercourse, they felt they needed to be close and in touch in some way nearly every day.

We talked about the fact that there were only two more visits before the end of therapy. Our instructions to the Parkers were: "Do whatever you want to do about touching."

May 10

As a couple approaches the conclusion of therapy, almost invariably they experience a sudden reversal. Their communication and sexual problems appear again, and they feel that they are back to square one. Our term for this phenomenon isn't like any of our other sex-therapy jargon. We call it the blue funk, and oddly enough, it is a sign that the therapy has been successful.

But Tom and Laurie felt devastated. The details of their difficulty aren't really important; they simply had a complete breakdown in communication of feelings. Laurie was furious, claiming Tom was "a slave to his work and was ruining his health." Tom was alternately snappish and silent. Two nights before their scheduled visit with us, they were so upset that they were on the verge of telephoning us.

"But we sat in the kitchen over a couple of beers instead," Tom told us, "and tried to remember all the rules you've been teaching us about how to talk. I think it was Laurie who put her finger on it when she said to me, 'I don't think I've said one sentence beginning with the word *I*. All I've been doing is telling you what's wrong with you.' "

Laurie added, "We sat there for I don't know how many hours. And then we went up to bed and just lay there together, talking and touching. It didn't matter to either of us whether we had intercourse or orgasms. We just enjoyed being together."

May 17

"It's been a good, hectic, hazardous, nerve-racking, upsetting, and wonderful few weeks," was Laurie's opening line.

They felt that sexually they were "a hundred and fifty percent cured." Tom no longer ejaculated quickly. In the lateral position or with Laurie above him, he could just let go and enjoy his own sensations and could prolong intercourse without trying to control himself. Laurie still found that she could have an orgasm most easily from manual stimulation, but combining intercourse with manual stimulation was something they were exploring and enjoying.

"But the best part," Laurie said, "is the fun and excitement we have the whole time. We're more tuned to each other, closer—it's so amazing. In the time we've been in therapy, I've decided that almost everything I always thought about sex was wrong—not just the facts but the whole attitude. I used to think it was this big, mysterious thing, but now I feel comfortable talking about it all."

Tom's final thoughts were simple but very moving. He said, "Over the past few years we've lost a lot—a lot of time and a lot of closeness. It's nice to be back."

10

Extramarital Sex

HUMAN BEINGS, unlike swans, are not naturally monogamous. Being sexually exclusive till death parts us is a religious/cultural ideal—an ideal most people believe in but many fail to achieve.

In our 1980 questionnaire, we found that 13 percent of the respondents said they were currently having sex with someone else in addition to their spouse or primary partner. Other studies show that 40 to 50 percent of husbands and 35 to 40 percent of wives have sex outside of marriage at some time.

There appears to be a difference between men and women in the timing of first extramarital sex. Most men start the practice fairly soon if they are going to engage in it at all. One study found that two-thirds of men who were ever unfaithful had their first experience in the first five years of marriage. Women were more likely to be unfaithful for the first time in their late thirties or early forties. These trends may change, of course, as social and sexual values change.

We are concerned here not with any and all experiences of infidelity but with those experiences that result in a sexual turning point—a moment that profoundly affects sex and/or the meaning of sex in our lives.

The impact of extramarital sex on the persons involved is influenced by so many variables; the permutations and combinations are almost infinite. The outcome will be determined largely by the context, that is, by the previous sexual experiences, the meaning of sex, of marriage, of fidelity, the timing of the infidelity, its social milieu, whether it is "open" or secret, the denouement of the lovers' relationship, and outside factors such as children, ill-

159

ness of a spouse, or loss of a job. We can only scratch the surface of the subject by telling the stories of a few women and men for whom extramarital sex proved to be a sexual turning point.

The first story was told to us in retrospect by a woman who had been married for almost twenty years. She explained how a brief affair had probably saved her marriage. She was thirty-two at the time, and had been married for five years. She was mildly depressed because she had quit work hoping to become pregnant, only to find that month after month, there was no pregnancy. Her self-esteem was at an all-time low, while her husband was enthusiastic about and busy with his work. They couldn't seem to talk about their fears of infertility. Neither could they talk about the fact that she rarely had an orgasm. He ejaculated very rapidly, but she attributed her lack of orgasm to her own failure to respond quickly. She thought her sexuality and her fertility were below normal.

One night she went to a "happy hour" with her former coworkers. Afterward, when one of the men she had always found attractive invited her to his apartment, she went. They had a brief affair that was an eye-opener for her. She had orgasms easily with this man. He seemed to think she was not only normal but rather passionate. The affair gave her courage to talk to her husband about her sexual dissatisfaction and her worries about not getting pregnant. They decided to do something about both problems. They sought sex counseling and that was successful. They went to an infertility clinic and she was able to become pregnant. She added, "That doesn't really tell you all that the affair with Bob meant to me. It's hard to put into words, but it was really my sexual awakening. I had sort of enjoyed sex before Bob but not all that much. I remember telling my best friend that I could think of about ten things I liked a lot better than sex, things like eating, walking on a nice day, listening to Mozart. I believed that the sex I saw in movies and read about in books was purposely exaggerated, and I thought my friends made a big deal about sex because it was the in thing to do. After the second or third time I made love with Bob, I was on a train going to New York. I remember it so clearly. I was remembering our lovemaking and the feelings of desire were so strong. It was like a revelation; this is what it's all about! I'll always be grateful to him for that."

Maria came for help because she could not have an orgasm with her husband but could with her lovers. She had been married for two years to Arthur, who was studying accounting and business while she worked as a waitress. In the past two years, she had had sex with three men in addition to Arthur, one of whom—a cook in the restaurant where she worked—was now her regular lover. She said, "I have a kind of split personality. The half of me that's married to Arthur is conventional and not very sexy. The half that has affairs is far out and goes wild in bed."

Maria's "split" could easily be traced to the two halves of her family. Her Puerto Rican mother had married a man from Ohio, and they lived in Florida. Marie had experienced the full force of two vastly different cultures, not only as embodied in her parents but also through direct exposure during long periods with both families. Her mother's family were poor, rural farm workers. When she stayed with them in Puerto Rico, she went barefoot, swam, played in the mud, was hardly supervised, played sex games with her cousins and other children, saw farm animals have intercourse and give birth. She lived with paternal relatives in Ohio for more than a year when she was about nine because her parents had briefly separated. There she experienced the discipline, work ethic, and success values of her father's family. She recalls being given the silent treatment for several days when she was caught reading a novel out of her uncle's library. She had been told not to read his books because they contained "the intimate details of marriage to which no decent child should be exposed."

Maria made a list of words that went with each of her halves. The paternal half included: *middle-class, uptight, verbal, white, consumer, sterile, constricted, prim, impotent, repressed, school, anxious, competitive,* and *cold.* The maternal side: *lower class, loose, ethnic, relaxed, earthy, sweaty, dirty, sexy, swearing, potency, dark skin, laughter, feelings, acceptance,* and *spirituality.* "But," she added, "this is a play world—not how you can really live your life."

Maria had run away from home when she was sixteen. She spent time in Puerto Rico and in Guatemala. She lived out her image of the lower-class, "loose" life and was even a prostitute for a few months. She usually enjoyed sex during those years, but the dangers of her life-style and the nagging voice of "reality" persuaded her to return to the United States.

She said, "Now I feel settled with Arthur. He represents a

world I think I *should* want to be in. He is safety and stability. I could have a family with him. I just don't find it exciting or fun. Sonny [her lover] is so different. He's not uptight like Arthur. He knows how to let go, laugh, tell jokes, get angry, make love like a wild man. He helps me to let go."

During the time Maria was in therapy, she discovered she had gonorrhea. Sonny admitted she had gotten it from him. Maria had to tell her husband so that he could be tested. His reaction surprised her. "At first he reacted in Arthur-style. He looked very cold and distant, put on his jacket, and said, 'I'm going for a walk.' I sat on pins and needles for an hour, thinking he might come home and very calmly say he was divorcing me. When he came back, he was furious. He screamed at me, called me a whore; he slapped me across the face and then he cried. We both cried. I told him about Carl and Mitch (the two other men with whom she had sex after marrying Arthur.) He was so hurt. I even told him I was able to have orgasms with them, not to hurt him more, but because I was sure the only chance we had was a clean slate. The whole scene with Arthur blew my mind. He had never let me see his feelings before. He said it surprised him, too."

This was a real turning point for Maria, and for the marriage. Maria began psychotherapy, "to try to integrate the two halves and be one whole person with Arthur." Six months later, she and Arthur felt they had made good progress.

You can read Maria's story on two levels. On one level, it is the unique story of a rather unusual woman. On another level, her split personality reflects a dualism many people feel, a dualism in which marriage comes to represent the unsexy side of life—the conventional, unexciting, nonplayful, the problematic and the constrained, while affairs represent all the sexy alternatives. If that is how one mentally packages marriage versus affairs, then affairs are likely to prove irresistible.

The third story is an excerpt from a sexual history told by a thirty-six-year-old woman named Sandra, who came for sex therapy with her lover, Lisa.

Sandra had been married for eleven years and had two children. She was not unhappy in her marriage, and her sex life with her husband, Richard, was mutually satisfying. "I considered myself heterosexual—absolutely. My first sexual experience had been with a girlfriend when we were about twelve, some breast fondling and petting, but that only lasted a few months and I never took it very seriously. Lots of girls do stuff like that. I was never seriously attracted to women, although I had fantasies about sex with unknown women and occasionally felt a sort of sexual awareness of some women. And I like to look at women's bodies—actual bodies or pictures. But I was completely unprepared for the effect Lisa had on me.

"The only thing I can think to explain it, and it's not really an explanation, is that I fell in love with her. I met her at a statewide convention and almost immediately felt something special. I certainly wouldn't have labeled it love or even attraction, just a kind of excitement about being with her. I thought she was beautiful. In fact, my first clue that something strange was going on with me was when I commented to two friends about Lisa being beautiful. They both said they thought she was just average. I began to wonder if I was infatuated.

"After the convention, she wrote me a long letter, telling me she was bisexual and was in love with me. I've never been so shaken to the core. I was scared but I had to see her. We talked and we made love. It felt natural to me. She couldn't believe I wasn't more awkward or maybe even repulsed, but I wasn't. I can't understand it myself.

"I tried to fight my feelings, and for a few months we had a secret affair. We spent a lot of time talking and doing things together, not just in bed. We're very intellectually compatible and have similar ideas, particularly politically.

"Eventually I faced my husband with it. You can imagine how shocked and devastated he was. He didn't want our marriage to break up. He cried. For a whole year he stood by, hoping it would blow over between me and Lisa, but she and I got closer and closer while I drifted away from him. We finally split six months ago. He's letting me have custody of the children but he sees them a lot.

"I think now that I will spend the rest of my life with Lisa, but it's pretty clear that life isn't always what you expect. I think of myself as bisexual. I still respond to men I work with in what I would call sexual ways, though I'm not even vaguely tempted to be unfaithful to Lisa. Her not having orgasms is a disappointment, more to me than to her. I suppose she's used to it, but I feel something is missing. It's a real issue for us, but I don't think it will break us up—no, I'm sure it wouldn't."

As mentioned earlier, a woman is most likely to have her first affair in her late thirties or early forties. This is a time when she is less tied down with small children, has greater freedom, may have begun or resumed working, and may feel more sexually confident than she felt in her twenties. Kinsey stated that these were a woman's peak sexual years, the years when she would be likely to feel the strongest desires and most intense responses.

The Summer Before the Dark, by Doris Lessing, is a very perceptive novel about a forty-two-year-old woman in which she explores, among other things, the meaning of an affair.

Kate Brown, the central character, reacts to the knowledge of her husband's repeated casual affairs. "Once upon a time she had known that her husband's life had been sustained by her, by what they found together, and the centre of that was bed."

When she has an affair, she reflects about it. "There had in fact been a delicious weekend, achieved at the cost of God knows what organization, and arranging and lying, but looking back, it was certainly not sex that had been the thing. For apart from anything else, no sane woman goes to a boy for sex, an area where ripeness is all: her sex life with her Michael was everything fantasy would choose. Or it had been . . . what was it now, then? Physically admirable, of course. Emotionally? But why should that matter?"

For Kate, the affair helps crystalize her emotions. It is through action that she experiences her feelings. Before there was only a blur, a numbness in routine.

Retrospectively, an affair is often seen as the turning point in a marriage. A forty-five-year-old divorced man told us, "I discovered that my wife was having an affair when I was thirty-six and she was thirty-three. She ended the affair, and our marriage continued as before. Now, looking back on it, I see that I never felt the same about her after that. Something had gone out of us. I don't know if it was trust or what it was we lost, but five years later, we got divorced. She was real sad about it. She said if she could turn back the clock and undo what had happened, she would gladly do it. And it isn't that I couldn't understand or forgive her, but it was just no good anymore."

One of the classic affairs is that of the old man who becomes infatuated with a much younger woman. Affairs of this type often lead to a man's divorcing his wife, and marrying the younger woman soon after. Daniel Levinson comments on this classic couple in *The Seasons of a Man's Life*. He thinks, "It reflects a man's struggle with the Young/Old polarity: he is asserting his youthful vitality at a time when he fears that the Young in him is being crushed by the dry, dying Old."

A variation on that theme emerges in the story of a sixty-two-year-old man, Harold, who sought treatment of sexual problems with his wife, Evelyn. They had been happily married for forty years and had three grandchildren. They were on the verge of a long-planned retirement, both having worked and saved a considerable sum. They had always been enthusiastic sailors and hoped to spend most of their time sailing around the world on a yacht they had bought five years earlier.

Evelyn told the story this way in their first consultation with us. "Everything seemed fine. I mean our marriage was content and our sex life was pretty good, though maybe not as frequent or exciting as it had been, but that seemed like normal aging to me."

Harold interrupted. "It may have seemed normal to Evelyn, but I was worrying because I didn't always ejaculate, and on just a few occasions, I lost my erection. It's stupid, but I got very preoccupied with thoughts of going over the hill. It wasn't helped by the discovery that I had mild arthritis. Boy, that really shook me because it could mean the end of sailing and our dreams for retirement."

Evelyn continued. "One day he got a letter from a woman he'd been in love with before he met me. She'd seen him on a TV talk show, she said, and just thought she'd drop him a line—just like that, after almost half a century. I don't know why it affected me the way it did, but I got upset, a kind of premonition, maybe. I knew that he idealized her in his memory, thought of her as a young vivacious girl. He had rejected her, you see; so she was, in Robert Frost's words, 'the path not taken'. And she had never married, so he had the idea she'd never gotten over losing him; very romantic, of course. That's what scared me—not the idea he'd have sex with her. We've each had brief sexual encounters, and they never seemed very threatening."

"To make a long story short," said Harold, "I met her for a drink. Of course she was almost sixty and looked very different, but the energy and, well, vitality were still there. I think I wanted to fall in love or at least have an adventure. The sex was—this is hard to say in front of Evelyn, but it was very good. I had no problems at all. I felt restored to health. All the gloomy thoughts I'd had about becoming crippled and dependent evaporated like magic. I agonized over it for months but finally told Evelyn about it and told her I was leaving. She begged me not to go, so I postponed leaving, and during that hellish time of indecision, the other woman was diagnosed as having cancer. She decided not to marry or even live with me. She went to live in New Mexico and paint."

Evelyn continued the story. "I forgave him, and we tried to pick up where we left off, but we haven't been able to—not yet. Harold has problems with erection, and I'm not really very interested in sex."

We were not successful in treating Harold and Evelyn. His underlying depression about aging and his reaction to losing his dream of rejuvenation made it difficult for him to engage in the therapy process. Evelyn began to face some of her suppressed rage, which was necessary, but it impeded sex therapy. They were referred for a combination of individual and conjoint therapy. The last news we had of them was that they were still together but had sold their boat due to Harold's worsening arthritis.

The next story is also about a failure of sex therapy. In this case, what therapy did not accomplish, a brief affair did. Martin and his wife, Judy, were referred for sex therapy by an infertility specialist when they told the specialist they had intercourse less than once a month. They had been married for four years, and Martin had only rarely been able to get an erection. Martin was a thirty-year-old accountant. Judy, thirty-five years old, had been a secretary until they married.

In their case, appearance seemed to speak volumes about their problems. Martin was slight, hunched, and timid-looking. His attaché case was like a security blanket that never left his side, but when he carried it, he seemed weighed down by it. Judy was taller, more muscular, and aggressive in style. She had a rather severe limp due to a congenital hip defect.

Judy had always been the odd one out, the "defective" sibling, the only "dummy" in the family. Her only hope to better herself, as she saw it, was to marry well, but she had always been overweight and not very attractive. In spite of all impediments, she brazened through, but very few men ever became interested, and by her late twenties, she felt panicked that she would be an old maid.

Martin was far less grand than the man of her fantasies— whose image had sustained her for so many years—but he was genuinely interested in her. His background had also undermined his self-confidence. He was the only child born to elderly refugee parents and was overprotected to the point of being completely controlled by his mother. He had shown almost no interest in girls until after his mother died. He found he was attracted to "strong" women. He attempted intercourse once before he met Judy, but when he was unable to get an erection, the woman became furious and actually hit his penis. He half believed that she had permanently destroyed his potency.

For both Judy and Martin the sexual problem met important psychological needs. Judy seemed to feel that Martin's potency problem balanced an equation in which her age, limp, and weight problem comprised the other side. She simply couldn't allow him to become potent and independent. Everytime he made some progress with erection, she would pull the rug out from under him with a (literally) withering comment. One time she "accidentally" hit his penis rather hard.

Martin had his own needs, which forced him to remain within the status quo. He needed to feel dependent and needed to have Judy run the show.

After trying to help Martin and Judy work through these difficult issues and seeing no progress, we told them that we thought the sex therapy should end and suggested either marital therapy or individual psychotherapy. They rejected both suggestions.

About a year later, we met the obstetrician-gynecologist who had orginally referred this couple to us. He told us that Judy was pregnant and, not only that, that Martin and Judy seemed remarkably changed. We wrote to them, asking if they would be willing to come in and tell us how they were getting along. Martin telephoned to say he would like to come in alone.

When he arrived, he seemed transformed; mild-mannered Clark Kent to Superman is only a slight exaggeration. His appearance had changed dramatically. He told us that shortly after the sex therapy ended, he took a part-time course in group relations. The course was actually an encounter-type group that met for long, intensive sessions. The people in his group reacted to his passivity first with anger, then with support. In the middle of the intense group process, he fell in love with a young woman in the group. They began to meet outside of session hours and gradually

began kissing and touching. She served the function that is sometimes served by sexual surrogates. She was gentle, undemanding,
encouraging, and very easily aroused. They had intercourse with
no difficulties on about ten occasions. The group and the affair
precipitated major changes in Martin. He became more assertive
with Judy. Fortunately, she didn't react too badly. The power base
in the relationship shifted considerably. Martin felt more desire
for Judy and started to have erections more predictably.

The pregnancy was very positive for both of them. Martin
thought she had mellowed once she knew she was pregnant, and
he felt a sense of confidence in his male role he had never felt
before. The final bit of good news was a promotion for him within
his firm. He seemed to fill the room with his presence now, and he
no longer carried the attaché case.

As the preceding stories have demonstrated, the issue of extramarital sex can be—and often is—complex and unpredictable.
More than any other form of sexual behavior, it has the potential
to create tremendous life changes—sometimes beneficial, sometimes destructive. On the other hand, it can also be a relatively
meaningless experience that takes place on the periphery of our
lives, leaving the center untouched.

For a while, in the late 1960s and early 1970s, Americans
seemed to want permission for extramarital sex. Books including
Robert Rimmer's *The Harrad Experiment*, Robert Francoeur's *Hot
and Cool Sex* and George and Nena O'Neill's *Open Marriage* sold
widely. These books held out the promise of having our cake and
eating it too. They suggested—no they preached—that happy
marriage and extramarital sex were not incompatible. Indeed,
couples could deepen their commitment to one another while
growing as individuals through sexual relationships with others.
And all of this, with little or no guilt, little or no jealousy. All you
had to do was keep the lines of communication open and maintain
your marriage as the highest priority relationship.

Apparently this works for some couples, but it is far from easy.
It does not seem to be a viable solution for the majority of married
couples. In fact, it wasn't even a solution for George and Nena
O'Neill. After the breakup of her son's marriage Nena O'Neill
wrote a book that is a hymn in praise of old-fashioned monogamy
and her parents' traditional marriage.

Is there a solution to the tension between monogamy and the desire for sex outside marriage? In our current, more conservative mood, more Americans seem to be reasserting the value of fidelity, although the statistics show that more than half of us engage in extramarital sex at some time.

When people come to us, troubled by conflict about extramarital sex, we often recommend that they read a book called *Becoming Partners: Marriage and Its Alternatives*, by the well-known psychologist Carl Rogers. It has at least one decided advantage; it tells the stories of a number of couples. The only conclusion Rogers draws at the end of the book is that lots of couples are struggling with issues of commitment, monogamy, and marital style.

We agree with Carl Rogers. The conclusion is that there is no conclusion. Probably, as long as monogamous marriage remains our norm, there will be no conclusion—no simple answer that will be right for everyone.

STAGE  FOUR

Making Babies,

Making Love

11

Deciding about Pregnancy

FOR the last fifteen years, we have taught a course in human sexuality for college students. The lecture topics include male and female sexuality, homosexuality, sexual problems, intimacy and love, venereal disease, contraception and abortion, pregnancy and birth. We always ask students to evaluate each lecture and at the end of the course to evaluate the entire course. Year in and year out, with no exception, the single most popular lecture has been, interestingly, the lecture on pregnancy and birth.

That lecture includes some special ingredients. In addition to a talk on some basic facts, there is a film of childbirth. There are also several young couples present with their new babies. They sit in the front of the room and talk about their own experiences of pregnancy, labor, and delivery. Usually one or more babies are breast-fed during the lecture. A father or mother may change a diaper. The babies cry, sleep, look around, reach up to touch a mother's face.

Before this lecture, the students have learned about masturbation, the clitoris, penis size, and pelvic examinations. They have seen films showing intercourse, orgasms, and same-sex lovemaking. And yet they overwhelmingly respond most to the discussion of pregnancy, birth, and babies. Every year it reminds us that sex and reproduction are psychologically and emotionally inseparable, even if birth control separates them in daily life.

How ironic, then, to realize that this remarkable turning point in the life cycle—becoming parents—so often interferes with a couple's sex life. Some of the couples who are holding their babies while talking to the students are already our patients because pregnancy has led to sexual problems.

It ought not to be true, but unfortunately it is; each step along the way includes traps and hurdles. Deciding whether to become pregnant, trying to conceive, and worrying about fertility can be very stressful. Then there are the physical and emotional changes of pregnancy to be negotiated. The postpartum months have their own special difficulties. Finally there is parenthood and childrearing, a phase in life studies have shown to be the *least* sexually satisfying for couples.

There are always exceptions—hundreds of thousands of exceptions—who find pregnancy to be the most erotic and fulfilling nine months imaginable, who shut the door on dirty diapers and screaming kids at two in the afternoon on a Sunday and make love as if they were spending a romantic weekend at a hotel.

For all the others, we believe that knowledge can help people avoid some of the traps, and that forewarned is forearmed.

To be or not to be pregnant—that is a question couples hardly ever asked themselves in the past. It was simply assumed that one married and had children. Now there seem to be more choices. Many couples are choosing to remain childless, and those who want to have children are timing parenthood to fit in with other life plans. This means that many couples are experiencing a new phenomenon—a period of time for decision making about becoming parents (for some, lasting years and filled with soul-searching), followed by a time of consciously trying to conceive.

Men and women who are moving toward the decision to have a child face a number of important psychological issues. One of these is anxiety about their ability to be good parents. A woman whose relationship with her own mother was poor, who rejects the idea of being like her mother in any way, or who is still in a struggle to separate psychologically from her mother may have a very hard time thinking of herself as a mother. Exactly the same may be true for a man and his relationship with his father.

This is not to say that people who decide to have a baby are always cool and confident about the kind of parents they will be. We all are nervous about this. But sometimes the anxiety becomes so great that it seems to interfere with going ahead. One way in which this anxiety may express itself is as a sexual problem that crops up during the time in which a couple is trying to conceive.

Having a baby together is a big step for a man and a woman.

Breaking up before there are children is one thing, but afterward it becomes infinitely more complicated. Parenthood changes a couple's status so profoundly that Margaret Mead once suggested that there be two different kinds of marriage contract—a prebaby contract that can be severed easily and a postbaby contract that is strongly binding.

Every couple considering a first pregnancy is aware of the increased commitment involved, but they don't always act rationally with regard to this commitment. Some couples, for example, imagine that by having a baby together, they can create a commitment where none has existed or improve a faltering relationship. In this situation, there may be no sexual or marital crisis during the decision-making time because the man and woman are feeling hopeful. The sexual problems are likelier to show up during pregnancy or after the baby is born, when they realize that their "solution" isn't going to work.

Another psychological issue that a surprisingly large number of couples have to deal with when thinking about pregnancy is fear of infertility. This may be a natural anxiety, but the circumstances of modern life have increased these concerns. For example, an increased number of women have had an abortion prior to their first pregnancy. Although an abortion does not increase the risk of infertility, many women fear that it may have harmed their reproductive capacity. Many couples have similar, unfounded fears about the effects of birth-control pills.

It is one thing to have a vague or preconscious fear of infertility while you are still using birth control; it is another to actually try to become pregnant and risk "failure." When the fear of infertility is strong—and particularly if it is associated in the person's mind with a sexual "transgression"—trying to conceive a child may stir up old feelings of guilt about sex. One young couple consulted us because although they wanted a baby and the wife had stopped using her diaphragm, they had not had intercourse in many months. They both were confused by her seemingly irrational withdrawal from sexual activity. In talking to us alone, the woman, who was in her early twenties, referred to herself as having been promiscuous when she was seventeen and eighteen. Because she had had a vaginal discharge and some pain with intercourse during this phase, she had worried that she might have had a venereal disease but had been too terrified to ask a doctor.

Eventually the discharge stopped, but she always secretly believed that she had VD and might be sterile as a result.

This young woman felt a great deal of guilt about her "promiscuity," and what she feared most was having to tell her husband "the awful truth about me." Several interviews with her alone helped alleviate her guilt to the extent that she was able to tell her husband about her past. He did not reject her; in fact, he shared some of his own past history with her. They felt a lot closer, and sex resumed quite naturally.

Still another psychological issue many men and women have to deal with when thinking about pregnancy is deep-seated insecurity about their sexual and gender identity. Becoming a mother is a statement of femaleness. Becoming a father is a statement of maleness. A young woman who has little or no sense of herself as a female or who still isn't sure she likes being female may have a hard time thinking about motherhood.

One graduate student in her late twenties was struggling with these issues. She and her husband were having complex sexual difficulties; they also were thinking ahead to her stopping her use of the pill.

This young woman—we'll call her Linda—had always been "too" intelligent, "too" physically large, and "too" unconcerned with her physical appearance. She had always struggled with the question, "How can I be myself and also be a woman?" The idea of motherhood forced her to face this question.

During the course of therapy, Linda had a dream that reflected her determination to resolve this dilemma. She dreamed that she was in a beauty contest, but that she was not dressed for it in a gown or bathing suit like the other contestants; she wore her usual clothes. The male judge picked one of the other women as the winner, but after the contest, he approached Linda and said, "I like you. I want us to make love." Linda thought her dream indicated her readiness to accept the idea that she could be an attractive, sexual female without having to fit a stereotyped image of female beauty. Coming to terms with what being female meant *for her*, she could feel more sexual with her husband and feel more confident about having a baby.

What happens when one spouse wants a baby and the other doesn't? This can be extremely difficult to resolve. Sometimes a couple can be aided in their decision making if they can discuss their feelings with a third party, perhaps a professional. When it is the wife who wants a baby, it is sometimes the case that she consciously or unconsciously arranges to become pregnant without her husband's consent. He may then feel tricked into fatherhood and withdraw both emotionally and sexually. In the case of one couple who consulted us for a sexual problem, the husband dated the onset of their difficulty to the wife's "tricking" him into pregnancy.

Nowadays there are more and more women who express serious reservations about parenthood, whereas their husbands are eager for children. These women do not see motherhood as the primary role in their lives or as their only route to fulfillment. Children may interfere with schooling or career and put an end to a style of independent living that is stimulating and fun. And even though many young men today are promising that they will "help out" with the baby, we hear women expressing doubts about how this will work in practice. Won't they—the women—still really have all the responsibility and have to make all the sacrifices?

As the age of thirty looms closer, a woman facing this kind of choice may begin to see marriage as a trap. She may stop being interested in sex with her husband and suddenly find other men more attractive. At the same time, she may be feeling pressured by some friends and her family to have a baby.

This is exactly the kind of intolerable conflict that so often leads husbands and wives into "accidental" pregnancies—leaving the diaphragm in the drawer or forgetting a few birth control pills. And sometimes there is a genuine contraceptive failure—no unconscious motives, just a truly unavoidable event.

When a couple hasn't made a fully conscious, much-discussed decision to have a child, it does not mean that they somehow magically by-pass all the normal conflicts and ambivalence about pregnancy. They just postpone them, to feel them during or after the pregnancy.

Since, in recent years, a sizable minority of couples are deciding not to have children, we feel we should say something about the implications of this decision for a couple's sexual life. Unfortunately, however, we can't say very much, because both our first-hand knowledge and research by others are scant. All we can do is speculate and raise a few questions. Since pregnancy and birth "prove" to the world—and often to oneself—that one is a sexual being, does the absence of this concrete confirmation undermine sexual self-confidence in some men and women? Is there an impact from continuous use of—and perhaps difficulties with—contraception? On the positive side, does a mutual commitment to a love relationship for the sake of that relationship alone create a special bond between a man and a woman in which intimacy and sexual satisfaction are enhanced?

It may be that the answers to these questions will vary with the decades. The pluses and minuses of childlessness may be one thing for a couple in their twenties but quite different for that same couple in their forties, sixties, or eighties. The answers to these questions will have to await the future.

What the future has in store for the great majority of couples who decide to go ahead and have children is more predictable—the pregnancy itself, with the physical and psychological changes it brings. At that point, a new passage in a couple's sexual life begins.

Trying to Get Pregnant

For the majority of couples today, a conscious decision to have a baby means stopping the use of birth-control devices. Depending on the method of contraception being discontinued, there may be some real physiological changes. Women who are coming off birth-control pills may experience changes that will directly affect their sexuality. Recent studies have confirmed the fact that a woman's interest in sex is influenced by her menstrual cycle. Since menstruation and ovulation have been suppressed by the pill, a couple may find that the fluctuations in a woman's libidinal cycle are greater once she's stopped taking the pill, and they may need to adjust to this fact. Coming off the newer low-estrogen pills, many women find that they have increased vaginal lubrication. For most, this is a positive change and makes intercourse more comfortable.

Having an IUD removed may have some beneficial effects on a couple's sex life if the woman has had any unpleasant side effects from her IUD, such as pain with deep penetration, unpleasant vaginal odor, or mid-cycle spotting.

Locking up the diaphragm, creams, foams, jellies, condoms, or suppositories has no direct physiological impact, but it does tend to increase sexual spontaneity and removes what for some couples is an unpleasant or inhibiting addendum to lovemaking. Some couples tend to refrain from cunnilingus (oral stimulation of the female genitals) because of the taste of spermicidal creams or jellies. The inclusion of cunnilingus, if the couple likes this, may be a distinctly positive change in their lovemaking.

In this contraceptive era, we all have it drummed into us from adolescence that we mustn't have intercourse without birth control. And for some men and women, the time of trying to conceive will be the first time they have *ever* had intercourse without some form of contraception.

If a woman is stopping her use of the pill or is having an IUD removed, we suggest, as do most doctors, that some alternate form of birth control be used until she has had two periods "on her own" before trying to conceive. One reason for this is that after discontinuing pills or an IUD, the time of ovulation is uncertain, so if a pregnancy should occur, it is usually more difficult to forecast the date that the baby is due. Women coming off low-dose pills should be aware that it may take several months for their periods to become established with any regularity. One not-un-common pattern is for a woman to have her period one month after stopping the pill, but then to go for six or more weeks until her second period. If she is trying to conceive, she may be very confused by this pattern.

Some couples make the mistake of immediately trying very hard to conceive, altering their sexual behavior in ways they believe will enhance the chances for pregnancy to occur. They try to time their lovemaking to coincide with ovulation; the woman tries always to have an orgasm. But some of these measures are unnecessary. A woman does not need to have an orgasm to conceive; neither does a couple have to have intercourse just at ovulation time. In fact, unless there is a known problem, couples should simply have sex as usual—whenever they want to—taking care not to *avoid* the fertile period.

If as months pass the woman doesn't conceive, it is difficult to avoid a sense of pressure. Although we know that 40 percent of couples will take six months to conceive and that there is no need to worry after just a few months, people *do* worry. And they begin taking more concrete steps toward conception. The woman may begin taking her basal body temperature daily or in some other way try to identify her time of ovulation.

This immediately places the couple under some pressure to have intercourse, including ejaculation, always at the "right" times. And it may create a new situation for some couples—a situation in which the woman determines when there will be sex. If the previously established pattern has been that the husband took all or almost all the initiative in sex, the change may be noticeable. Because we believe that there is value in having both partners able to initiate sex, we believe this change is potentially very positive. For some couples, however, it may create a problem.

One husband and wife who consulted us did have such a problem. The woman was considered by her husband and by herself to be sexually shy and inexperienced. He had always assumed the role of teacher and initiator. When she began taking the lead, saying, "We should have intercourse tonight," he felt pressured and insecure. He had some difficulty maintaining an erection, which, of course, made him more anxious. It was significant that the husband's only previous sexual experience had been with a woman described by him as "very aggressive" and with whom he had felt overwhelmed and frightened.

One option for this couple would have been for the wife to retreat once more into passivity. But we helped them try another option—for the man to feel comfortable saying no or even stopping midway if he felt anxious. This worked for them. Eventually this couple, like 90 percent of couples who want a baby, conceived.

Infertility

At the end of one year of intercourse without contraception, 80 percent of the women will have become pregnant. At this point, many couples who have not conceived will consult a doctor, sometimes a specialist in fertility, about why they haven't become pregnant. This ushers in a phase of tests, repeated pelvic examinations, timed intercourse, and high levels of anxiety. Virtually every couple involved in a so-called infertility workup for any period of time will feel the impact on their sex life.

Many women involved in infertility workups report a decreased interest in sex and say that they are less likely to have an orgasm. Some men report transient impotence or an inability to ejaculate. These sexual symptoms may be caused by depression and worry, loss of self-esteem because of the fertility problem, or increased tensions in the marriage, including a tendency toward mutual blame for the infertility. As mentioned before, the need to have sex on demand rather than spontaneously is a notorious antiaphrodisiac.

When it is shown that the infertility is on the part of the male, the question of artificial insemination arises. There are no studies of the effect of this procedure on couples' sex lives, but one expert believes that the frequency of sexual activity often plummets.

Couples whose problem is repeated spontaneous abortion or miscarriage are likely to abstain from intercourse and even from sexual arousal every time there is a conception, although this is usually not necessary.

Doctors and nurses can be of help to couples undergoing the stress of infertility studies. Just having a chance to talk about your feelings and hear that they are shared by others in the same situation can be helpful. There should probably be more use of discussion groups for couples during this time. It can be helpful to take a holiday from all the tests and doctors and from the ovulation calendar. It can also help to remind yourselves that sex *isn't* just for making babies and to indulge in the "luxury" of making love without intercourse.

Fewer than 5 percent of couples remain unable to conceive. These couples will need to resolve their feelings about not having a child together. Some will adopt a child, and that will at least relieve the pain of childlessness. Again, there are no data. Do these couples have more sexual difficulties than their peers or are they able to put the stresses of the infertility phase behind them? The greatest hope would seem to lie in minimizing those stresses in the first place.

12

Pregnancy

THE TEST has come back and it's positive. You are going to have
your first baby. Both you and your husband are excited, even
ecstatic, but there's also a flutter of fear about this new and awe-
some experience. When you make love that evening, there is a
heightened awareness that this sexual sharing between you has a
new dimension—it has started a new life. Your entire relationship,
including your sex life, will be affected by this pregnancy and by
the process of becoming parents.

During the coming months, much of the impact will result
from the physical changes that accompany the different stages of
pregnancy, and from concern about the growing fetus. We hope
to make some of these changes less mysterious and to put some
aspects of this sexual passage in perspective, in the belief that
understanding helps people cope better and more creatively.

The First Trimester (Months 1 to 3)

Virtually all studies agree that early pregnancy is not a sexy
time. The majority of women say that they are turned off, just not
interested in sex. They don't want to make love and they tend not
to masturbate. Yet, as for every generalization we make about sex
and pregnancy, there are numerous exceptions. Some women feel
no diminution of interest in the early months, and a few report
increased sex drive and response. We want to stress this fact of
individual variation, lest all the women reading this come away
with the message, "This is exactly what happens during this phase
of pregnancy," because such ideas have a way of becoming fixed
and then turning into self-fulfilling prophesies.

Women attribute their low libido in the first trimester to fear of hurting the fetus, plus fatigue and perhaps nausea. Yet there are other bodily changes occurring during these months that may contribute to a lack of sexual interest. Because of the surge in hormone production, there is a marked increase in vaginal lubrication. While this lubrication potentially can facilitate intercourse, many women report a negative psychological impact. The steady, rather copious discharge makes them feel messy and creates in some a vague uneasiness.

In the early months of a first pregnancy, the breasts enlarge, and during lovemaking, when a woman's breasts normally tend to become engorged with blood, they will enlarge even more. Many women complain that this is painful, especially in the area of the nipple. If a woman anticipates that sexual arousal will cause pain, she is less likely to have intercourse. For most women, this breast pain diminishes or disappears altogether after about the third month.

Another common occurrence in early pregnancy—frequent urination or leakage of urine—also contributes to a woman's feeling less sexual. In the first trimester, the enlarging uterus presses against the bladder. Some women find that coughing or sneezing, for example, will cause some leakage; a number of women have told us that they also experienced leaking of urine if they had an orgasm during this phase of their pregnancy.

As we mentioned, in addition to body changes, many women—and men—avoid intercourse during pregnancy because they fear injuring the fetus or precipitating a spontaneous abortion. But under ordinary circumstances, intercourse is not dangerous during pregnancy. Sometimes, however, a doctor will recommend that a couple not have intercourse during the early months. Usually this is suggested only when a woman has previously had one or more spontaneous abortions. When there is bleeding, there should be no sex—not only no intercourse but also no orgasm for the woman by any means. Orgasm induces uterine contractions that may cause increased bleeding. If the doctor does not specifically prohibit sexual response, and if there is no bleeding, a couple may have sexual relations and a woman may masturbate during the first trimester.

Notice that we specify no orgasm for the *woman*. There is no reason for the expectant father not to have orgasms. If there is a need for the woman to refrain from being aroused, it does not have to mean the end of all sexual activity during this period. Couples can still "pet"—they can kiss and caress each other, and the woman can stimulate her partner's penis, or he can rub against her, until he experiences orgasm. Some couples have never had the experience of the man ejaculating anywhere but into the vagina, and it can be very nice to share this new kind of sexual intimacy. So often couples think that sex means only intercourse and that petting is just kid stuff. We believe lovemaking should not *always* include intercourse. Neither should it always include orgasm. Pregnancy can be a good time to explore the options.

The Second Trimester (Months 4 to 6)

Studies of sexual activity during pregnancy present conflicting data about the middle trimester of pregnancy. Two studies show a general decline in activity from the time pregnancy is discovered; two others, including one by Masters and Johnson, found increased sexual activity during this phase.

In Masters and Johnson's study of 101 pregnant woman, 82 reported increased levels of sexual desire and responsiveness during the middle months of pregnancy. By the fourth month, the entire pelvic region, including the genitals, is engorged with blood. This is similar to the engorgement caused in the nonpregnant woman by sexual arousal. Many pregnant women are aware of a feeling of genital fullness and of a chronic level of sexual tension.

During this trimester, a woman may have the most intense orgasms she has ever experienced. Some women who are not ordinarily multiorgasmic have multiple orgasms. The orgasmic contractions in the outer third of the vagina and in the uterus may last as long as a minute—quite a rare happening for the nonpregnant woman. It sounds like bliss, but not every couple reacts with unalloyed joy. A few women we have talked to were frightened by the intensity of their response. They felt too out of control and found the chronic sexual tension a distraction. A husband may also feel overwhelmed by these changes in his wife's sexuality, although most either accept or welcome them.

Ironically, the woman in mid-pregnancy may not feel that her pent-up sexual tensions are released even after one or more orgasms. In the nonpregnant state, a woman's feeling of release of tension comes during the resolution phase (following orgasms or when stimulation stops), as blood congestion in the pelvis rapidly decreases. By the fourth month of pregnancy, however, this decongestion process is reduced. The pelvic area remains congested, and the woman may still experience sexual tension.

The second trimester is usually the time when a pregnancy begins to show. Relatives and friends know. They also now know— for sure—that you have had sexual intercourse. Almost half of us in this country grew up hearing that sex was dirty and sinful. Thus it isn't surprising to find that pregnancy can still feel embarrassing.

One woman we treated found that she was completely turned off sexually after announcing her pregnancy to her parents. She had delayed telling them until the fifth month, when she began to wear maternity clothes and could no longer hide her condition. She reported a series of dreams in which her mother was criticizing her for being dirty. She realized that her mother had always conveyed a vague feeling that genitals and sex were dirty, and she remembered that when she was five or six, her mother had caught her touching her genitals and had made her wash her hands three times. These memories helped her to understand where her negative feelings about her pregnancy were coming from and enabled her to initiate a discussion with her sister, who also had some sexual problems, about the attitudes toward sex that they had learned from their mother. Our patient overcame her lack of sexual interest—and so did her sister.

Women and men react very differently to the various changes that accompany pregnancy. Some women see in pregnancy a kind of natural, earth-mother beauty that is rich with life and sexuality. Others see the large belly and breasts, the stretch marks and nipple changes as distortions of their usual appearance. One woman said that she enjoyed most aspects of her pregnancy but could not combine her image of her large body and her image of female sexiness. When she got into bed each night, she had a fantasy wish of removing her belly and then making love.

Husbands may find their pregnant wives very appealing sexually or they may not—and this, too, is complex. A man who seems turned off during pregnancy may be reacting to the big belly as unsexy, but more likely his feelings run deeper. Many men fear that intercourse will hurt the woman or the unborn baby. There have always been unconscious connotations of the penis as a weapon or instrument of aggression.

One couple, pregnant with their second child, consulted us because of the man's complete lack of interest in sex that was due to his fear of injuring the baby. The same thing had happened during their first pregnancy; they had talked to their family doctor about it then and the doctor had reassured him. But apparently this anxiety ran deep, because the problem recurred. Now, during the second pregnancy, he told us, "I know in my head that intercourse is safe, but my gut seems unconvinced."

His wife tried not to take his sexual coldness as personal rejection, but that is hard when you are already feeling unsure about your own attractiveness. She became depressed and threatened to leave him. The couple somehow held together until the baby was born, and just as it had with the birth of the first child, the problem vanished.

The husband who is sexually turned off by pregnancy doesn't always turn back on again this easily. There is a classic psychological conflict, sometimes called the *madonna complex*, that makes it necessary for some men to keep sex and "good woman" or "mother" in two very separate categories. When a sexual partner becomes pregnant for the first time, and as the physical evidence of that pregnancy becomes inescapably obvious, her category (in the man's mind) shifts from lover to mother. Virtually all men have a strong internalized taboo against sex with mother, but most can integrate the concepts of wife-lover-mother. The man with a madonna complex can't integrate these ideas. For such a man, a mother cannot be an object of sexual feelings. This sort of unconscious conflict usually requires professional help.

Luckily, the majority of men find their wives' pregnancies to be a joy—a happy confirmation of their shared life and the beginning of a new family.

The Last Trimester (Months 7 to 9)

There are no conflicting data about this trimester. All studies agree that sexual activity declines in the seventh, eighth, and ninth months of pregnancy, and most sharply of all in the ninth month. An English study found that by this trimester, 93 percent of the women reported a decline in frequency of intercourse. One extensive study found that 72.7 percent of pregnant women had no intercourse at all during their ninth month. Masters and Johnson found that 20 percent of the *husbands* who participated in their study lost interest in sex during the last trimester.

Discomfort during intercourse is one commonly given reason for decline in intercourse toward the end of pregnancy. A couple's usual positions during sex may now be difficult or impossible to achieve. At the same time, in the last month, the baby's head moves down into the lower pelvic region, causing more sensations of pressure in the legs, lower back, and rectum. Knowing that the baby is closer to the vaginal space may increase concern about injury to the baby, and many couples worry that sexual activity may cause premature birth. What are the facts?

At the beginning of the seventh month, during her regular checkup, a woman should ask the professional who will deliver her baby if there is any reason for her to restrict her sexual activity over the next three months. A woman who has no history of premature births, whose cervix is firm, and who shows no signs of impending prematurity probably will be told she can continue to have intercourse as long as she and her partner wish—right up until she goes into labor.

A woman who has a history of prematurity is usually advised to abstain from intercourse and from reaching orgasm by any means, including masturbation, between the twenty-sixth and thirty-fourth weeks. After that time, sex usually can be resumed.

The other group for whom sex may be restricted during this trimester are those woman with so-called high-risk pregnancies because of some possible impairment of blood flow to the fetus (for example, due to diabetes or toxemia). Orgasm in the mother may lead to a slowing of the fetal heart rate, and when blood supply is already compromised, this could be serious. If, during her pregnancy, a woman is consulting a professional who is not a medical doctor, an obstetrician should be asked to advise her in such situations.

Unless they are otherwise prohibited, then, a couple may have intercourse during the last trimester and it is not harmful for the woman to experience orgasm. Women should be prepared, however, for the fact that some uterine contractions following orgasm during this stage of pregnancy—and even earlier—may last as long as several hours. Unless the contractions settle into a regular pattern or intensify, though, one needn't worry that labor has begun.

Having intercourse and experiencing orgasm in the last month may even be helpful for a woman. A study done by Phil found that women who had been having sex regularly up to the time of labor had shorter and easier labor than those who abstained in the last trimester. In that study, 105 women who had intercourse within two weeks of delivery (almost three-fourths of whom had intercourse within 72 hours of delivery) were compared with 123 women who had not had sexual relations for at least one month prior to delivery. There were no differences between the two groups in the incidences of prematurity, infection, rupture of membranes, bleeding, or any other complications. However, among the women who had had intercourse who were pregnant for the first time, labor lasted an average of six hours less than among those who had abstained.

Labor and Delivery

Some people may be surprised to find that we mention labor and delivery in a chapter on the sexual implications of pregnancy and birth, but we believe that the physiology of labor and delivery can be seen as sexual and, more important, that labor and delivery shared by a husband and wife can be one of their most intensely intimate experiences.

There are many similarities between the physiological changes in a woman that lead up to orgasm and those that lead to birth. Some women have described the birth of a baby as a kind of orgasmic response, both physically and psychologically. And even though most women would not describe birth in this way, they sense that birth is a sexual event. It is the culmination of an act of intercourse, the product of male-female union, and unless there is heavy sedation or a cesarian delivery, it is a moment of surrender to natural body rhythms and processes.

Most obstetricians encourage the father to be present during labor, and in more and more hospitals, he is allowed to stay with his wife through the delivery itself. If the couple have been taking childbirth-preparation classes together, and particularly if they have opted for natural childbirth, they will share the timing of contractions and breathing exercises. *They* can give birth to *their* child. When a couple can comfortably share this experience, they have added new strength to the bond between them.

Does Intercourse During Pregnancy Cause Uterine Infection and Fetal Death?

Media reports throughout the world resulted when an article published in the *New England Journal of Medicine* in November 1979 indicated that sexual intercourse during pregnancy was potentially harmful to both mother and child. Much confusion has been caused by a general misunderstanding of what the article reported, and we hope we can clarify some of the points at issue.

The article, by Dr. Richard Naeye of the Milton S. Hershey Medical Center of Pennsylvania State University in Hershey, is based on data collected between 1959 and 1966 from more than twenty-six thousand women giving birth at twelve different hospitals. All the women were at least twenty weeks pregnant. Most of the information the women gave about intercourse in the preceding month was elicited when they were admitted for delivery.

Dr. Naeye concluded that infection of the amniotic fluid surrounding the unborn child is more common among women who had intercourse during the month before delivery than among those who did not have intercourse. Moreover, he stated that two to three times as many babies died as a result of infection in the group of women who had intercourse than in the group who did not.

The same issue of the *Journal* carried an editorial about this article. The editor pointed out that there is no statistically significant difference in the number of infections and fetal deaths between the two groups of women when pregnancies were between thirty-three and thirty-eight weeks advanced. Statistical significance is attributed mainly to the differences between the groups when the pregnancies ended early—between five and eight months. As might be expected, those babies born at five months did not survive in either group.

We think the most serious problem with the study is that it was done between eighteen and twenty-five years ago, and that today's statistics concerning maternal infection and fetal death are considerably lower. (The infant death rate was twice as high among the women in the study as in the general population today.) The author himself makes this point and did indicate that his study was but an early one—the results of which might well have been different if the data were gathered today.

Another serious problem is the reliability of the answers to the question, "When was your last coital act?" We wonder about this because the question was asked in twelve different places, and mostly when women were in labor and obviously under considerable stress.

There is, however, one part of the Naeye study that was confirmed by other studies: Women who have a history of premature delivery or of a complicated pregnancy should avoid sexual stimulation of any kind during the precarious middle months of pregnancy. The last eight weeks seem to be a safer time.

Our conclusions: there is no significant statistical correlation between infection or loss of babies and sexual activity for women who are between thirty-three and thirty-eight weeks pregnant. For some women, intercourse during the twentieth to thirty-third week of pregnancy may lead to premature labor and infection, but even this conclusion is uncertain. As for specific recommendations to couples concerning sex during pregnancy, as the editor of the *New England Journal* concluded, we will have to await the outcome of further studies.

Husbands' Extramarital Sex During Pregnancy

One image in the American consciousness is that of Stanley Kowalski having sex with his sister-in-law, Blanche Du Bois, while his wife is away giving birth to their first baby—the *Streetcar Named Desire* scenario. A popular myth is that men often stray when their wives are pregnant. But is it true? Oddly enough, we cannot locate any data that prove or disprove the myth.

The only relevant statistic that we could find is Masters and Johnson's study of pregnant couples, which they reported in their first book, *Human Sexual Response*. They found that twelve of the seventy-nine husbands said they had had sex with other women when the doctor prohibited sex with their wives. Three more men had extramarital sex in the weeks after delivery when, again, sex with their wives was medically off limits. Does this suggest that it is only the medical prohibition on intercourse that motivates husbands toward extramarital sex during pregnancy? This seems unlikely.

It also is not clear how many husbands are likely to have extramarital sex during any given nine-month period. Kinsey found that more than a third of married men reported extramarital affairs within any given five-year period, so the approximate rate of 15 percent reported by Masters and Johnson may not be much above the typical rate.

While they are not offering statistics, Arthur and Libby Coleman have speculated on the psychological factors behind husband's extramarital sex while their wives were pregnant. In their 1981 book, *Earth Father/Sky Father*, they offered the following possible reasons:

1. Husband feels jealous of the female's creativity.
2. Husband feels pushed away by his wife's involvement in the pregnancy.
3. Husband is reluctant to have intercourse during the pregnancy because his pregnant wife represents "mother" and is felt to be an inappropriate object for lust.
4. He is repelled by the wife's pregnant body.
5. He is frightened of new sexual demands his wife is making.
6. Husband fears hurting his wife and/or the baby.
7. He is uncertain about the logistics of intercourse in later stages of pregnancy.

This subject, like the more general subject of extramarital sex, is clearly underresearched. Is there, perhaps, a stigma associated with the subject that keeps researchers away? It is interesting that Kinsey felt his data on extramarital sex were his *most unreliable* data because of pervasive reluctance to admit to extramarital sex. Hopefully, future research will prove more fruitful.

13

Postpartum Sex

ONE MOMENT you are a couple, and the next you are parents. It is exhilarating and terrifying, but there is also a demanding new *person* on the scene who takes time, attention, and love, and who wakes you up at night. You and your husband are entering a new stage of your life together.

In the first few months after your baby's birth, your relationship undergoes important changes—emotionally, psychologically, and socially. The sexual aspect of your relationship will also be affected during the postpartum period.

How quickly do couples get back together sexually after the baby is born? One study at Yale showed that the majority of doctors are still recommending "no intercourse until after your first checkup"—usually at six weeks. There never has been a clear-cut, scientific rationale for this recommendation. It is a kind of medical folklore. More than half the women in the Yale study said they had had intercourse by the fourth week.

Couples can have intercourse when they feel ready, taking into consideration that there may be discomfort in the area of the episiotomy (the incision at the vaginal opening that is usually made at the time of delivery and then stitched). It takes one to two weeks for the episiotomy to heal. After two weeks, there may still be some residual discomfort or tightening, so penetration should be careful and gentle. An English study published in 1981 revealed that twelve months after delivery, 40 percent of women said intercourse was sometimes painful due to soreness. It is most likely that such pain is *not* due to the episiotomy but to vaginitis or vaginismus. Ovulation can occur as early as four weeks after delivery if a woman is not breast-feeding and as early as six weeks if she

192

is. Unless you want children *very* closely spaced, contraception is a must for the postpartum period.

For the first six weeks after delivery (and longer in those who breast-feed), there is relatively little estrogen produced by a woman's body. The lack of estrogen causes vaginal changes that frequently affect feeling during intercourse. There may be little or no vaginal lubrication, in which case an artificial lubricant may be used to avoid pain. The vagina may be tighter and more sensitive. Also because of hormonal changes, monilial vaginitis may flare up, causing itching and burning. This can be a factor in causing a lack of feeling during the first intercourse experiences or an inability to respond sexually, and it should be brought to your doctor's attention and treated immediately.

For a number of reasons, then—the episiotomy, lack of estrogen, or perhaps a monilial infection—the vagina is more vulnerable to pain at this time, and women tend to anticipate some pain when intercourse is resumed. When there is actual *or* anticipated pain, the muscles at the vaginal opening may tense at the moment of penetration (vaginismus). In most couples, the degree of tightness doesn't make penetration impossible, just difficult and uncomfortable. Once a diagnosis is made, treatment is usually quite simple and the couple is able to have intercourse without discomfort in two weeks' time.

Although a woman may be very eager to resume sexual relations, for her own sake and/or her husband's, it is important not to resume sex with negative, painful experiences. In the long run, this can erode a basically good relationship. If there are physical problems with intercourse, it is far better to make love without including insertion of the penis until the problems correct themselves or can be treated medically.

In Dr. William H. Masters and Virginia E. Johnson's study of sex and pregnancy, 47 of 101 women said that they had little or no interest in sex for the first three months postpartum. They mentioned fear of pain or injury to the vagina as important reasons for their feelings. They also mentioned fatigue as a major causative factor.

Interestingly, breast-feeding mothers reported a higher level of sexual interest and response than nonnursing mothers, even though it takes longer for estrogen levels to return to normal when a woman breast-feeds. One possible explanation for this lies in the close connection between breast-feeding and sexual response. Many women are aware that suckling their infant can arouse distinctly erotic sensations. Some women have not understood that this is a normal physiological reponse and have been very upset by these feelings. Actually, such pleasurable feelings may aid in the formation of a close and loving mother-child bond.

Another sign of the close connection between sexual response and breast-feeding is that at the time of orgasm, milk will usually come from one or both nipples. This is entirely normal.

A new father can have concerns about sex, too. He often has the same problems as his wife—fatigue and worry about hurting her with vaginal penetration. Because of a combination of abstinence (which predisposes a man to climax quickly) and fear of inflicting pain, premature ejaculation is not uncommon when intercourse is first resumed. In addition, there may be heightened fears of pregnancy because of an uncertain contraceptive method and the strong wish not to become pregnant again immediately after the birth of one child.

The English study mentioned before found that new parents are likely to show a decline in intercourse frequency throughout the first year after their baby's birth. Before the pregnancy, only 6 percent of couples had intercourse less than once a week. In the first postpartum year, 20 percent of the couples reported having intercourse less than once a week. At the time the baby was one year old, 57 percent of the couples were having intercourse less frequently than before the pregnancy, while between 3 and 13 percent reported an increased frequency.

This is an important time to keep the lines of communication open. One couple who had been in sex therapy before their first pregnancy returned to us in a panic when their baby was three months old. They thought they were back to square one; both felt turned off.

When they resumed intercourse after delivery, he noticed that her vagina was always dry. He was reluctant to discuss her dryness for several reasons. He didn't want to pressure her if she was feeling sexually uninterested; he felt sexually rejected by the dryness but didn't want to admit it; he was afraid the difficulty in penetrating would cause him to lose his erection, a fear he preferred to keep to himself; and his style was to act rather than talk.

There was something else he wasn't talking about. He had

always been strongly aroused by feeling his wife's large breasts, but now when he touched them, milk often leaked or spurted from the nipples. It repelled him.

At first, the dryness didn't bother her, but when it persisted, she became confused. ("I thought I was aroused but my body seemed to contradict me") and then defensive. She eventually spoke up and suggested they return for a "sex-therapy refresher course."

We did four things: We got them to talk (including a discussion of his feelings about the breast milk); we explained about breast-feeding, low estrogen levels, and lack of vaginal lubrication; we suggested they use an artificial lubricant; and we had them go back through the sequential steps of touching used in sex therapy, but this time in rapid succession during the course of one week. We saw them two weeks later, and they felt things were working out.

This couple came for professional help quickly. Others choose to wait. Sometimes a sexual problem that originates in the postpartum months may resolve itself as hormone levels return to normal and the baby becomes integrated into the family. Some-times, however, the sexual problem persists or worsens. If the problem is troublesome, we recommend that couples get profes-sional help right away rather than waiting a year or two in the hope of somehow working it out themselves.

One problem often associated in people's minds with childbirth and the postpartum period is a loose vagina. This problem can arise if the vaginal muscles are badly torn during delivery. With modern obstetrical care, this rarely happens unless it is a very precipitous delivery. The episiotomy, a small incision along the midline of the bottom wall of the vagina, allows the baby to emerge without causing damaging tears in the vagina.

A loose vagina can also result from deliveries that occur too close together in time. When children are spaced at least two years apart, the vaginal tissues have a chance to return to a firm state before the next delivery.

Perhaps the most important information comes from the re-ported observations of vaginal response when a woman is sexually aroused. With sexual stimulation, there is an increased blood flow to the vagina, which leads to congestion in the vaginal wall. This congestion is such that if there is no penis in the vagina, the walls of the outer third come in contact with one another. With the introduction of the penis, the walls adjust, snugging around it. These changes do not lessen after childbirth and in some women are even more pronounced. The result is that a sexually responsive woman may actually be more snug after childbirth than before.

If there is a slight feeling of looseness after childbirth, Kegel exercises can help. You simply practice contracting and relaxing the vaginal muscles repeatedly every day. You can tell if you are contracting the right muscles by seeing if contraction will stop the flow of urine.

In unusually severe cases, which are relatively rare these days, there is a surgical procedure that reinforces the vaginal muscles. We suggest getting more than one opinion before having surgery.

Within two months or so of delivery, the majority of couples find that their sex life is back to normal. They now are well launched into parenthood, which, with its enormous demands and equally enormous rewards, is one of life's richest experiences. Parenthood and the continuing marriage represent a time of sexual readjustment and potential growth toward the ideal we all hear so much about but less often see realized—the happy, lasting marriage of a couple, with children, who manage to keep their relationship and their sex life vital, loving, and exciting.

Parenting—

New Roles,

New Challenges

14

Parenting

MOST STUDIES seem to agree: being Mommy and Daddy is anti-erotic. A study done in California in 1970 and two magazine sex surveys revealed the same thing: Couples with children at home rate their sexual satisfaction lower than others.

Here is a letter that seems to say it all.

Dear Sarrels:

We are the parents of five children (all planned) and enjoy every one of them; however, we frequently wonder what happened to time for us. Often we find that when everyone has been tucked in, those ideas we had at four in the afternoon give way to much-needed sleep.

You could suggest weekend getaways, but the one time we found somebody willing to sit with five, going away to an empty motel room seemed deliberate and almost desperate.

I'm sure we're not alone in wondering what happens to intimacy between husband and wife during the child-rearing years. But unlike many, we're still very much in love after twelve years of marriage, and we'd like to be able to do something about it more often. *Help!*

We replied:

Thank you for stating a common problem so warmly and so well. Our first response to your letter was: "Sigh . . ." It's a truly universal dilemma.

We are glad you phrased your question in terms of missing intimacy, not simply not having time for sex, because it is the special intimate emotional bond between husband and wife as well as the sexual one that tends to take a backseat during the child-rearing years. It isn't only the presence of the children, their demands and interruptions and the time spent with them; it's also the fact that so much time between husband and wife is spent discussing the endless nitty-gritty of budget, school problems, the broken toilet, or Johnny's stomachaches. Not that this

199

sharing of life's fabric is meaningless; on the contrary, it too can be a special bond. But it does tend to nudge out time for talking about feelings—feelings about each other, a book, a fascinating dream, sex, or where life is heading.

In doing sex therapy with a couple, we place a major emphasis on their taking time every day to talk about feelings. Many couples find that they need to plan very carefully to manage thirty minutes or an hour. It may be when they are jogging or exercising together between 6:30 and 7:00 A.M., having a drink at six in the evening, or passing up the late-night news.

Couples also need to find a way to make their bedroom a private place where the children won't intrude. A lock and a Do Not Disturb sign help. Some parents feel too guilty about taking time for themselves and saying no to their children to do this. Others are simply not comfortable enough with sex to deal with the fact that slightly older children may understand what Mommy and Daddy are doing behind the door.

We think that parents are actually giving something very valuable to their children when they convey in spoken or unspoken terms such messages as "Mommy and Daddy love each other and want private time" or "We value sex—it's good and nothing to be ashamed of, but it's private." If more parents managed to communicate these attitudes, there would be many fewer sexual problems.

The weekend getaway is a good idea, but you are so right in describing its pitfall—great expectations that turn it into an anxious situation, a kind of demand for sexual performance and special feelings. One solution is to get away more often. (Have you thought of swapping baby-sitting with another couple one weekend every other month?) Another solution is to recognize the pressures and tensions and talk—even laugh—about them. Then try to put the emphasis on sharing time and fun. The sex is likely to follow, but if it doesn't, you've still had a nice time.

This issue of obtaining privacy from the children seems to be a universal dilemma. When we give talks about sex, it is one of the questions most frequently asked. Once, after a lecture to a group of parents, a father stood up and asked, "What should you do if your five-year-old bursts in on you in the middle of sex?" You could feel a sympathetic shudder pass through the group. Phil's reply was a surprise to most. He said, "It shouldn't ever happen. If you teach respect for privacy in a family, the five-year-old won't burst in. And one of the best ways to teach privacy is to respect your children's right to it. Never burst in on them. Always knock before you go into a child's room. Start when they are very small and it will be second nature." Alternatively, you can have a lock.

Some people are so acutely aware of their children's presence in the house that they never fully enjoy sex unless the kids are away or they are away from the kids. One woman said her anxiety about being overheard during sex started when her first child was an infant. "It seemed like she had ESP or some sixth sense. Whenever we'd make love and really get into it, she'd start to cry like mad and I'd have to stop and go to her." This woman couldn't even relax when her children were out of the house because she always feared they might come home unexpectedly. She was able to relax and enjoy sex in a hotel or motel or a borrowed house. One interpretation of her problem could be that she was projecting her own feelings of guilt and shame about sex onto her children and thus imagined them to be potentially judging and condemning her.

There is also the problem of housewife syndrome and depression among some women who feel stuck at home with the kids and miss working, with its built-in daily stimulation. In recent years, housewife/mothers have had to face the added burden of a devalued role. They often feel defensive and embarrassed about "only" staying at home. One woman said, "I think my feeling less sexy is directly related to my being home with the kids. When I worked [as a librarian], I met people, even flirted some. I dressed nicely every day and felt good about how I looked and about how I did my job. Now [being home with sons age 3 and 5] I wear any old thing. I can't even *imagine* flirting. It's as if a whole piece of me that includes my sexuality got lost somewhere. I wish I could get it back." Actually a part-time librarian's job, losing ten pounds, nursery school for her three-year-old, and some long talks with her husband made a big difference for this woman.

House-husbands, who are becoming more numerous, can have problems, too. Julia and Don were firmly committed to the idea of sharing the job of parenting. When Franny was born, Don quit his job and stayed home to write detective stories, something he had always wanted to do. Julia kept her full-time job as a dental hygienist.

For a while, things seemed to be going smoothly, but trouble began when Franny was five months old. Don's parents visited, and Don's father was scornful of Don for "not taking the responsibilities of a husband and father." After this, Don began to have trouble keeping an erection. Soon he was unable to have an erection at all. They came for a consultation with us and were consid-

2 0 2 Parenting—New Roles, New Challenges

ering sex therapy. A few months elapsed, and one day Don telephoned to say there was no longer a sex problem. He had gone back to work, and that had made the difference. He felt upset that he had been unable to live up to his own ideals. He said, "I guess I was born about a decade too soon. The traditional male image got too deeply into me for me to be able to transcend it."

A few hours later, we got an unexpected telephone call from Julie. She said, "Don told me about his conversation with you, and I felt badly that he took all the blame for the failure of our arrangement. I thought you should know that I think I was part of the problem. Looking back on it, I realize I actually lost some kind of respect for Don when he was staying home with Franny and not earning money. On the one hand, I thought it was terrific, even heroic. But it's as if some other voice in me said it wasn't manly. I got less sexually turned on by him."

Julia and Don's experience with nontraditional parenting arrangements is certainly not universal. Many couples have no problems and, in fact, blossom when the male takes some or even most of the parenting responsibilities. As Don suggested, he and Julia are part of a transitional generation, with one foot in the past.

15

Our Children's Sexuality

BEING PARENTS means dealing with our children's sexuality. Most people choose to ignore it, keeping an image of the child as "innocent," that is, free of sexual impulses and curiosity. This image persists in spite of Freud's descriptions of childhood sexuality and in spite of modern psychological and sexological research that leaves no doubt about it; children are intensely sexual beings in their own way.

We confront our children's sexuality from infancy on. Diapering sons, we notice an erection; nursing, we sense an erotic response in ourselves and perhaps in the baby; we find our two-year-olds touching their genitals with obvious pleasure; they want to touch our breasts, see Daddy's penis and Mommy's vagina; they play doctor. Most of us choose to ignore these manifestations of sexuality in our kids. Why? Probably because we simply aren't comfortable with sex and, particularly, with our children's sexuality.

Some parents are able to get past the mental block and are aware of their children as sexual beings. They may even observe that they sometimes have erotic responses to a child. This can be very frightening. Isn't that incest? No, incest is acting on the feelings. Simply having the feelings from time to time is normal.

Some of us would find it easier if our children weren't sexual. We wouldn't have to *deal* with it, teach them about it, make decisions about what is healthy or moral. The questions are perplexing, and "experts" disagree on how we should handle things.

Obviously we believe that confronting the facts about children's sexuality, dealing with the issues thoughtfully, and providing sex education for our own children should be a high priority for parents. Unfortunately, it is definitely *not* a priority for most American parents today.

A recent survey of families in Cleveland found that 85 to 95 percent of the parents *never* discussed sex or intercourse with their three- to-eleven-year-old children. Forty percent hadn't even discussed menstruation with their daughters. Those are incredible statistics—and very sad. They tell us that for some people, sex is so far outside the realm of ordinary human experience that we dare not speak of it.

Probably the single most valuable sexual lesson any parent can teach a child takes place in infancy. The lesson is simply that it is wonderful to be close, body to body, in a loving embrace—to make eye contact, to play and make sounds together, to love and to trust. Monkeys that are deprived of a mother or mother substitute in infancy are usually unable to mate when they mature. In that sense, sex is not truly instinctive. It is a human potential that must be activated through touching and bonding.

In addition to expressing our love for our children in a warm, physical way, we can answer questions about our bodies, babies, and sex in a way that is understandable to a child. For some parents, this is easier said than done. Many adults have never had a candid and relaxed conversation about sex, so how are they supposed to begin? If this were the best of all possible worlds, all parents would be offered an opportunity to attend some seminars designed, among other things, to help them deal with their own feelings before they discuss sex with their children. The group could also share advice and air anxieties. (Organizing such a seminar would be a marvelous project for some concerned parents.)

Short of holding seminars, parents can still do something; they can simply try their best, even if their best includes blushing, stammering, and lots of "I don't knows." After a child is six or so, parents can say, "You know this isn't an easy subject for me to talk about. Grandma (or Grandpa) and I never talked about it when I was your age. But I think it's important and good, so I'm trying my best to make it something our family can discuss."

What can we do to help our children feel better about their bodies? Apart from encouraging a healthy diet, exercise, and good health-care practices, we can teach our children to feel at ease with the way they look, smell, move, and feel. Illness or pain should not be unmentionables; they are part of life. If aches and pains are an admission of failure, children learn early to ignore signals from their bodies—to feel the body as some "thing" they drag through life, a source of nothing but problems.

Many negative lessons about genitals are communicated through toilet training, when everything "down there" can become associated with "dirty"—and Mommy and Daddy's displeasure. It is important for our children to learn that urine and feces are not horrible or disgusting. Children should not be made to feel ashamed of their bodies or of natural body odors. The genital area is not a germ-infested place and should not be treated as such.

When we call a nose a nose and an arm an arm but the penis "Charlie" or "little wee wee" or "thing," we are communicating something. We are saying that the genitals are different from other body parts that have universal names. More important, it's confusing when you call your penis "Peter" and your friend calls it his "weenie."

Although most people refer to the female genitals as the vagina, that is not really correct. A little girl may be taught that she has a vulva (the outside part of her genitals, including the clitoris) and a vagina (the inner part). While she may have some trouble with the concept of the vagina, since she can't see into it, she can safely insert a finger if she's curious.

Actually, all animals, including human ones, seem to have some natural curiosity about their own bodies. All little babies explore their bodies, working gradually downward from head to toes. Boys usually discover their penis at about ten months; girls find their genitals at about twelve months. As with the eyes or the knees or the toes, the genitals are explored, and then the child moves on.

Most infants and toddlers do engage in some genital stimulation, although usually in an absentminded way, during other play activities.

As reported by Eleanor Galenson and Herman Roiphe, careful observation of children in nursery settings has enabled psychiatrists to note that between the ages of fifteen to seventeen months, there is a shift from more aimless exploration to vigorous and deliberate genital stimulation. Both boys and girls will touch their genitals in a purposeful way and generally appear to be enjoying their feelings. Some seem to experience orgasm.

After twenty-four months, the self-stimulation usually continues, but with somewhat lessened intensity. It often becomes a more private, solitary experience as the child learns more about social expectations.

Genital pleasure is *not* harmful or wrong. Unless a child is particularly anxious or upset, this early kind of self-stimulation will not be excessive, and it should never be punished. If a child touches his or her genitals in a public situation, he or she can be told, "It's all right to touch your penis (or vagina/vulva), but it's something you should do when you're by yourself—not in front of other people." There are many things we do in private, and most children can easily accept this idea.

The majority of children will play doctor or house at least once, which may include looking at and/or touching another child's genitals. They may do this with a child of the same or opposite sex, or in a group. This is a normal expression of curiosity and, like self-touching, should never be punished.

Many of us dread the thought of discovering our children in sex play or masturbation. We may remember our own guilt or our parents' disapproval. In spite of knowing in our heads that it's really okay, we may find ourselves reacting with anger. A colleague of ours, a sex educator and counselor, told us that when he first noticed his three-year-old son touching his penis, he had an impulsive response. He started to say no and pull the boy's hand away. "Luckily," he remarks, "I caught myself in time, but the experience showed me that it's a continual struggle to reconcile our own negative childhood messages with the positive ideas we now hold."

When parents do offer sex education to their children, they usually think of it as a one-time explanation of the process of reproduction. One study found that most parents talked only in terms of animal or plant life. Fewer than one-third talked about human beings! Talking about animals and plants is appropriate at a certain age, perhaps for preschoolers, but the concept of both male and female being involved in reproduction, and even the idea of sperm and egg, can be grasped by young children.

Even the most basic facts can be confused in children's minds. They often spin their own fantasies about how babies get started, where they grow, and how they are born. They need to learn about sex and reproduction many times, not just once, so an open flow of communication, one that permits questions to be asked and asked again, is important.

There comes a moment when most children who know about the sperm and the egg and about babies growing in the uterus will ask the next logical question: "How does the sperm get into the mother to meet the egg?" Our own son, who knew many technicalities from the books and teaching models we had around the house, asked this when he was five. We explained sexual intercourse. He was quiet for a moment and then said, "I suppose you do that in private."

Many parents are uncertain how to describe sexual intercourse to children. Books for children on the subject are extremely helpful for several reasons: (1) pictures help children understand; (2) having a book is reassuring and can help parents feel less anxious about what to say; and (3) when reading a book together is a common, everyday occurrence, this will be just one more reading time rather than a slightly tense "Talk About Sex."

Since sexual intercourse and making a baby involve both parents, we think both should talk with their children about these subjects, either together or separately. Children often have a hard time fully understanding and remembering facts about sex. They need to be able to hear the same facts a number of times, perhaps even many years after the first explanation.

The following is one possible way of describing sexual intercourse to a child. This explanation is geared to a five-year-old, but a three-year-old could certainly listen in and grasp some of the ideas. For the seven to nine age group, one might add even more facts—for example, more information about the female internal reproductive organs, the uterus and ovaries.

"A husband and wife love each other and they like to be close together—to sleep together, to hug and to kiss. The way they make a baby is a special way of being close and loving. It's called sexual intercourse. A woman has a vagina—do you remember what that is? No? Well, it's the place I told you about, where the baby passes through when it is born. The vagina is near the place where urine (or pee pee) comes out, but there's a separate opening just for the vagina. The vagina is a space that changes its size. It can become larger or smaller depending on whether or not something is in it. It adjusts to the size of a baby but that's not very often. Much more often it adjusts to the size of Daddy's penis so that he can be close inside me without it hurting me.

"In sexual intercourse, the husband's penis is placed in the wife's vagina. They move back and forth for a while. Then the sperms come out of the penis in a white liquid and the liquid stays for a while in the vagina. When one of the sperms joins with an ovum (a very tiny egg) made by the woman, a baby will start to grow inside the woman's uterus (a special place in the woman's belly). It will grow from a tiny speck to the size of a newborn baby in about nine months, and then the baby is ready to be born. Since we don't want to have a baby every time we have sexual inter-course, we use birth control to keep the sperm from getting to the ovum. Husbands and wives have sexual intercourse not just to start a baby but at other times as well, because it's a way of loving each other that is special and because it feels so nice."

Some common questions from children arise when sex is dis-cussed:

1. Do you and Daddy have sexual intercourse?
   ANSWER: Yes, we do.
2. Can I watch?
   ANSWER: No, it's private. But we can tell you anything you want to know.
3. How does the baby know when it's time to come out?
   ANSWER: The mother's body knows, and she can feel her body starting to help the baby come out.
4. Does a man have a vagina (or uterus)?
   ANSWER: No.
5. Does a woman have a penis?
   ANSWER: No.

The way we talk about sex and the way in which it's described in books for adults and children is usually with the male as the active agent and the female as the passive recipient. The penis *always* enters the vagina, and the sperm are pictured as swimming furiously toward and then penetrating the egg. The fact that the egg moves through the genital tract and plays an active role at the moment of fertilization is usually left out. We really should say, "When the man and the woman join together," or, "When the egg and sperm come together." We should try to avoid sex-role stereo-typing in describing sex and reproduction because we want to emphasize female and male—not something a male does to a female.

As our children approach the time when their bodies begin to change, we have an obligation to prepare them so they won't be frightened or bewildered. Between the ages of nine and eleven, girls need to be told about the normal vaginal discharge that begins one to two years before the first menstrual period, about breast growth, pubic and underarm hair, menstruation and the paraphernalia of menstrual periods, such as pads and tampons. If a girl is frightened about the idea of inserting something into her vagina, she should be reassured that it is all right not to wear a tampon until she is comfortable with the idea (and it may take time for this to be so).

Our sons need to learn about hair growth, voice changes, enlargement of the penis and testicles, onset of the ability to ejaculate, and wet dreams. At about the age of eleven through fourteen, boys often lag behind girls in growth and pubertal development, and they may need reassurance about that.

We are often confused about what our children need around the time of puberty because they often seem to be saying, "I know all that sex stuff. Don't talk to me about that." They may also seem intensely embarrassed. As parents, we walk a fine line between respecting our teenagers' right to privacy and their need for information and communication. Privacy means practical things like not bursting in on them in the bathroom or bedroom, not reading their diaries, as well as allowing them some secrets. It does not mean not educating them or not talking about subjects that may make them uncomfortable.

If talking doesn't seem to be working, books can be helpful because older children can read them on their own, reread the parts that concern them particularly and not expose more of themselves than they want to.

Either from parents, books, or some other authoritative source, young adolescents should learn about the kinds of sexual feelings and sexual experiences that are typical of their age group. They need reassurance that sexual feelings, fantasies, crushes, and intense curiosity are normal and common.

It helps to understand that some kinds of experimentation also are common. It's estimated that about 37 percent of teenage boys and 10 percent of teenage girls have some sexual experiences with same-sex peers. These do not predict adult homosexuality, necessarily; they are simply a part of adolescent development.

Not all teenagers masturbate, but most do. Among boys entering college, about 90 percent masturbate and most others begin around the same age. Among women in college, between 65 and 80 percent masturbate. Most of us know that masturbation is not physically or psychologically harmful; however, some parents may disapprove on religious grounds. If so, this belief should be shared with a child. Parents who do not object to masturbation for specifically religious reasons may just feel vaguely that it is wrong; others simply don't know what to think. Most psychiatrists, psychologists, and sex therapists believe masturbation to be entirely normal. It can be a good way to learn about one's body and sexual responses, and it does not impair one's capacity to love another person or to share sexual pleasure.

Similarly, some parents, because of religious or moral beliefs, may not approve of contraception. If so, their attitudes should be discussed with their children, and perhaps other sources of information should be provided. Parents who do not object to birth control owe it to their youngsters to help them find out as much as possible about contraception or to guide their children to informative and up-to-date literature.

As you read this you may be thinking, if only there weren't so much talk about sex, maybe our children wouldn't get ideas or be involved in so much sexual activity. Well, in one sense, we agree that there is too much irresponsible talk and too many exploitative visual images of sex today. Sex is used to sell, and as a result, our culture sells sex. But that only makes our job as parents more important. Our discussions with our children about sex are not going to push them to experiment on their own. In fact, studies have shown that children whose parents discussed sex openly with them were more likely to postpone first intercourse to a later age than those whose parents never talked with them. And when these young men and women had intercourse, they were more likely to be responsible about contraception.

One thing that continually amazes us in talking with young people about sex is learning that they don't really know just what their parents believe about sexual behavior. Why don't we discuss sexual morals with our children? One reason is that we have given up all hope of controlling them. And that's correct—we can't control what they do. But we can influence them. Believe it or not, many young people welcome the chance to discuss the pros and cons of different behaviors. Now more than ever, teenagers need to be told it's okay to say no—because of religious beliefs, because they're scared, because they're not ready—for any reason.

The best way to learn about sex, to enjoy it both now and later on in life, is to go slowly, to think about what is happening, to make conscious decisions that are compatible with one's values. If we can communicate these ideas to our children, we will be helping them to deal intelligently and morally with one of life's most complex tasks—growing up sexually.

There is one final concept we should bear in mind. That is, simply, that our children see us as role models. If Mom and Dad are never affectionate, if they are heard fighting about sex, if Mom tells her daughter that all men are "out for just one thing and can't ever be trusted"—these messages are a form of sex education.

By contrast, we parents can give positive messages if we sometimes hug and kiss or snuggle when the children are present. And because sex is one form of intimate communication, we can demonstrate good, open communication about feelings. We can say, "We've been working so hard lately that we don't have much time together. I miss you," or "I feel hurt by what you said." It's particularly valuable for our children to hear their fathers talk about feelings so that they learn that feelings aren't peculiar to females.

We have a job to do. We must try to raise a generation of children who are loving and open; comfortable with their feelings, their bodies, and their sexuality; able to make thoughtful decisions about sexual behavior and relationships; and eager to pass their wisdom and sense of fulfillment on to *their* children.

16

The End of Fertility

ORDINARILY, fertility ends at menopause, but it may also end surgically by way of a tubal procedure on either the male or the female—a vasectomy for a man or a tubal ligation or hysterectomy for a woman. Loss of fertility is certainly a turning point in the life cycle, but it is one to which the vast majority of people adapt easily. The exceptions tend to involve involuntary sterility, as when a young woman has a hysterectomy. In fact, voluntary sterilization is often a positive sexual turning point because it eliminates anxiety over pregnancy and the mess and inconvenience of situational contraception and may usher in a new era of spontaneity.

Tubal Occlusion and Vasectomy

"What I like best about having my tubes closed is not even having to *think* each month if I could be pregnant. Since a third child now would absolutely wreck my career [which involved extensive travel], I find it a great relief. Before I had the surgery, I know I was uptight sometimes around mid-cycle, knowing I could be ovulating. I trusted my diaphragm, but it's not one hundred percent, is it? My sex life with my husband? It's either the same or maybe a bit better. The one problem I sense is just the hint of a thought on my part, when I'm out of town, about maybe having sex with someone else, but I don't think I will. I'm just reacting to this new sense of freedom."

This thirty-six-year-old woman is fairly typical in her reaction to having tubal surgery. In a recent British study of women one year after tubal occlusion, 58 percent of the women who had undergone surgery reported no change in sexual satisfaction, 34 percent said sex was better, while 8 percent said it was worse.

Other studies have usually revealed an even lower rate of decreased sexual satisfaction—between 3 to 5 percent. And after all, we would expect a small percentage of couples to report some deterioration in their sex life in any given year. Tubal surgery is clearly not a threat to one's sex life. Even women who have no children who elect to have tubal surgery do not have adverse afterreactions. They are no more likely to have regrets than are women who have completed their desired childbearing.

Now, with microsurgery, even the irreversibility of the procedure may not be a problem, since more than half the women who want the procedure reversed can have their tubes reopened.

There is always the exception that proves the rule. Not long ago, we spoke with a married couple in their mid-thirties who had experienced great difficulty following the wife's tubal surgery. She, a doctor herself, had made the decision on her own and had announced it to her husband rather than their jointly arriving at a decision. He hadn't objected too strongly because he felt it was her right and because they really hadn't been planning to have any more children. It was only in the weeks and months after the procedure that he became aware of his resentment and of a very strong wish for another child. He persuaded his wife to have her tubes reopened, but the surgery was unsuccessful. The husband became mildly depressed and began having trouble keeping an erection. After consulting us, he entered individual psychotherapy, so we aren't able to say how things worked out for them.

A study of voluntary sterilization demonstrated that couples are likely to proceed with tubal surgery without intensive discussion or counseling, whereas couples who decide to use vasectomy tend to share a more thoughtful decision-making process and are more likely to seek professional counseling before the procedure. One very interesting study compared women who had tubal occlusion with wives of vasectomized men. The sterilized women reported a significantly lower frequency of sexual intercourse and more sexual problems than the wives of the vasectomized men. Apart from the differing ways of approaching the decision, the other significant difference between these groups was that in the vasectomized couples, the husband was obviously more involved in sharing responsibility. In the marriages of the sterilized women, the wife's responsibility for fertility control was generally taken for granted.

In contrast to tubal surgery, vasectomy, at least in its early days, raised a hue and cry about "castrating" men psychologically and caused some alarm about possible hormonal side effects. It has now been shown, as reported by author Robert Kolodny, that vasectomy does not alter pituitary function or testosterone production either in the short or the long term. The studies of psychological and sexual aftereffects of vasectomy have also been reassuring. Only between 1 and 4 percent of men have reported a deterioration in their sex life.

Men often seek vasectomy less as a method of fertility control than as a means of enhancing their sex lives. This is particularly true of men over thirty-five. Many of these men have tended to use condoms, and the vasectomy is a way out of continual condom usage. As with women, there are the exceptions that prove the rule. An occasional man will, to his own surprise, feel less sexually assured after a vasectomy. One study did find that 19 percent of the men said they found their orgasms were now less intense. But this has to be weighed against the fact that exactly the same percentage (19%) reported *more* intense orgasms after their vasectomy. In this same study, 12 percent of the men felt they now had less ejaculatory control, but 25 percent felt they had more control. In general, those men who had sexual difficulties before the operation were more likely to report adverse sexual consequences. It seems logical that men who are already concerned about some aspect of their sexual functioning should have counseling before they proceed with a vasectomy.

Hysterectomy

Hysterectomy means removal of the uterus, including the cervix. Removal of the uterus plus the ovaries and tubes is called total hysterectomy and bilateral salpingo-oophorectomy.

Removal of the ovaries induces an immediate and sharp decline in estrogen. It creates a surgically induced menopausal state in which the symptoms may be more severe than in normal menopause. Although the current medical literature states that a hysterectomy without removal of the ovaries does not affect subsequent ovarian function, there is some clinical evidence which suggests that premature ovarian failure may be triggered in some women by simple hysterectomy.

Contrary to popular myth and expectation, removing a woman's uterus does not appear to cause severe psychiatric or sexual difficultues. In fact, three very recent studies done in England showed considerable *improvement* in sexual function and enjoyment after hysterectomy. One of these studies found that 44 percent reported improvement, 31 percent no change, and only 19 percent indicated a deterioration in their sex lives. Another study found improvement in 42 percent, no change in 52 percent, and deterioration in only 6 percent.

This does not mean that women who have a sexual problem should imagine that a hysterectomy will improve the situation. The reason so many women report an improved sex life after hysterectomy is that so many had been suffering from tumors, excessive bleeding, infections, endometriosis, or some other uterine condition that was adversely affecting their sex lives. Women often endure a year or more of distressing symptoms before deciding on hysterectomy. Then the relief from symptoms is a tremendous boost physically, psychologically, and sexually.

Not everyone follows the statistical norm. Some women and their partners will react adversely to a hysterectomy. For some women, the loss of the uterus decreases their sense of femininity. If sex has been valued largely for the sake of making babies, then the woman may find her sexual interest declining when she can no longer reproduce. Even if she does not feel she is less of a woman, her partner may see her in that light and may withdraw sexually. Husbands are sometimes simply mystified by a hysterectomy. They don't really understand female anatomy and they aren't sure just what has been removed. One very highly educated man confessed his utter confusion. He didn't understand the difference between the uterus and the vagina and assumed that intercourse would be impossible after his wife's hysterectomy.

A few women claim that removal of the uterus changes the intensity of orgasm. They say, for example, "I used to have a deeper feeling that is missing now," or, "I can still have one kind of an orgasm, but there's another kind I used to have sometimes and now I don't." Possibly these women had experienced sensations when the uterus contracted rhythmically during orgasm, and now they miss these contractions.

In a small percentage of women who have a vaginal hysterectomy (removal of the uterus through the vagina rather than through an abdominal incision), the vagina ends up being too tight at the opening because of the surgical repair of weakened muscles in the vaginal wall. If intercourse is then uncomfortable, the woman may develop vaginismus and/or withdraw from sex. Her husband may also react negatively to the difficulty in penetrating the vagina by developing a problem with premature ejaculation or problems with erection.

Sexual problems may also occur if a hysterectomy triggers premature ovarian failure. For example, if a thirty-seven-year-old woman has a hysterectomy and at age thirty-nine or forty begins to have menopausal symptoms, she is likely to dismiss them or, at best, be confused. Her doctor may not think in terms of low estrogen levels causing her problems. We have seen a great many couples whose sexual relationship faltered in just this way. The wife's lack of vaginal lubrication or decreased sexual feelings were apparently inexplicable—that is, until tests revealed the wife's low estrogen levels. Then the couple at least understood what was happening and why. They could then decide whether to use hormone replacement therapy.

The one situation in which a hysterectomy is likely to be a severe psychological trauma and perhaps adversely affect sexuality occurs when it is a medically necessary procedure done before a couple has completed their childbearing and particularly if they haven't yet had any children.

The impact then is the same as that of any infertility problem, but with one difference: In many cases, infertility is not absolute—there is always a small ray of hope—but a hysterectomy is absolutely final. On the other hand, the sexual problems associated with infertility usually arise during the year or two of active testing and trying to conceive. With a hysterectomy, there is no such period. The emotional trauma is perhaps closer to that of loss—the loss of hoped-for, imagined children. As we know from parents who lose a baby at birth, this loss can be every bit as painful as the later loss of a child. We know, too, that loss of this magnitude can certainly affect every aspect of a couple's relationship, including the sexual.

STAGE *Six*

Making Love

the Second Time

Around

17

The Effects of Divorce

on Sex

WHEN a man and woman divorce, they experience changes that affect almost every aspect of their social and psychological behavior. Because the changes wrought by divorce exert a profound impact on sexual functioning, we feel that divorce is one of those events in the human life cycle that signal a sexual turning point.

Divorce might not have been on the list of sexual turning points even as recently as ten years ago, but according to demographers from the United States Census Bureau, four out of ten marriages are now ending in divorce. And we know from individuals and couples who come to see us about their problems that divorce often has a major impact on a person's sexuality. Sexual dysfunctions may initially signal a setback, but in the long run, it may prove to be the starting point for new growth.

We want to describe three stages that commonly occur during and after the breakup of a marriage, and some of the meanings of these stages with respect to sexuality: (1) breaking up; (2) dating—a transition; and (3) moving toward a new commitment.

Breaking Up

A couple's sexual life often is affected for months—or possibly years—before the divorce occurs. There may be a sexual problem of some duration, or in the face of a deteriorating relationship, a once-adequate sex life may become a problem area. To the couple, the sexual problem may feel like the central issue.

A husband and wife in their late twenties came to the United States from Latin America so that he could get a graduate degree. The culture shock was severe. She became interested in feminism and wanted to change their life-style completely. He had trouble with his courses. In the midst of this, he became impotent and was so traumatized by his impotence that he could not think or talk about any other issues. They were divorced, and he stayed to finish his studies. He was able to work but was unable to function sexually. Although he had not masturbated in years, he tried to do so now and found he was unable to repond. He felt that his "sexual powers" were gone forever and was quite frightened when he first came to talk to us.

A twenty-two-year-old woman saw us in consultation a year after her divorce. After two years of marriage, her husband had announced that he was leaving because she was "totally frigid and uptight." She was completely surprised. Although she hadn't had an orgasm, she had felt that she was becoming more and more responsive. Her husband apparently was unable to discuss his concern about their sex life, although he must have had very strong feelings about it, which finally burst out when it was too late to do anything about it. The young woman was so devasted by his accusation of frigidity that she felt she could never venture into a sexual relationship again.

The two examples we have just cited may sound extreme, but in fact they represent a level of sexual trauma we often encounter. The traumatized individuals must try to face the realities of being divorced. They would like to meet potential sexual partners or mates, but their anxieties about their sexual functioning may keep them from taking even the first tentative steps.

By contrast, a number of couples we have counseled were able to work out their sexual problem with professional help before splitting up. When the sexual problem was resolved and the total picture was clarified, some of these couples saw that there were many other fundamental problems that seemed unresolvable, and they decided to divorce. But—and this, we feel, is a very large *but* —they were breaking up for the "right" reasons, and from positions of greater individual strength and sexual self-confidence.

A couple in their thirties, both of whom are business executives, sought help with the wife's problem of "frigidity." They used this now-outdated word in an outdated sense, meaning that she was unable to have vaginal orgasms. She had been in psycho-analysis with a Freudian analyst because of this so-called defi-ciency, and neither the analyst, the wife, nor the husband knew that research has invalidated the concept of the vaginal orgasm.

Although a more thorough sexual history revealed that the husband had a problem with premature ejaculation and occa-sional loss of erection, this couple had established a myth in which they both believed: that he was sexually adequate and that she had a severe sexual problem.

She had come from a Southern family in which her large physical size, intelligence, ambition, and assertiveness had been labeled unfeminine. She was so insecure about her femaleness that she easily assumed the blame for their difficulties. Seeing the realities of their situation was painful for this couple, but they were able to work together on it, and for some months, it seemed their marriage would continue. At that point, however, other dif-ferences in temperament and outlook became more apparent. The sexual problem had served to deflect attention from those issues.

Eventually the couple split up, but after talking with each of them individually, we were certain they encountered much less difficulty in the postdivorce period than they would have had their sexual problem not been resolved.

To avoid giving the false impression that divorce is likely to follow sex therapy, we want to stress that sex therapy usually strengthens a relationship, both sexually and emotionally. When a sexual problem is a central issue and threatens to undermine a marriage, sex therapy may well be the most appropriate form of help.

Dating—a Transition

In the year or two following divorce, there comes a phase of readjustment, a transitional time that has psychological and social aspects. Psychologically there is a need to mourn and gradually eliminate the myriad attachments to a former spouse. It is impor-tant to remember that resentment, hurt—even hate—can be forms of attachment, so that the process of emotional disentangle-ment means easing away from both loving *and* angry feelings.

The social side of the transition involves adjusting to a new social status—being one of the formerly married. For many divorced persons, this means single parenthood and perhaps also a new home, job, and geographic location. Friends, relatives, and co-workers redefine you.

One of the major changes in the social situation is the resumption of dating. In his book *The World of the Formerly Married*, published in 1966, Morton Hunt reported that 75 percent of divorced persons begin dating during the first year following the termination of marriage, 90 percent by the end of the second year. Although there are no statistics available, we can assume that a high proportion of divorced persons have at least one new sexual relationship in this year or two.

A new sexual relationship can be one of life's greatest, most enriching experiences, or it can simply be fun; it can also be complicated and difficult. For almost everyone, beginning a new love affair means being vulnerable. If it doesn't go well, feelings of failure or rejection can be very intense. Even when the feelings and the sex seem to flow easily, there are necessary accommodations to the other person; there are also practical realities, such as contraception or the possibility that one's children may intrude.

The recently divorced individual may be even more vulnerable than the never-married to the pitfalls of a new relationship. To begin with, dating and all it implies is a thing out of the past to be experienced again, but in a new time and place with new rules. For men as well as for women, finding out how to fit comfortably into current norms and expectations—while meeting their own needs and satisfying their own values—can take quite some time.

Many divorced people complain about the pressure they feel to become sexually involved soon after meeting someone. A thirty-year-old divorced woman, Jacqueline, described it graphically. "I went back into the world of men and sex like a lamb to slaughter. I was sure I'd never survive. Sex with Todd, my ex-husband, had been pretty terrible most of the eight years we were married. I rarely had an orgasm. I thought I was undersexed. When Todd told me I was hopelessly frigid, I believed him. Then he walked out on me, and my friends started introducing me to men. Some were single and some were divorced, but they had all been around—the singles bar scene, affairs with married women, you name it. Some of them were straightforward about it; they expected sex. Others were more subtle, but they still expected it.

After three or four men spent exactly one evening with me saying no and then disappeared, I knew I was going to have to choose— either play the game or be a nun. Then I met Arnie, and I really liked him. He's a smooth guy, but I sort of trusted that he liked me. I wanted to hold onto him—for a while, at least. So I decided to go ahead and sleep with him. Did I tell you he's a pilot? He's been all over the world. I had the image of him that he's been with every kind of woman from Swedish stewardesses to Japanese geishas. I didn't want to disappoint him, but I was so sure he'd be able to tell I was frigid, that I couldn't relax at all. Eventually I just faked it, the way I used to, in the beginning, with my husband."

Jacqueline came for sex counseling. The counseling concentrated on building her sexual self-esteem. She was encouraged to explore her own sexuality by writing about her past, finding out what kinds of situations she could respond to, exploring her fantasies, and learning to enjoy masturbating to orgasm. Eventually she had enough confidence to tell Arnie that she hadn't really been having orgasms. She told him about her unsatisfying sex life with her ex-husband and about her sex counseling. Arnie reacted positively to her honesty and was eager to help. In the next two months, Jacqueline was more and more sexually responsive with Arnie. The relationship ended when Jacqueline took a job in the Midwest. Before she left, she told us, "The next time I get involved with a man, I'm going to be honest about everything even before we go to bed together. If the guy gets scared by that—well, he wouldn't be very good for me in the long run anyway."

Even sexually secure women may find the sexual world of the formerly married to be rough sailing. A thirty-three-year-old medical illustrator told us what happened to her just a few weeks after she left her husband. "I met a doctor at a party. He told me he was separated from his wife. Now I wonder if that was true. Anyway, he was a bit of a sexual bragger—made me think he would be a fantastic lover. We ended up having sex and it was really strange. I had never had a problem having orgasms, but I just couldn't with him. Looking back on it, I think the problem was his making *too* big a deal out of satisfying me. He sort of stage-managed it, telling me what to do, how to move. I realized he expected me to have some tremendous orgasms, and he awed me by his technique. But it backfired. I felt really pressured, like I had to have an orgasm for his ego. Once I started trying to force an orgasm, it was almost unpleasant. Finally I told him I wanted to stop. He was upset. I only saw him one more time after that. My self-confidence was shaken for a while, but now I think it was a normal way to react to his pressuring style."

Very recently the press has been telling us that things are changing, that sexual pressures are easing somewhat among young unmarrieds and among the divorced. After a decade or more of sex on demand and sex as recreation, people are now saying, "Enough; what I want is a relationship."

We have been hearing some statements from people in counseling that do corroborate a change in sexual climate. One man said, "After my marriage broke up, I didn't know how to meet women in my not-so-large town, so I did something that really was awkward for me; I went to the singles bars. But I wasn't interested in getting laid. I wanted a relationship. I was pleasantly surprised to find that there were women who also wanted to get to know a guy. I actually met several women. I dated them all and only had sex with one, and that was after we'd spent a lot of time together."

Another man, a dentist in his early forties, made this interesting observation. "My wife walked out on me for another man, with no warning at all, and she got herself a shark of a lawyer. I was in shock. One of my strongest feelings was a desire to screw any woman I could. Luckily I went into therapy right away. The therapist helped me to see that my sexual desires were like ninety percent anger and ten percent lust. Once I started to get my anger out—at my wife and women in general—my sex drive simmered down. I found that what I craved then was sympathy, understanding—a *nice* woman; you might call it mothering. Anyway, sex certainly wasn't my top priority, and I found that the women I met responded well to that—once they started believing that I really meant it."

A woman in her late twenties said, "At first [after her marriage ended], I thought I would have a great time seeing lots of men, but I got tired of that really fast—in maybe three months. It was exhausting and it took too much away from my time with Kim [her four-year-old daughter]. It also took energy I needed for work, and it just wasn't satisfying me. So I just stopped—didn't date at all for a few months. Now I see one man at a time, and I'm looking forward to getting married again."

In marriage, there is some degree of predictability about sex.

The frequency, location, and who does what to whom are, after a while, more or less settled, even if not totally routine. (Indeed, one of the values of marriage may be the comfort of a routine.) In a new relationship, everything is open to question and negotiation. This can add piquancy or anxiety—usually both.

One woman described her reluctance to suggest that her new lover stimulate her orally—the only way she had ever been able to reach orgasm. For several weeks, she felt too shy to say anything; she hoped he would just do it spontaneously. Both of them became uptight about her not coming. She was beginning to think she would never be able to have satisfying sex with another man and was even on the verge of telephoning her ex-husband when one of those nice things that sometimes happen in a new relationship happened to her. She *relaxed* and had an orgasm while he was stimulating her clitoris with his hand.

Another woman, who had been a virgin when she met her husband and who had been monogamous for eight years of marriage, had understood from him that a man must always ejaculate once he is sexually aroused. He had never allowed lovemaking to stop until he had an orgasm. After her divorce, the woman began a sexual relationship with a man who was *not* accustomed to ejaculating every time he made love. The first time he didn't reach orgasm with her, she was sure she had failed him sexually and after that occasion was anxious to make him come whenever they made love. He sensed her anxiety, which he felt as pressure to ejaculate whether he wanted to or not. They never talked about what was happening, and sex became less frequent and more tense. The relationship ended. A year later, after reading a magazine article on normal male sexual response, the woman understood that what she had learned from her husband was not correct for all men.

We are telling her story to underscore the point that many divorced persons have learned what sex is all about in the context of their marriages. The attitudes and "facts" they learned with their spouses sometimes ill prepare them for sexual experiences with others.

What about the small percentage of persons who do not date in the year or two after divorce? They often are the most upset and frightened. One man in his mid-thirties had not dated for four years. He was wary of women and convinced he couldn't function sexually. He said he felt dead sexually. He had tried to masturbate but found that he ejaculated rapidly—even before he became erect. He was very frightened by this, unaware that it is not such a rare variation in male sexual response. After this experience, he was afraid to masturbate and, as a result, did not experience a full cycle of sexual response for more than three years. As sex therapists, we know that not using the sexual system for such a prolonged period may make it difficult to resume sexual activity.

We feel it is important for divorced men and women to keep in touch with their sexual feelings, fantasies, and responses. Masturbation is a useful alternative for those who are not willing or able to find partners. (It is also fine for those who do have partners.) Some divorced individuals have never or have rarely masturbated and need to be able to learn or relearn how—not so much how to do it as how to enjoy it. (For women, we can recommend a book that may be helpful: Lonnie Barbach's *For Yourself: The Fulfillment of Female Sexuality*.)

It is possible that masturbation will help keep sexuality alive and vital, not just psychologically but perhaps also hormonally. The biological factors involved in sexual response are not completely understood, but there does seem to be a connection between remaining sexually active and maintaining hormonal equilibrium. It is known, for example, that in males, there is a definite rise in testosterone levels in the blood following ejaculation.

Moving toward a New Commitment

The U.S. Census Bureau estimates that 80 percent of divorced persons eventually remarry. Some move very rapidly into a new, committed relationship (which may have begun even before the marriage ended), but most go through the transition phase and experience several relationships along the way. We have observed an interesting pattern among many of the divorced persons who have consulted us about a sexual problem. After an initial period of dating a number of people casually or for a fairly brief time, a "serious" relationship develops. To the persons involved, to close friends and relatives, this often looks like the beginning of a permanent relationship, but, in fact, this relationship ends and is followed by a relationship that does lead to marriage or some other long-term commitment.

It is our impression that for these people, the first serious relationship after a divorce serves as a testing ground for many things. Can I really trust someone of the other sex? Can I accommodate my life pattern to a new person? Can my children accept a new father (or mother)? Can I even think about marriage again? Can I sustain an emotional and sexual bond over any length of time?

This relationship tests the waters of recommitment. If the waters are calming, or at least not too turbulent, it will probably be possible in the future for the woman or man to form a new primary bond. In this testing relationship, sexual problems that have persisted since the divorce are often resolved. The man who has been impotent tells *this* woman all about it and she is not put off; she wants to help and, somehow, it works out. They both are elated.

Or the woman who has been fearful of men and sex since her divorce meets a man who seems gentler and more sensitive. He is sympathetic about her fears and her need to go slowly. She never feels that he is using her. He is the kind of man who wants to please women, not hurt them. She discovers that she can relax with him, get turned on, have an orgasm.

The fact that these relationships seem not to last is very interesting. They could be regarded as an example of parasitism—one person growing at another's expense and then abandoning the source of nourishment—but it hasn't appeared this way to us. The helpful partner is attracted to a person who is in need. Being a rescuer has its own rewards. After trust and a good sexual relationship have evolved, the needy person has changed—he or she is stronger, more independent, more sexually assertive. The helpful partners have not seemed to be very upset. They, too, have moved on to a new and often permanent relationship.

When a divorced person begins to consider remarrying, it is almost always with some ambivalence. This is a moment when sexual problems may recur or doubts about the sexual relationship may surface. A twenty-nine-year-old woman who had been divorced for four years began to think that she and her current lover might get married. She started to worry about the fact that their sex life wasn't all that good. Recently she had been less likely to have an orgasm, and she didn't feel free to be as "sexy" with him as she wanted to be.

She recalled the history of their sexual relationship. He had problems with erection at first. Thinking that she was being too demanding and maybe overwhelming him, she let him take the lead in initiating sex and during lovemaking. This seemed to work; at least he had erections. But over time, they had settled into a pattern that she felt constrained her sexuality. The alternatives seemed clear. She could back off from the relationship, or she could tell him her feelings and see if they could work it out. (A third alternative, of course, was to continue with things as they were, saying nothing and hoping the situation would somehow get better. This, she knew, had been the pattern in her first marriage, and she had learned it just didn't work.)

She chose to discuss the issue with her lover. He was surprised and a bit taken aback, but he was able to talk about it. Over the next few months, they were able to work things out between them—and they did marry.

Did they live happily ever after? We don't know. Did they continue to feel satisfied with their sexual relationship after several years of marriage? We don't know. Actually, we can find no statistics comparing sexual satisfaction or the rate of sexual problems in first versus second or third marriages. It would be nice to know whether couples who are older and wiser can achieve more satisfying sex lives or whether the experience of marital breakdown and divorce makes future sexual adjustment more difficult for them.

In any case, statistics aren't much help to the individual living through a situation. We want to emphasize the importance of divorced persons making some sense out of their former marriage—to put it, their own feelings, and their former spouse in some perspective, preferably before venturing into serious dating. Some divorced couples go for counseling together or have individual therapy. Many find a great deal of help through support groups such as Parents Without Partners or the groups (often called transition groups) geared for the recently separated or divorced.

We would encourage those who feel that the ending of their marriage has left them feeling sexually inadequate to consider a support group or counseling. A time of upheaval and change—a sexual turning point—can be sexually disabling or it can be an opportunity for growth.

18

Remarriage after Divorce

HOPE springs eternal; If at first you don't succeed . . .; Love is lovelier the second time around; Get right back on the horse after you're thrown. So, nursing their barely healed wounds, 80 percent of divorced people walk down the aisle again. This time she is probably wearing beige or pastel, but the excitement of a new beginning is just as intense.

Most people entering a second marriage think they are making a wiser choice, having learned something about their own needs and about the realities of being married. One of the most important lessons is simply to have more realistic expectations. We have heard people express this in a variety of ways: "I honestly don't think I'm that much more compatible with my new husband, but I don't get so upset over differences and I don't expect to be happy and in love all the time. In my first marriage, I see now that I expected a fantasy, so I went around disappointed and angry all the time. The main thing that's changed is me." Or, "I was unprepared for marriage the first time. I was too young—just twenty-one. My career was all I cared about. When my wife said we weren't communicating, I didn't even know what she was talking about. To be honest, I used to fall asleep whenever she tried to talk about feelings. I was a zero when it came to relating, but I didn't know it. I spent ten years between marriages; some of that time I was in a therapy group. That, plus living, I guess, opened my eyes. Now, with Joanne, my second wife, we have what Nancy, my first, always wanted."

After a divorce people often clarify their ideas about what they need sexually. A thirty-five-year-old woman, a gynecological patient of Phil's, said that her first marriage had been a failure in many ways, but one of the most important was that it hadn't met her sexual needs. "I've always been, well, you might say highly sexed. My first husband was not. I wanted sex at least four or five times a week; for him, once a week on Sunday was the ideal. He turned me down a lot, and sometimes when he'd try to go along, he'd lose his erection. At the time, I felt rejected and hurt. Now I think it was just a different level of need for sex and not his fault. After my divorce, I didn't consciously set out to find a younger man but I did gravitate that way, I think for sexual reasons. Sal, my second husband, is eight years younger than I am. We're well matched sexually, and that is something we both think is important."

Another woman explained that her first husband's style of lovemaking had left a basic need unsatisfied. "It took me five years of marriage to be able to express what was missing. Vic and I made love frequently, and I almost always had an orgasm. So why did I feel so empty and even miserable after sex? Funny enough, it was a novel that woke me up—a sex scene that was so beautiful that it brought tears to my eyes. I thought, 'What's missing is tenderness.' Vic never even looked at me. He didn't touch me except like a checklist of buttons to press. After we had our orgasms (usually at the same time), he'd grunt and that was that. I don't know why it took me so long to recognize that this was painful—emotionally, I mean. I tried to talk to him about it, but it didn't help. I have a theory that he secretly thought sex was not very nice. He had a superstrict upbringing. Anyway, with my second husband, it's different. He's a toucher, and he talks to me while we make love. He's sometimes satisfied just to give me pleasure and not even ejaculate himself. He knows how to give in lots of ways."

It would be wonderful if all the tales of second marriages sounded this hopeful. Unfortunately, the statistics don't bear out the idea that second marriages are more likely to succeed. In fact, an even higher proportion of remarriages than first marriages fail—about 60 percent. We have been seeing couples in their second (sometimes in their third or fourth) marriages who are trying to work out sexual problems. We have been impressed by the fact that some of these couples have learned a great deal about themselves and about intimate relationships from their first marriages and from the pain of divorce. They have grown to a new level of maturity at which they can at last find a sense of satisfaction. Even when there is a problem, they can work together to resolve it. Other couples seem to be stuck in a rut, repeating old self-defeating patterns. Or, having realized that they married for all the wrong reasons the first time around, they have avoided the old pitfalls, only to fall into newer, deeper pits. What are some of the factors that may influence sexual and emotional compatibility in a second marriage?

Could the length of time between the end of one marriage and the beginning of the next be a factor in the success or failure of second marriages? There is no study that answers this question, but there are some provocative statistics. Interestingly, divorced men rush to the altar in greater numbers, and much faster, than divorced women. United States government statistics indicate that divorced men are one and a half times as likely to remarry as are divorced women, and that they remarry within two years, while women, on the average, wait four to five years. One psychologist, Peter Mayle, studied divorced people and discovered that he couldn't locate men who were, in his words, "living full, creative, single lives." He came up with an interesting hypothesis—that men remarry quickly because when they find themselves alone, they feel lonely and frightened; they recognize their own dependency on women, and this makes them feel unmanly, so they quickly bond to a new woman. This may not hold up as a general theory, but it is certainly an accurate description of some divorced men. Divorced women tend to remarry less quickly than men, partly because of their circumstances. They are more likely to have children living with them and to be less free to meet new partners. They may have to go to school and work at the same time to prepare themselves for independence. They are also at a disadvantage in the "competition" for available partners, since men their own age or older may be looking for younger, perhaps never-married women.

Some women we have spoken to thought enforced delay could be an advantage. As one woman put it, "My husband married the woman he'd been seeing for three years behind my back, and their relationship is on the rocks already. When they got married, I envied him so much I could hardly stand it. I was stuck with the two kids, on the verge of emotional collapse. I looked so awful and was so depressed, it's no wonder no men were interested in me. It took me more than two years to begin to get my act together. I changed a lot during those years. When I finally started to date, I could really see men—and myself—clearly. If I had remarried right away, it would have been a disaster—just an escape."

This woman, Vera, found that the sexual experiences she had before she met her second husband helped change her attitude toward sex so that when she met Alex, she was a lot less hung up. She came for one session of counseling about a month after meeting Alex, to ask if it was normal to need clitoral stimulation in order to climax during intercourse.

She explained that in her marriage, her sex life had been a source of major conflict. She was only able to have orgasms with oral or manual stimulation, not with intercourse. Neither she nor her husband thought to combine forms of stimulation. Both of them assumed that her failure to climax from the movements of his penis was a form of frigidity. Her husband also thought it reflected badly on his sexual prowess. "Believe it or not," Vera said, "that was one of the things that led to our divorce. He couldn't ever discuss it with me, but I know it ate away at him.

"After we split, I had a few experiences that made me think. One guy I went with for a while bought me a vibrator, and he used it on me during intercourse. I used to actually come too fast that way! Then another man I slept with just once told me to touch my own clitoris while we were making love. I did, and it was fantastic. These experiences made me think maybe I wasn't sexually abnormal. I started asking a few women friends and some of them seemed to be like me, you know, the penis didn't do it all for them either.

"With Alex, he stimulates me with his hand or his mouth. He doesn't think I have to have my orgasm during intercourse. If it's before or after, that's okay. It's fine with me, too, but I just wanted—I don't know—some official stamp of approval, I guess, from an expert."

About six months later, we got a letter from Vera. She wrote, "I thought you might like to know, Alex and I got married. Our sex life is terrific. I realize now that what made sex go wrong in my first marriage wasn't a physical or even a deep psychological problem; it was my stupidity (and my husband's) plus blaming ourselves and overreacting. Maybe every couple should be required to take a sex education course before they get married. Alex says he volunteers to teach it!"

There is a wise old saying, 'Marry in haste, repent at leisure.' There is nothing like falling madly in love to make people act hastily. Sometimes a second marriage begins as an idyllic, passionate extramarital affair. The romance of the affair is like fairydust, blinding the couple to each other's realities. They leave their spouses, marry, and suddenly wake up to what they have done.

A thirty-five-year-old psychiatrist met a beautiful woman on a flight to Chicago on his way to attend a medical convention. She was a glamorous, highly paid photographer-journalist from France. Both the doctor and the photographer were happily married, but they were intensely attracted, sexually and intellectually. Their affair, begun during the four days of the convention, continued for a year via the mail and with four or five trysts in all parts of the world. Each tryst was a tour de force of planning and an adventure. The sex was spectacular. They would make love for hours and then have dinner in their hotel room. They had the money and the imagination to have the "perfect" affair.

Perhaps the affair would have burned itself out, but she wrote him a letter, saying she loved him more than ever but wanted to end it to save her marriage. Fear of losing her inflamed his passion. He flew to Paris and begged her to leave her husband and marry him. She agreed. They had three wonderful days in Paris. He flew home and began divorce proceedings. Eight months later, having seen each other only twice more, they married. Two years later, they came for counseling for lack of sexual desire on her part and premature ejaculation on his. In fact, he had always had a problem of premature ejaculation, which had been disguised by the frequency of lovemaking during their trysts. Their psychological (not to mention sociocultural) incompatibility was profound. The outcome was a second divorce for both of them.

We have seen a number of men and women over the years who seem to make a habit of marrying in haste and repenting slowly. This is the way they go about their first, second, third, fourth, and even fifth marriages. These men and women remind us of another well-known line, this time a song lyric: "I fall in love too easily."

The men we have seen with this syndrome all have a sexual problem (but, remember, we see a selected group). They appear to be particularly vulnerable to women who are maternal, caring, and uncritical. When they meet a woman like this and she accepts their sexual performance or, on one or two occasions, they find they *can* function sexually, they are instantly head over heels. The new woman seems to be the embodiment of all virtues. These marriages often take place a few months after the initial meeting and sometimes after just a few weeks.

The women who follow this hasty nuptial pattern are a very diverse group. Some seem to be seeking cuddling more than sex. Others have managed repeatedly to select men who turn out to have sexual problems and/or sadistic tendencies.

The basic psychological problem for both these men and women is a tendency to "fuse" too quickly and intensely with someone of the opposite sex. There is a euphoric sense of having at last met one's true soul mate. As one man said exactly two weeks after meeting his third wife-to-be, "She's a mirror image of me. I start a sentence and she ends it. She knows what I think and what I need without my having to say anything." Breaking out of such a self-defeating pattern usually requires some psychotherapy, but the first step toward a new approach to mate selection is recognizing that this is your pattern. That is why we have described it in some detail.

We have probably all heard or read about couples who divorce and then remarry one another—a peculiarly fascinating sequence perhaps because it seems to be a bizarre confirmation of the monogamous bond. It also piques the curiosity. What led to the divorce? How did they change in the period apart? How and why did they get back together? What might make the second time better than the first?

One couple who came for help with an unusual problem after they remarried one another presented a remarkable variation on the story; during the time they were divorcing, she (Tammy) sexually assaulted her then ex-husband (Chuck).

Before we tell this story, we had better say a word about reverse molestation (when a female molests a male), since many people have never heard of such a phenomenon and, in fact, believe it to be an impossibility. Phil first reported reverse rape at a professional meeting in 1980. At that time, he had counseled eleven men who had been physically forced or intimidated into intercourse by a woman. The common assumption is that men cannot or would not get an erection against their will, but apparently at least some men do. Some of the men even ejaculated, although the overall experience was not at all pleasurable; it was terrifying, humiliating, and confusing. Phil also co-authored a paper on the subject with Dr. William Masters in which five additional cases, seen by Dr. Masters, were described.

Returning to Tammy and Chuck: they had been married for five years when Tammy literally walked in on Chuck while he was in their bed with another woman, Mary-Ann. Tammy was stunned. The children, aged three and four, were only steps behind her. She barely had time to close the door and prevent the children's seeing. Chuck then announced that he was in love with Mary-Ann and wanted a divorce.

After he moved out, Tammy was in emotional turmoil. The divorce and custody battles over the next year were intense. Tammy, near the breaking point, persuaded Chuck to visit her to try to work out some of the differences. Tammy sent the children to stay with friends and made a lovely dinner. She told us, "My own motives weren't clear to me. I told myself I was being nice to him in order to win some concessions from him. I think I was also being seductive because my own sexual self-confidence and pride were so badly shaken." After dinner and wine and brandy, Tammy kissed Chuck, who "sort of" responded. In Chuck's words, "Suddenly Tammy seemed to go wild. She started pulling off my pants. I was so shocked I didn't really resist. When I did object, verbally, she swore at me. I became helplessly passive, as if I were watching it all on a movie screen. She mounted me, had a quick orgasm (I think) and then got off. I actually was crying.

"I've thought about it a lot since then. I think I was paralyzed by seeing her tremendous—her towering—rage. She had held it all in. I should have known, but I didn't. It was like I was a small bad boy and she was my mother, punishing me."

In the months that followed, Tammy and Chuck went into therapy together in order to try to work out their feelings about the children and custody. Neither one saw this as therapy to reunite them, and, in fact, they went ahead with legal proceedings and were divorced. The therapy process helped Tammy express her hurt and rage more appropriately. Communication improved, and Tammy and Chuck felt fairly friendly toward one another.

Then Tammy and one of the children were in a car crash. Tammy had a broken leg and the child had serious internal injuries. Chuck and Tammy were brought together over concern for their son's life. About a month later, they decided to try to get back together. They went back to their therapist, this time to work toward reuniting. Three months later, they married. They continued in therapy. After a year, they felt they had made good progress in all areas but the sexual. Chuck became very anxious as soon as they began touching or kissing. On the occasions when they did have intercourse, he couldn't ejaculate. Most of Chuck's problem with Tammy could be traced to his reaction to the sexual assault. Sex therapy was helpful, and they overcame their sexual problems.

Reflecting on their two marriages, Tammy and Chuck agreed that "it's like four different people. We thought we had closeness when we first fell in love, but that was some sort of halo effect. When it was gone, we had just habit, the kids, the house—but no real communication." Chuck said, "I never told Tammy what I was thinking or feeling. I thought she should understand me without words." Tammy added, "I never got to know him, not really, until the divorce and our therapy. Then I heard him saying all sorts of things—feelings I never knew he had. It's ironic. One of the things he objected to in our first marriage (but he never told me this) was that I was too sexually passive! Now at least we can tell each other what we need."

Our sexuality, as part of our personality, is unique and individual, but it is certainly not immutable. The die is not cast forever at age twenty or age thirty—not even at age eighty. A new partner is possibly the most important opportunity for sexual change that life offers. A new person brings his or her own unique sexual likes and dislikes, values and attitudes. New dimensions of passion or playfulness or experimentation can open up. It's nice to know, after the pain of divorce, that there *is* the possibility for this kind of newness.

STAGE SEVEN

Keeping Sex Alive

(and Lively)

19

Positive Changes at

Mid-Life or Later

OUR CULTURE tends to reinforce the idea that sex is for the young, and *young* seems to get younger all the time (as witness the teenage models in some jeans commercials). Television, which often tends to exaggerate cultural stereotypes, makes it very clear that only young females are sexual. No fewer than 85 percent of all women on television are under forty, and the other 15 percent are likely to be shown as asexual.

Most of us know that the stereotype is a myth, and yet we aren't sure what the facts really are or just how we do feel about "older" people and sex. Do men "go over the hill," and if so, when? Does menopause affect a woman's sexuality? Do older couples still need and want sex? *Should* they want sex? Is it all right to masturbate at any age? Can people past forty still improve their sex lives or is it too late for them? What about people past seventy?

When we are young, these questions may not interest us very much, except perhaps academically. Yet younger people's attitudes toward their elders' sexual lives do influence the way the elders are viewed as persons and sometimes affects their lives significantly. For example, if a grown son or daughter makes it clear to a widowed mother that she is seen by them as asexual, she may be reluctant to face them with a different reality. She may even choose to reject potential lovers rather than spoil their image of her. Or, a doctor may neglect to advise his sixty-five-year-old patient who has had a heart attack about when to resume sexual activity if the doctor thinks that no one over sixty has sex anyway.

239

We believe that people of all ages should be intelligently informed about sex and aging, but obviously it is most relevant and important for people who are themselves entering or passing through these years. The main point is that sexual functioning and desire are not immune to the aging process, but when we understand the changes of aging and know how to cope with those changes, we can stay sexually alive for as long as we choose—and for many of us that means for as long as we live. In fact, many couples whose sex life slumped during the child-rearing years find that they rediscover sex in the more relaxed and private life of a home without children. Older couples can make fresh discoveries and enrich their sexual lives, and may even find that sex becomes *more* important in later life.

In Masters and Johnson's book describing sex therapy, *Human Sexual Inadequacy*, the average age of the couples seeking therapy was fifty-one. We, too, see a great many couples in their forties, fifties, sixties, and seventies. Getting older doesn't have to mean putting up with a sexual problem—even if that problem has been a very long-term one.

Let's start with a particularly dramatic illustration—the unconsummated marriage of a couple who has *never* been able to have intercourse. This problem is not as uncommon as most people imagine, and it can happen to couples who, in other respects, are as normal as anyone. Even when a couple has been completely unable to have intercourse for fifteen, twenty, or more years, the problem can often be treated successfully. Then, in their forties or fifties, the couple can *begin* to have intercourse.

We worked with one couple in which the husband had been unable to have intercourse with either his first or second wife. Still unable to maintain an erection sufficient for intercourse, he came to us with his third wife. He (Martin) was fifty-eight; she (Sonya) was forty-three. She was also a virgin. Martin's difficulties had begun when he was born almost three months premature and with a variety of physical handicaps. The doctors held out little hope for his survival, but his mother never gave up hope. When he finally went home after six months in the hospital, she devoted herself to his care and nurturing. He had severe problems with vision, balance, and coordination, but with her constant support, he developed and was able to attend a regular public school. He even participated in some sports.

But Martin felt the impact of his handicaps in his social isolation. He had no friends. His entire world was a struggle for self-improvement, plus his mother. His father was distant and peripheral to the mother-son pair. He rarely dated during adolescence, and his first marriage, at age thirty-three, was arranged. By then, Martin was working, but he was socially and sexually immature. When the couple couldn't have intercourse, his wife had the marriage annulled. At thirty-nine, Martin married again—with similar results. Two attempts at intercourse with prostitutes also failed.

When he was fifty-two, his mother died, and Martin became very depressed. Psychotherapy for two years helped his depression and deepened his determination to achieve a stable marriage. At fifty-eight, he met and fell in love with a very shy schoolteacher who had almost no sexual experience although she was past forty. Sonya's background was of strict religious orthodoxy, but a move from a residential religious school to teaching in a city public school had opened her eyes to new paths she might follow. She also fell in love with Martin.

Love is a powerful sexual stimulus, but it couldn't overcome so many years of failure, inhibition, and accumulated anxiety. They married anyway and then sought sex therapy. As is so often true with couples starting therapy, a great deal of the psychological growth has already taken place before they cross the threshold of the office. Martin had finally separated emotionally from his mother; Sonya from the cocoon that had sheltered her from sex and a full, enriching life. By the end of the therapy, they were having intercourse and enjoying their sexual relationship.

Another couple came to see us when she was fifty-seven, he sixty. They had never had intercourse. In addition, he had never been able to ejaculate while awake, and he even managed to stifle most of his wet dreams. After therapy he was able to overcome his problem partially, to the extent that he could at least ejaculate from masturbation or petting, and they were able to have intercourse, albeit without his ejaculating in her vagina.

In another instance, a couple in their early forties were referred to us from an infertility clinic because they had never had intercourse during their eighteen years of marriage. Someone in the clinic had told them, "If you can't have intercourse you aren't fit to be parents." They felt humiliated and demoralized but eager to try anything that might help.

Their inability to have intercourse was due to her severe vag-

inismus. Since adolescence, she had been terrified of vaginal penetration. Her fear was at least partly rooted in a severe vaginal
infection she had had at age fourteen and the repeated, painful
pelvic examinations that were done at that time. Whenever intercourse was attempted, she felt frightened that it would hurt, and,
in fact, attempts at penetration in the months after their wedding
had hurt a lot.

This couple had settled into a pattern of sexual relating in
which she would stimulate him to orgasm with her hand and he
would fondle her breasts. Since any approach to her genitals made
her very anxious, they had simply eliminated any contact below
her waist.

During therapy, they were able to overcome the problem and
to have pleasurable intercourse. They even went on to have a baby,
who is now a healthy two-year-old. Their sex life continues to be
problem free and satisfying for both of them.

Perhaps the most common complaint among couples at or
beyond mid-life is lack of sexual desire. The problem can be very
long term, sometimes dating to the early years of the relationship.
Although the results of sex therapy in treating lack of desire have
not been spectacular (one well-known clinic reports only a 25%
success), nevertheless, therapy can sometimes reverse even long-
entrenched desire problems.

One couple, Marge and Donald Jones, sought our help when
they were approaching fifty. Good friends of theirs had overcome
a problem through sex therapy, and this gave the Joneses the
courage to try therapy. For sixteen years (since they married in
their early thirties), they had been having intercourse very infrequently—about half a dozen times a year—but often enough to
have two children. There was constant tension between Donald
and Marge over sex. Donald would have liked sex more often, but
initiating it made him so extremely tense that he preferred to
avoid the situation. Marge told us, "The funny thing is, when we
do have sex, it feels good to both of us and afterward we often say
to each other that we should do it more often, but then we fall back
into the same traps and a month or maybe two or three months go
by and we don't do it again."

The Joneses' story is sad because for so many years, each of
them was locked in a silent torment of self-blame, guilt, and fear
of inadequacy. They both agreed that the problem had started

early in their relationship, during their engagement. We asked them to recount the story in some detail.

Marge had not experienced any orgasms during the early months of their lovemaking. She was fairly inexperienced and assumed that she would eventually start to have orgasms. Meanwhile she enjoyed lovemaking with Donald and showed her enjoyment very openly. Unfortunately, Donald misread her moans of pleasure as signs of orgasm, so that when she finally decided to mention her lack of orgasm, he was flabbergasted and felt betrayed and deceived. Donald was also fairly inexperienced. He had no sexual self-confidence and immediately assumed that he must be a terrible lover. Unfortunately, about the same time, she allowed him to read an old diary of hers in which she wrote about having had an orgasm during petting with a former boyfriend. This, of course, was another blow to his sexual self-esteem.

Donald became obsessed with the need for Marge to have orgasms. "After lovemaking," she said, "he would want to know exactly how it had been for me. I knew he was expressing concern for my pleasure, but it felt like a grilling—as if I had to give a progress report. I started holding back on showing when I was aroused because I thought he might mistakenly think I was coming and then afterward be disappointed!"

Marge quickly lost interest in sex and found subtle ways of putting Donald off whenever she thought he might be planning to initiate it. The lack of frequency was yet another blow to Donald's self-confidence.

They never dared to be really honest with each other after this period. Marge said, "I was honest when I told him I wasn't having orgasms, and that was a complete disaster. I was just too scared to open my mouth again. I started to think of Donald as too fragile in this area to handle my directness."

Fourteen years of silence about sex and, in fact, about most emotionally tender subjects meant that more than anything else, Marge and Donald needed to talk. But this was extremely hard for them. We asked each of them to make a list of ten topics they were reluctant to discuss and then to start talking about two of the *easiest* topics on the list. It took them several weeks to have the courage to make the lists!

Gradually, as they worked down their lists of undiscussable topics, each came to trust that the other could listen and not be devastated by the truth. There was a major breakthrough when Marge told Donald that she had been masturbating to orgasm for many years. When she told him that she thought she could show him how to touch her genitals in a way that might lead to her having orgasms, his enthusiasm and curiosity outweighed his anxiety and self-doubt.

Talking and beginning to trust each othere were what mattered for Marge and Donald. Once they could share their feelings, the anxiety about failure and rejection faded. Sex became more relaxed. Initiating sex became easier. They started making love more often, and with more unalloyed pleasure.

At their six-month follow-up visit, Donald commented, "I feel so much lighter now. The sex problem was a kind of weight I carried all the time, for years and years. I only wish we had had the courage to get help sooner."

It does take courage to seek help for a problem that has been part of the fabric of your life for decades. The prospect of saying to someone, "I (or we) have had this problem for thirty years" can be so daunting that tackling it gets put off again and again.

We have been particularly impressed by the courage of women in their forties, fifties, sixties (and one woman in her eighties) who join groups for women who want to learn how to have orgasms. In the face of internal and external opposition, these women have decided that orgasm is a human potential they want to experience, and they are willing to try to change. And they *can* change; they *can* learn to have orgasms. It may be that there is no upper limit to the age at which a woman can experience her first orgasm.

We would like to tell the story of one of these women in some detail, because her struggles and her growth seem to us to say very important things about the sexuality of the older woman.

Claire came to talk (to Lorna) when she was two months shy of her sixtieth birthday. "I've never had an orgasm in my life—well, maybe one—and I wanted to find out what sort of treatment is available." Lorna described couples' sex therapy and also an alternative treatment, a group for women. Claire listened carefully, and then said, "I'm not sure I can go through with it. I want to and I don't."

One of the main reasons for Claire's reluctance was her fear that "exploring this area could wreck my marriage. Maybe I'll find out that our marriage has been a sham, that I married the wrong man—one who doesn't attract me sexually. I've told myself for thirty-seven years that Stewart and I have a good marriage. We've raised four terrific kids. Part of me wants to leave it at that—not risk what has seemed good."

Claire also felt that it might be presumptuous of her to try to "expand myself sexually at this age. I mean, if people, like my friends or my sister, knew what I was doing, wouldn't I be making a fool of myself?" At this stage of her life, Claire was involved in a variety of interesting activities—a course in Italian, volunteer work, and caring for two grandchildren one day each week. She was accustomed to justifying what she did as "worthwhile." "I've always felt good about doing things for others. I was a very busy mother. Really, my life was my kids. Now I'm free to do things just for me, and it feels good, but also part of it feels strange. And, I mean, it's okay to study a language. I can see that; anyone could. But a sex group? I just don't know."

Claire came back for a second visit just to talk about her mixed feelings. As she got off the elevator for her appointment, she bumped into an acquaintance, a nurse who worked in the gynecology clinic across the hall from Sex Counseling. The nurse said, "Oh, hello; what are you doing here?" Claire made some excuse and fled. She sneaked back a few minutes later. She told Lorna about it. "I'm not sure I have the guts to go through with this. I was so embarrassed. What would she think—someone my age?"

As we talked, it became clear that Claire thought of sex as not quite nice—not filthy, but not really clean, either. She was surprised that she felt that way. "I'm more liberated in my head than I am deep down. I hope my kids have heard my words when I've talked to them about sex and not my negative feelings."

In her struggle to decide whether to pursue therapy, Claire's greatest support came from her husband, Stewart. He said he would gladly join her in sex therapy or would help in any way he could if she chose to enter a women's group.

A few days later, Claire telephoned to say she had decided to join the women's group.

This group of seven women (led by Lorna and another woman sex therapist), met weekly for two-hour sessions. In the first meeting, each woman talked about herself—why she was in the group and how she felt about sex. Claire told us that she had been very curious about sex until she was ten, when she and two boys were caught playing doctor. The mother of one of the boys caught them, screamed, carried on, and called Claire's parents. Claire was forbidden to play with these boys again. She thought everyone in their small Southern town must have known what she had done. She felt humiliated and also very guilty about "disappointing" her parents.

"After this incident, I just seemed to lose interest in the subject for years. I do remember my mother cautioning me repeatedly about what not to do with boys . . . I never tried to masturbate, and I had only a little fooling around. Once, I think, I may have had an orgasm with a boy when he was touching me. . . . I married my husband because he was 'right' for me. I knew he'd be a good provider, father, and husband, and he has been. I was just never attracted to him physically, you know, no chemistry there for me, though he never has a problem getting excited. He's sort of straitlaced. If he'd been a different type, more adventurous with sex, maybe things would've been different."

In the early stages of group therapy for women learning to have orgasms, each member is given "homework"—to look at her body in a full-length mirror from many angles, to look carefully at her genitals, and to make a drawing of her external genitals. Different women react in vastly different ways, but almost all women have at least one bodily feature they dislike intensely. Claire actually felt good about her body. She was an active person and was in good shape. "To tell you the truth," she said, "what I don't like is my face—the wrinkles and spots and sags. Southern women are supposed to know better, but I've always been a sun lover, so now I look my age plus a few years." Lorna asked, "Does it affect how you feel about yourself sexually?" Claire thought it did. "I've always had an idea way at the back of my brain that maybe I'd have an affair and that would do the trick for me sexually, but now, if I'm honest about it, the way I look, I don't think there's much chance of it. Of course, I never did do it and probably I never would, but it's a hope I've lost. On the other hand, maybe it helped push me to join this group, and that's probably more realistic than looking for Prince Charming!"

In the next phase, the women's "homework" is to explore genital sensations, without any goal, for an hour at a time. Claire said she had been too busy to give it the time we suggested. It turned out that her week had been spent giving to others. In fact, her son

had telephoned one day when she was just beginning her touching homework. Rather than tell him she was busy, she talked to
him for almost an hour and then had to go out. The other women
in the group told her she was too used to being in fifth or sixth
place in her family. Hadn't she said it was time now to meet some
of her own many needs, to give a little to herself? Many of the
women identified with Claire's feeling. One of the other women in
her fifties said, "In her generation, we were taught that a woman's
value was in her unselfishness and sensitivity to others' needs. It's
not easy to stop that after forty years and say 'I need.' "

As we neared the halfway point in the meetings, Claire's attitude toward sex began to undergo a transformation that was
amazing—and sometimes amusing. She once more met the nurse
she was acquainted with on her way into the sex counseling office.
This time she chatted for a few minutes and then said, "I have to
go now or I'll be late for my group." She told us she had a twinge
of embarrassment—just a twinge. She also told us about being at a
play with some "stuffy" friends who were not pleased with the
nudity in the play. Claire said, "Until now, I would have shut up,
but I told them I liked the nudity and I thought it was a pleasure
to look at nice, naked bodies." She added, "I don't care if they do
think I'm a dirty old woman. It's their problem if they view it that
way."

When the women all brought examples of erotic books, magazines, and pictures to the group, it was Claire who suggested they
all go to see a local male striptease act. Claire organized the out-
ing, and all seven women went. Then, in the next session, when we
talked about vibrators and several women said they wouldn't have
the courage to buy one, Claire volunteered to buy several, at a
discount price!

Meanwhile, at home, Claire was doing her "homework" more
regularly and discovering new sensations. She was actually the
first woman in the group to report having an orgasm. Her husband continued to be helpful and encouraging. They began to
talk about sex, something they had rarely done. Claire told Stewart about some of her sexual fantasies.

She told us about an important change in her sexual behavior
with Stewart. "I don't know if it's my age or my Southern upbringing, but I never felt right to be the one who initiated sex. The
other night Stewart and I were watching a movie on TV and he

said, 'Did you ever think about having sex in front of the TV?' I said no, I hadn't. Then I waited for him to do something, but he didn't. I started to get into my usual funk, thinking what's wrong with him and if only he were more aggressive, when suddenly it dawned on me, I could ask him. So I did and it was really nice."

In the group's last session, Claire said, "I've gotten so much out of this group I hate to see it end, and I really want to share what I've learned. I had a long talk with my youngest daughter, who is twenty. I told her about this group and we talked about everything—orgasms, masturbation, vibrators, everything. She's only had one boyfriend, but she hasn't had an orgasm with him. She said she felt relieved to hear it was common and that there are groups. She asked me if I'd ever talked that way with my mother. I said, are you kidding? That generation of women, at least the ones I grew up with, probably never said the word *orgasm* to anyone their whole lives."

Claire is unusual but not unique in her ability to change her sexual attitudes and behavior. Women in their fifties and beyond can, if they choose, shed lifelong prohibitions and anxieties and become more sexually alive than they have ever been. As one almost-seventy-year-old woman put it, "I feel as if I'm like my fourteen-year-old granddaughter, just discovering this whole new dimension of life."

20

Menopause

MENOPAUSE is a time of biological change that has profound implications in many areas of life—psychologically, interpersonally, and socially—which means that it is a very significant sexual turning point. Reproductive capacity ends. Ovaries markedly reduce the production of estrogen and stop producing progesterone. For the majority of women, these hormonal changes produce some immediate symptoms and also initiate gradual bodily changes. We react both to these changes and to the idea of being menopausal. Sexual partners also react.

We know from our work as sex therapists and from talking with hundreds of women attending general menopause clinics that menopause and sexual problems often go together. In 1982–83 Dr. Sarrel conducted a study of the sexual concerns of 200 women attending a menopause clinic in London. Fifty-seven percent were found to be having sexual difficulties that had begun during the climacteric (the years of hormonal change leading up to and including menopause itself), while another 18 percent had long-standing sexual problems that predated the climacteric.

The cause-and-effect relationship between menopause and sexual functioning is complex. How much should we attribute to hormonal changes? How much to physical aging? How much to psychological factors, to changes in the male partner, to cultural values, and to other life events? In order to clarify the causes and the meanings of sexual problems associated with the menopausal years, one needs to understand something about this phase of life, the commonest symptoms of menopause, the direct and indirect effects of low hormone levels on sexual functioning, and the effects of aging on sexual functioning in both sexes.

The menopausal years typically span the eight to ten years from age forty-five, when the ovaries are slowing down their production of estrogen, to about age fifty-five (and certainly by age sixty), by which time most women have stopped having the more classic menopausal symptoms such as hot flashes. Biological changes resulting from ovarian shutdown continue for the rest of a woman's life, but beyond age sixty, women are not usually thought of as "menopausal." Menopausal symptoms can also be induced when the ovaries are removed surgically, or made nonfunctional by radiation. Because the hormonal changes then are more abrupt, the symptoms are often more pronounced than in natural menopause, unless, of course, hormone-replacement therapy (HRT) is begun immediately, in which case there should be no symptoms of hormone depletion.

Our emphasis in these pages is going to be on the biological aspects of menopause, but it would be foolish to think that this sexual turning point is only biological. Women between the ages of forty and sixty are also confronting change and challenge in their families and often in their work. They are at an age when society's perception of them is changing, causing internal reappraisal. Simply by virtue of age and life expectancy, old age and death loom as personal realities, not something that happens only to other people.

The age of fifty, statistically, is an age of loss. The "average" fifty-year-old woman may expect to lose one or both parents at about the same time her children marry. The loss of parents means that she is now the senior, responsible matriarch. Whatever psychological protection the presence of parents provided is gone, and the mourning process uses psychological energy.

Meanwhile, the nest has been emptying. Many couples actually move from one nest to another—from a large family home with a garden to a small apartment with a few potted plants. Life is contracting. The so-called empty-nest syndrome hits some women harder than others. For the woman who has defined her worth largely in terms of family roles, it may lead to a sense of being useless and aimless. On the other hand, a woman is freer to leave an empty nest untended—to work, travel, paint, play, read, and be with her husband. It can be a bittersweet time. And let's not forget that fathers are deeply affected by their children leaving home. The family has been the father's nest too.

If a woman's parents are still alive, this may be a time when they become ill and possibly dependent. Decisions have to be faced. Just as she is thinking about launching herself totally into the outside world, the woman at forty, forty-five, or fifty may find that she needs to devote considerable energy to caring for elderly parents.

If she hasn't been working, she may feel frustrated now, trying to enter a job market without experience or special training. She feels prepared to manage people, make decisions, use her acquired wisdom, but all most employers want to know is "Can you type?" If she has had a career, she is subject to the same mid-life career stresses as a man—pressure to get an important promotion, burnout, boredom, facing up to her own limitations. Or perhaps she is just hitting her career stride, mingling an excited sense of accomplishment with the stress of new demands.

There are, of course, the marker birthdays. If you want to understand our society's attitude toward such birthdays, spend ten minutes scanning the birthday cards in a stationery store. Recently, at a surprise forty-fifth birthday party for a friend of ours, more than half of the cards referred to being over the hill, and the jokey gifts included a box of over-the-counter medication such as antacids and sleep aids, a huge magnifying glass for reading, and a cane!

Our Swedish and Danish friends tell us that the attitude in their countries is exactly the opposite. The fiftieth birthday, by long tradition, is a genuine celebration. There is a sense of entering a new, exciting, vital part of the life cycle, of hitting one's stride, of being able to make a special contribution now, by virtue of experience and wisdom. One friend, recalling the weekend-long bash her friends gave her when she reached fifty, said it was possibly the happiest moment in her life.

We all want to be one of those women who are almost unaffected by menopause, who march through to age fifty-five and sixty as zestful and sexy as ever. Hormones are one of the factors that will influence our well-being and state of mind during these years. But, apart from hormone levels, life-style and attitude appear to be crucial variables. The research isn't very solid, but sociologists tell us that in some societies, women are extremely eager for menopause and seem to have many fewer symptoms and complaints. The society usually cited is in India, where, traditionally, women are segregated from men and kept out of the mainstream of life until menopause. Menopause equals liberation, status, possible power—a whole new life. With these rewards ahead, who would even notice a hot flash?

Psychologists tell us that what we think and believe about our experience can change that experience. Menopausal signs and symptoms are no exception. One seventy-six-year old woman who told us she never had any trouble with menopause added, "Well, I guess it is true I had what you call hot flushes, but I always associated that feeling with getting sexy, I mean aroused, and I liked the idea that I was so sexy at that time in my life, so the feeling was really kind of nice."

A few studies suggest that the so-called nervous symptoms associated with menopause such as irritability, depressive moods, and insomnia may be more severe among housewives than among women who work, although in a Belgian study, lower-class housewives who worked actually had *more* symptoms in the years leading up to menopause. In general, women in the lower socioeconomic group and women with less education have been found to have a more pessimistic view of menopause, and it is hypothesized that this pessimism increases "nervous" symptoms.

Changes in Menstruation and Fertility

Most people are not aware that the hormonal changes that lead to menopause usually begin five or more years earlier. Menopause (which simply means the cessation of menstruation) occurs, on the average, at age fifty-one or fifty-two in the United States today (about two years earlier for smokers). That means that almost all women in their late forties and many in their early or mid-forties are already experiencing a decline in ovarian hormone production, and some of these women will experience symptoms.

Some women are completely unaware of any changes. They feel the same as they have always felt, and their periods remain regular. And then, one month, their period doesn't come, and it never comes again. Much more commonly, however, there are gradual changes in the menstrual pattern that clearly signal a change. Periods may come closer and closer together. For example, if a woman had a thirty-day cycle for many years, she may shift to a twenty-seven-day cycle for a while and then to a twenty-four-day cycle. Later the pattern may become very erratic, with some cycles as short as three weeks, others as long as six to ten weeks apart.

Another change will be that more of her menstrual cycles will be anovulatory (when no egg is released by the ovary). Because the hormone progesterone is not produced by the ovaries in anovulatory cycles, premenstrual symptoms are usually absent, but her periods may start quite suddenly and be heavy and pro-longed. Heavy bleeding, sometimes with blood clots, is usually a sign of normal change in hormone production. Still, such bleed-ing should be brought to a doctor's attention.

An irregular menstrual pattern is not ordinarily upsetting, al-though any change in our usual biological cycles can be unsettling. However, for women who rely on the rhythm method of birth control, irregular cycles make it more difficult to predict and iden-tify the time of ovulation. For the user of "situational" contra-ception—diaphragm, foam, sponge, suppositories, or condoms—the problem is simply one of worrisome late periods.

One woman in her late forties who came to see us was so unnerved by repeated "late" scares that she began using more and more diaphragm jelly and her husband started using a condom as an added precaution. The quantity of jelly made intercourse less enjoyable, and stopping to put on a condom sometimes caused her husband to lose his erection. Sex had become an increasingly anxious time for both of them. Some reassurance and contracep-tive advice were all this couple needed to resume a satisfying sex life.

Women who are on birth-control pills will not experience the menstrual changes we have been describing, but few women over forty-five or fifty are using the pill now. Women on the pill usually stop menstruating within a year or two of when they would have stopped had they not been on the pill.

Whatever a couple's method of contraception, they should be alerted to the fact that sometimes a very last period can occur as long as nine to twelve months after what seems to be the end of menses. Thus doctors usually recommend using birth control methods for a full year after the "last" period.

The end of fertility at menopause may be a joy and a release for one woman, a depressing loss for another. One mother of eleven, who for religious reasons had never used birth control, found that she started to really enjoy sex in a relaxed way only after her menopause, at the age of fifty-four.

Another woman from a similar religious background had the opposite reaction. As her periods waned and then stopped, she lost all interest in sex and thought it was somehow "improper" for an "older" couple to have sex. Talking to her, we learned that in her mind, sex was for creating babies. Once she was no longer fertile, there was no rationale for sex, and she became flooded with feelings of shame for her continued sexual interest.

During their forties, many women are aware of times when they have an intense desire to become pregnant—an "irrational" desire that conflicts with their firm conviction that they don't want any more children. There is a German expression that seems to capture the flavor of this craving for pregnancy—*torschluss* panic, the panic "before the door closes." Knowing that the door of fertility is about to close, you may think, "This is my last chance," and decide to have a child. This can be very fulfilling, but it may not always be the right decision.

Changes in a woman's menstrual pattern may be her only sign of decreasing ovarian function, or she may experience one or more symptoms—the sort of symptoms one associates with menopause. Because they are still menstruating, many women don't realize that their symptoms are hormone related, and they may be unnecessarily anxious or confused.

SYMPTOMS OF THE CLIMACTERIC

The subject of the symptoms associated with decreased ovarian hormone production is large and complex, but it is important to understand. Some of the changes directly affect sexual function; others have an indirect impact on sex. Together, these changes spell one of the most significant sexual turning points in the life cycle.

It is important to reemphasize that menopause is a very different experience for different women. Social, psychological, and life-style factors can be more important than hormonal ones. The woman who is happily busy, active, and content with her sexual relationship may wonder what all the fuss is about because she hardly notices any change. Even hormonally, there are important individual differences. After menopause, adrenal gland hormones are converted into estrogen, primarily in the body's fatty tissues, for at least ten to twenty years. The amount of estrogen produced this way varies considerably. Fatter women usually produce more estrogen and generally have fewer menopausal symptoms than thin women. For whatever happy combination of reasons—hormonal, social, or personal—about one women in four will have an easy time of menopause, without any major symptoms. The other three out of four will experience one or more symptoms.

The following story of one woman's experience of menopause is used to illustrate some of the more common symptoms.

Pamela is an attractive fifty-two-year-old woman, petite and vivacious. About eight months after her last menstrual period, she came to a menopause clinic because she had a variety of symptoms—hot flashes up to three times a day, disturbed sleep, irritability, lack of energy, and loss of interest in sex. She said the symptoms had actually started more than two years earlier but it took time for her to decide to seek medical help. Blood tests confirmed what her symptoms suggested—a very low estrogen level and also a low level of biologically active testosterone.

Low hormone levels were apparently not the only consideration in Pamela's story; they rarely are. She also described life events and intense feelings about her family that were relevant. Three years earlier, her father had died, and in the same year, her daughter had married. Now her daughter was pregnant after three years of trying but was bleeding, and Pamela was very worried she would miscarry.

Pamela's relationship with her husband had undergone significant changes. He had received a major promotion within his firm and was busy many nights and weekends. Their son, now twenty-three, still lived with them. He was just starting out in business. Pamela said, "I don't feel like the same person in my family. My kids and I were close, but now Gilly is gone and Matthew has shifted from me to his father. They talk business and the economy in ways that shut me out. Matt used to tell me about his life and his feelings, but not anymore. I feel ignored and unimportant. I don't say anything because I don't like to make waves. I've never been able to tell people when my feelings are hurt."

Sexually Pamela felt both physical and emotional changes. "I do think there's some change related to hormones. All my life I was aware of my monthly cycle affecting me sexually. Now some internal thing is gone. There's no desire that gives me those feelings down there that I used to get. And gradually my orgasms got smaller and smaller until now, well I haven't had one in almost a year, I think. My clitoris doesn't seem right, not as sensitive as it should be, and there's less lubrication. My husband and I haven't really talked about it, but when I told him I was coming here, he said he was glad and maybe you could do something to get me back to my sexy old self. That was the first I knew of his reaction."

In addition to hormone-replacement therapy (HRT), Pamela was given some counseling. She was encouraged to tell her husband and son when she was feeling left out and slighted. She was also encouraged to discuss her changed sexual feelings with her husband. He, of course, would be welcome to attend the clinic with her if he wanted to.

There were three follow-up visits about six weeks apart. Pamela's symptoms responded well to HRT. Her hot flashes stopped, she slept well, felt less fatigued and irritable, and, more gradually, her sexual desire and response returned. She made good use of the counseling suggestions and began to feel better about her relationship with her husband and son. Her daughter's pregnancy was proceeding normally. Pamela had also decided to return to school to get a master's degree. She had just one reservation: "I think my new assertiveness and independence are making my husband anxious."

Now let's take a look at the symptoms Pamela experienced and some others she did not, but that are common menopausal symptoms.

Hot Flashes (or Hot Flushes). Between one-half and three-quarters of all women experience hot flashes (or flushes) associated with menopause. This rather infamous and most common side effect of decreased estrogen may be anything from a barely noticeable warmth to a very intense sensation of heat (usually focused in the upper torso, neck, and head), sometimes accompanied by profuse sweating. Hot flashes may last for from a few seconds to up to three minutes, and they may occur from once a month to twenty times in one day. Sometimes a hot flash is followed by a shaking chill.

When they are intense and frequent during the waking hours, hot flashes can interfere with a woman's daily routine. She may find them inconvenient and embarrassing at her job or in social situations. Some women tend to curtail their social activities and stay at home to avoid having a hot flash in public. Some women say their hot flashes can be triggered by strong emotions, particularly anger. One woman said, "I've learned to count to ten and calm down. It prevents a hot flash, but I think it's not good for me in the long run to hold in my feelings." Another woman said, "It's so frustrating. I begin to express my anger, but suddenly I feel myself starting to boil over, the heat spreading along my chest and my face. Instead of getting upset at him, I get upset at myself."

When hot flashes occur at night, they tend to interfere with sleep. Many women get hot flashes only at night, and some are not even aware that they have them; they are only aware of sleeping very badly and waking up tired. When asked if they can remember anything about their restless sleep, they are then able to recall waking up, briefly feeling hot and sweaty, and throwing off their nightclothes. Since the value of sleep is determined not so much by its duration as by its quality (a good night's sleep should be uninterrupted), nighttime hot flashes can be extraordinarily debilitating, causing not only chronic fatigue but mood swings and irritability. Disrupted sleep also effects several different hormone production systems that are active during sleep. Included are the release of adrenocorticotropic hormone (ACTH) and cortisol; renin, a kidney hormone related to blood pressure regulation; growth hormone; and parathyroid hormone, which affects calcium metabolism and bone integrity. Doctors now recognize that sleep disturbance resulting from night hot flashes may play a central role in a variety of menopausal symptoms. The subject is now receiving research attention.

Hot flashes respond well to hormone replacement therapy for some women, but even without therapy, the flashes usually persist for no more than two to five years. However, more than 25 percent of women may continue to have this symptom for longer than five years and, for a very few women, for as long as twenty or more years. We have recently seen a woman in her seventies and another in her nineties suffering from sleep disturbance due to hot flashes. Minimal amounts of hormones were able to control these symptoms.

Changes in Memory and Concentration. There is evidence that decreased estrogen levels affect the short-term memory capacity of the brain in some women.* This usually shows up in such ways

---

*A study reported in Uppsala, Sweden, in 1981 found that women who were not given hormone replacement at menopause and whose estrogen levels were low did significantly less well than women taking hormone replacement on two tests of memory and concentration involving arithmetic and visual search.

as forgetting a telephone number one has just looked up or suddenly asking oneself, "Now why did I come upstairs?" or "What did John just ask me to do?"

The memory loss is not usually debilitating, but it often creates anxiety about senility. Over and over again, women tell us how anxious they became when they noticed a problem with their memory because it reminded them of something they had observed in their mothers. Often they are confusing the "normal" memory changes associated with menopause with a mother's later senility. The symptom looms out of all proportion. It means being old, helpless, disabled, dying. Of course, the anxiety then interferes with memory function, and every little event of forgetfulness becomes a small moment of panic. Although too early to be sure, it appears that HRT improves short-term memory. Equally significant, however, may be reduction of anxiety about this symptom.

Difficulty with Balance. A common complaint among women attending a menopause clinic is that they have a problem of missing a step and falling. Menopause can be accompanied by dizziness or wobbliness. It is not unusual to see a woman staying close to a wall as she walks down the hall to the clinic.

Falling is frightening. In some women, the tension necessary to maintain balance is exhausting. Since most women have not learned that balance can be related to hormone levels, the loss of body control they are experiencing can conjure fears of undiagnosed disease or of senility.

The cause of balance problems is not established. Changes in nerves that sense vibration may be important, or these may be inner ear or brain changes affecting equilibrium.

Depression. Although studies show that there is no statistically significant increase in the incidence of serious depression during the climacteric and at menopause, about one in five women do complain of feeling depressed.

Skin Changes. Skin cells use estrogen. When the estrogen level is low, there are a number of gradual changes, and some women develop specific signs and symptoms such as bruising easily, dryness, itching and burning, numbness and tingling (usually in fingertips), and *formication*, which is described as a sensation of ants crawling under the skin. Wrinkling may also be influenced, although most wrinkling results from aging and sun exposure.

Joint and Muscle Pain. In a 1974 Belgian study of menopause, one-quarter of the women complained of joint and muscle pain. This affects small joints (fingers) in particular, as well as the vertebrae in the neck. The cause of this pain is not known, but it does appear to relate sometimes to estrogen levels, as hormone replacement can improve the symptoms.

"Fragility." In her book *Menopause: A Positive Approach*, which gives a feminist perspective on menopause, Rosetta Reitz describes a symptom she calls fragility—a combination of forgetfulness, moodiness, and a sense of being easily overwhelmed. If you add to this list some of the other commonly expressed complaints of dizziness, palpitations, and fatigue, it isn't surprising that a small percentage of women actually become afraid to leave home—a condition technically called *agoraphobia*. In the group of two hundred women seen in London, 13 percent had developed agoraphobia around the time of menopause, and all of them related their fear of going out to a sense of fragility or vulnerability brought on by menopausal symptoms. A combination of hormone replacement therapy and reassurance and encouragement to venture out significantly helped about 80 percent of these women.

The symptoms described so far indirectly affect sexuality. Fatigue, irritability, and anxiety about one's body and one's capacity to cope with life are almost certain to affect sexual interest and response. The remaining symptoms have a more direct impact on sexual function. Women with one or more of these symptoms usually have fairly serious sexual problems and may have stopped relating sexually altogether.

Altered Touch Perception. Our recent clinical research has found that between 20 and 30 percent of women attending a general menopause clinic are aware of an altered perception of touch. They are aware of not wanting to be touched by anyone. Many say that the sensation of clothing on their skin is unpleasant and they look forward to being at home, in a nightgown or wearing a loose robe. For a few women, the impairment of touch is so extreme that they say, "I could scream if anyone touched me." They don't mean just their husbands' touching, which would lead to sex; they mean that anyone—husband, children, grandchildren—coming into their body space makes them very anxious. One woman said that it was her hairdresser who first noticed a change in her. He said, "You used to enjoy a shampoo and having your hair done, but lately I get the feeling you don't like me to touch your hair or your head." Another woman said she became aware of a negative feeling about being touched when she found herself sleeping at the edge of the bed to avoid contact with her husband's body.

It is known that estrogen influences the time it takes for an impulse to travel along a nerve. Numbness and tingling of the skin are commonly reported by menopausal women. It is possible that a change in the way touch is perceived is directly attributable to changes in nerve-impulse transmission time or to other physiological and/or psychological factors.

It isn't surprising that a negative feeling about having your body touched can dampen sexual interest and response. A woman who was forty-nine and who had stopped menstruating at forty-eight said she thought her aversion to touch had ended an important relationship. She was divorced at forty-five and started living with a man shortly after that. They had a good sex life for a year or so, until she began to resist his caresses. "I just didn't like the way it felt when he touched me, and we both misinterpreted what that meant. The fact that my vagina didn't lubricate anymore was sort of a confirmation." Their relationship ended. After beginning hormone replacement therapy, this woman commented, "I think now that my not wanting him to touch me or make love to me was definitely related to my estrogen being low. I even went back to him recently and it [the sex] was like old times, but now he's pretty involved with someone else, so I guess there's no future there for us. It makes me furious, actually."

The symptom of touch impairment appears to be quite responsive to hormone replacement. Approximately 90 percent of the women who complained of this symptom when their estrogen level was low said the touch impairment disappeared after starting hormone therapy. However, this was not a controlled study, and the effect of suggestions or the therapeutic effects of talking may have played an important part in these apparent cures.

Studies of other effects of hormone deficiency (primarily estrogen) on perception are being carried out. Vibration sense depends on special nerve fibers in the skin, and it is known that these nerve fibers show degenerative changes when estrogen levels are low. Our vibration sense helps us determine where we are by way of subtle vibrations from air pressure, ground movement, and so on. Disturbances in vibration sense have been reported to be associated with abnormal psychological conditions. The study of vibration sense in menopausal women is a research project now in progress as part of our work at Yale.

Other nerve functions that may be affected by low hormone levels include vision, smell, and hearing. All these areas are currently being considered for scientific research.

Vaginal Changes. When there is an adequate estrogen supply, vaginal lubrication takes place within ten to thirty seconds of sexual arousal, whether the arousing stimulus is a kiss or a fantasy or a touch. When circulating estrogens diminish, lubrication takes one to three minutes, and there may be very little lubrication. These changes in lubrication have been studied in the laboratory by Masters and Johnson and others, using volunteer subjects.

If the vaginal opening is dry, attempts at penetration will be uncomfortable. This symptom is most destructive when a couple doesn't know that it is physiologically caused but assumes that the woman is not getting turned on. In our sex therapy work, we see many such couples. Once the cause of the dryness has been explained, they may decide that the woman will try hormone-replacement therapy, which is almost always effective in alleviating the problem, or they may choose to use a commercial vaginal lubricant.

In the series of two hundred women who were interviewed in the menopause clinic in London, 45 percent complained of vaginal dryness leading to pain with intercourse. Women were often confused by the discrepancy between their turned-on sexual feelings and their turned-off vaginal response. Partners were equally confused, often reacting to the vaginal dryness as a sign of sexual rejection.

In women sixty years of age and older, those whose estrogen level is low are likely to experience changes in the vagina that interfere with sexual function. The walls of the vagina become thinner and less elastic. The vagina becomes more vulnerable to irritation, infection, and trauma. A small percentage will experience bleeding from the vaginal walls after intercourse, which can be frightening. Gradually the vagina shortens (from 7 to 8 centimeters to from 4½ to 6 centimeters) and narrows (from 2 centimeters to 1½ centimeters).

These changes may sound frightening, but it is important to understand that they are not universal. Adequate estrogen levels, from your own body or from hormone replacement, will usually prevent most of these changes. So, too, it appears, will regular, uninterrupted sexual stimulation and vaginal penetration, although there is no certainty as to why this should be the case. The women who are most seriously affected by vaginal changes are those with low estrogen levels who go for a long period of time without sex. In these women, the vaginal opening may shrink so much that intercourse is impossible. Treatment with estrogen cream in the vagina and/or oral estrogen plus gentle dilating can reverse the problem rather quickly.

In a younger woman, the outer third of the vagina becomes swollen as she approaches the moment of orgasm. Masters and Johnson called this the orgasmic platform. After menopause, there is a general decrease in genital congestion during sexual response. The orgasmic platform, therefore, is less extensive. And at orgasm, the rhythmic contractions of this part of the vagina become fewer, changing from an average of from five to ten contractions to an average of from three to five contractions.

Clitoral Changes. Masters and Johnson reported a wide variety of physiological changes during sexual response in older women. They did not report any clinically significant changes in the clitoris. However, in our clinical experience with menopausal women, they have frequently mentioned clitoral changes.

They have complained of decreased sensitivity of the clitoris, sometimes saying, "It's dead." Pamela, the woman whose menopausal symptoms were described earlier, mentioned absence of clitoral sensitivity. One lesbian woman was particularly disturbed by loss of sensation in her clitoris, because for her, the clitoris had always been the primary source of sexual stimulation (as it is for many women who are not lesbians).

Careful examination of the external genitals of women attending a menopause clinic has shown that a significant percentage appear to have clitoral atrophy. The organ has shrunk from approximately half the size of a pinky finger to the size of a pea. With hormone-replacement therapy, the clitoris enlarges to its premenopausal size, and sensitivity usually returns.

Urinary Tract Changes. There are cells in the bladder and urethra that depend, in part, on estrogen for their growth and functioning. When there is very little estrogen available, these cells do not function as efficiently. This can lead to changes in the bladder and loss of "tone" in the urethra, which leads to frequent urination (seven to ten times each day) and urge incontinence (urine may leak soon after you become aware of the need to urinate). Some incontinence is taken in stride by many women. Others find it so upsetting that they are reluctant to go anywhere unless they can be near a toilet. Some women also complain about odor and about embarrassment over losing control. This symptom can affect a woman's sexuality by reinforcing ideas about "down there" being a dirty and smelly place.

Approximately 10 percent of menopausal women who are asked about it say that they have begun to leak urine during sexual response, usually just before or during orgasm. We know that ordinarily during orgasm, the urethral opening will relax. With the changes in the urethra caused by low estrogen levels, this relaxation apparently causes leakage. As with urge incontinence, many women and their partners are not bothered by this; they put a towel on the bed and deal with it as a minor inconvenience. Other women and/or their partners find it inhibiting. One woman said that since one episode of leaking urine during lovemaking, she and her husband had sex very infrequently, and when they did, she was very preoccupied by her anxiety that it might happen again. She had become fearful of letting go and hadn't allowed herself to have an orgasm.

With low estrogen levels, the urethra and bladder become more vulnerable, and thinned vaginal walls provide less tissue between the vagina and the urethra. As a result, intercourse can irritate the urethra and bladder, causing burning after intercourse and sometimes cystitis (infection in the bladder). Any regular association between intercourse and pain and/or illness can make a woman lose her enthusiasm for sex.

Change in Sexual Desire and Response. A number of studies have found striking evidence of a decline in sexual interest among women over age forty-five. Eric Pfeiffer and his co-workers studied men and women between the ages of forty-five and seventy-one from the middle and upper socioeconomic classes in a southeastern state. They found that only 6 percent of the men said they had no interest in sex, while one-third of the women said they had no sexual interest. Brecher's research for *Consumer Reports* also found that one-quarter to one-third of the women studied (in their fifties, sixties, and seventies) said they had little or no sexual interest, but his study found that male sexual interest also declined sharply during those three decades.

There is no evidence that estrogen level directly affects sexual desire. However, common sense tells us that a woman who has pain with intercourse due to vaginal changes brought about by a lack of estrogen or a woman who doesn't want skin contact because she dislikes the sensation of being touched (a change that appears to be estrogen linked) is more likely to report little or no sexual interest. In that way, then, estrogen level probably has an indirect effect on sexual desire.

When the ovaries slow down they also may produce less testosterone. We usually think of testosterone as a male hormone, which it is. But women normally have a much smaller quantity of circulating testosterone. It is believed that testosterone influences sexual desire in both sexes, but we don't yet understand how or to what extent. Clinical evidence suggests that some menopausal women who complain of lack of desire feel more desire when they receive estrogen alone. Others don't respond to estrogen alone, but, when testosterone is also given, they report increased sexual desire. This is an area in which more research is needed.

In the previously mentioned study of two hundred women in London, 24 percent said they had been having orgasms until around the time of menopause, but now they were no longer able to have an orgasm. Over 80 percent of these women experienced return of orgasmic ability when hormone-replacement therapy was instigated. Unfortunately, the study did not clearly evaluate whether it was the estrogen and/or the testosterone that affected the ability to have orgasms. One or the other or both may well have contributed to this change. It is also possible that simply talking about the problem had a beneficial effect.

The loss of the ability to experience orgasm was not an unexpected finding. Although most of the writing on sex and aging says that female orgasm is unaffected by aging, there is one early study (by Hallstrom) and a more recent one (by Ballinger and Howe) that have shown an increase in women complaining that they were not experiencing orgasm.

Hormone Replacement Therapy

Between puberty and menopause, a woman's ovaries play two important functions: They release eggs, and they manufacture hormones. The ovary produces estrogens, progesterone, and testosterone. One of the estrogens, estradiol, plays a role in cell function in many parts of the body—nerve cells, the skin, the vagina, the bladder and urethra, and the breasts. Ovarian hormone production starts declining during the thirties, but there are usually no symptoms of the decline until a few years before actual menopause. By menopause, the average woman will have less than a tenth the amount of estradiol she had in her twenties and thirties. This single hormonal change, directly or indirectly, probably causes most of the signs and symptoms associated with menopause.

During the 1950s and 1960s, doctors and women alike thought they had a safe cure-all for menopausal troubles—estrogen replacement. It seemed to hold the promise of prolonged youth and well-being. Then came the bad news. In the 1970s, some studies suggested that taking estrogen pills might increase the risk to women of developing cancer of the endometrium (lining of the uterus). Many women discontinued taking estrogen pills, and since then, many others have declined to take them. At least ten different studies have been done to investigate the relationship between estrogens and cancer of the endometrium. Important findings include:

- Among women who take no hormones, endometrial cancer occurs at the rate of 2 per 1,000 women.
- Among women taking estrogen pills, the rate varies (depending on the study) from 3.6 per 1,000 to 15.2 per 1,000 women.
- Among obese women not taking any hormones, the rate is between 6 per 1,000 to 18 per 1,000 women. This is thought to be due to continued estrogen production and storage in fatty tissue.

Continuing research in the late 1970s and up to the present has revealed that the problem of uterine cancer was related to high doses of estrogen and to the fact that no progesterone was given to counter the effects of estrogen stimulation on the uterine lining. It has now been shown that if a progestin (a substance similar to progesterone in its chemical structure and biological activity) is taken for twelve days each month and estrogen is not discontinued, the risk of uterine cancer is not increased and, in fact, the incidence for women taking these hormones may prove to be *less* than the incidence among women who take no hormone. There is *no* indication that this kind of hormone-replacement therapy (HRT) increases the risk of breast cancer.

Most women on HRT take it orally. However, new methods are being tried because some complications of taking estrogen, such as elevated blood pressure and the development of stones in the gall bladder, appear to be reduced or even eliminated if the estrogen is not taken orally. The two new approaches being tried are (1) estrogen cream applied to the skin or inserted in the vagina; and (2) estrogen implants beneath the skin, which release hormones continuously for about six months.

Most doctors who specialize in the treatment of menopause are including a supplemental progestin, taken orally, twelve days each month.

Testosterone, taken either orally or in implant form, is used for some women in addition to estrogen and progestin. Testosterone is tried when other approaches fail to relieve the symptoms of low sexual desire and/or muscle fatigue, which are thought to relate to testosterone levels.

What, in fact, will HRT do? HRT is usually helpful in preventing hot flashes, loss of urethral tone, and some of the changes in skin described earlier. In our own studies, it has usually reversed women's aversion to touch.

HRT can be very important sexually. Numerous studies have shown that HRT will reverse atrophy of the vagina and the external genital structures; that it will eliminate the problem of scanty or absent vaginal lubrication; that it will change the chemical environment of the vagina and help prevent postmenopausal chronic vaginitis and vulvitis. Edward Brecher's survey for *Consumer Reports* found that women taking hormone replacement differ from those who do not in several significant ways: Women on HRT are twice as likely to be involved in a sexual relationship; they are somewhat more likely to masturbate and to reach orgasm; they are more likely to report a strong interest in sex; and more likely to rate their current sex lives as very enjoyable.

One Solution for Women?

We have already mentioned that in the study of two hundred women seen in a London menopause clinic, only 13.5 percent did *not* have a sexual problem. The obvious and intriguing question is: "What did those women have in common?" In reviewing their records, it didn't take long to spot a common denominator. One out of three of the women had new sexual partners—either new husbands or new lovers.

This is a finding that is by no means definitive, since there is no control group and the number of women studied is small and self-selected. But it does lead to some interesting speculation. Could it be that a new partner revitalizes sexual interest and that, in turn, keeps sexual problems at bay? We know that in animal studies, introduction of a new sexual partner brings about an increase in sexual activity. This is called the novelty effect. Or perhaps these women were already more sexually oriented and interested, and that predisposed them to find a new partner. Masters and Johnson found that some women reported an increased interest in sex after menopause. Perhaps these women fall into that category.

It may also be that many of the male partners of middle-aged women have sexual problems of their own (which would help account for the high incidence of sexual problems reported in the menopause clinic). The women who say they do not have a a problem may simply have moved away from a dysfunctional part-ner to a new partner, whose sexual functioning is fine.

Here we enter an old debate in the sexuality field. Everyone agrees that sexual activity and interest decline gradually with age, but why? Is it because of the female or the male? Kinsey and his colleagues felt that menopause had *no* effect on female sexual response. They believed that the drop in levels of sexual activity after menopause was primarily caused by declining male sexual interest. Other research (by Pfeiffer, for example) suggests that aging women are more likely than men to lose interest in sex. One well-known sex therapist (Kolodny) speculates that boredom in a long-term couple may account for lack of sexual enthusiasm and activity in older couples.

What conclusions can we draw from all this conflicting data? It seems futile to try to blame the male or the female. It seems to us that the story of sexuality and aging reaffirms one of Masters and Johnson's propositions: There is no such thing as an uninvolved partner. We have seen how men can react to biological changes in women. We also know how sensitive people are to psychic shifts in their partners. Certainly, at least as far as couples are concerned, we need to look at the interactive effect of biological and psycho-logical changes in both sexes.

21

Male Sexuality and

Aging

MENOPAUSE is *the* marker event for a sexual turning point in the aging woman. The decline of estrogen production from the mid-forties onward, the identifiable cessation of menstruation and fertility, the well-known effects of the climacteric on a woman's sexuality all give clarity to the subject. Whatever our feelings about the process, at least it has a certain predictability.

Popular belief notwithstanding, there is probably no equivalent event in men. Hormonal and age-related changes in male sexuality are more gradual and more idiosyncratic. What, then, are the sexual turning points in the male as he moves past forty? At age forty or forty-five, some men experience a mid-life crisis—one of whose hallmarks is often a sexual crisis—an affair with a younger woman, a spell of impotence, even a divorce. The next turning point, usually seen among men in their fifties, is a sexual dysfunction or sexual withdrawal, which is triggered by a wife's menopausal symptoms—usually a specifically sexual symptom, such as lack of lubrication. Finally, among men sixty years old and older, there are specific changes in the physiology of sexual response that may precipitate serious sexual problems because of the man's psychological reaction to the changes.

The Mid-Life Crisis

According to Gail Sheehy in *Passages* and Daniel Levinson in *The Seasons of a Man's Life*, the years from about thirty-five to forty-five are characterized by a man's reappraisal of his life, confrontation with his own mortality, and a fuller integration of the masculine/feminine polarities within himself.

Recently, novels, plays, and films have been full of stories about men's mid-life struggles, from John Updike's books about Rabbit as he ages and *Bech is Back*, to Dustin Hoffman in *Kramer vs. Kramer*, who is transformed from an insensitive workaholic to a nurturing father and human being. In this film, a subplot shows Dustin Hoffman developing a noneroticized loving relationship with a woman neighbor. Levinson says that by the age of forty or so, a man is more likely to be capable of such a relationship "with less intrusion of his masculine values and sexual needs. . . . He can learn from her and have a more equal relationship. He is freer to enjoy the erotic aspects of their relationship without having to be directly sexual."

This newfound harmony within a man may translate into a more comfortable relationship with his wife, in which male-female role distinctions can blur without creating anxiety. He can accept her desire for independence and strength and welcome it when she becomes more sexually assertive.

Some men, as Sheehy emphasizes, aren't able to adapt to assertive women, particularly when sex is concerned. These mid-life men seem to run in panic from sexually initiating women, feeling their "waning" potency threatened. But, in fact, potency is not waning at thirty-five, forty, or forty-five—at least not for biological reasons. If there is a mid-life-crisis impotence, the problem is likely to reside in a man's own inner turmoil, blows to his self-esteem in the wider world, or emotional problems in his marriage.

Gavin, who came to see us at age forty-four when he found he frequently lost his erection as he was about to enter his wife, is an example of a man at mid-life whose confrontation with his own limitations, plus envy of his wife, led to sexual dysfunction. Gavin is a tall, unusually handsome man who had generally had what he wanted in life until, as he put it, "life finally started to test me the way it tests most men by twenty-five." He had been a successful scriptwriter until a series of disastrous flops led to doors closing in his face. He found himself having to make new contacts and struggling to get his material read by producers, just like the younger people breaking into the field. It meant financial pressure and, much worse, self-doubt, as well as the fear that he was being laughed at behind his back.

Meanwhile, his wife's sculpture had begun to sell. She was

offered a one-woman show. He was delighted for her and relieved about the money she was bringing in, but at the opening of her show, he found the role of "husband of the star" unbearable. He said, "Probably a few years ago, when I was more confident, it wouldn't have hit me this way, but I felt so invisible there, so unnecessary. The only attention I got was from a few women flirting with me. God, it must be how women feel. Who wants to be *just* a sex object?"

After this occasion, Gavin found that he was preoccupied with concerns about failing his wife financially, socially, and sexually. First the number and intensity of her orgasms was his focus, but gradually anxiety about his own potency entered the bedroom and then, predictably, he sometimes lost his erection. Within six months, the problem of losing erections was a pattern.

Fictional mid-life men almost all have affairs as part of their search for meaning in life or as a defense against the pain of facing their own mortality. There are no reliable statistics to go by, but we all seem to know plenty of men who fit the stereotype—the quick affair that becomes public gossip, the sudden divorce and remarriage. Piers Paul Read, whose novels are very popular in Great Britain, has written of the humiliating self-deception so often involved in these affairs.

In his book *A Married Man*, Piers Paul Read describes John Strickland's mid-life-crisis escapade with the nineteen-year-old niece of good friends. She is a pretty but childish and insipid girl, yet he becomes infatuated. "Every time John saw Jilly Mascall he became more obsessed by this pretty but otherwise ordinary girl until everything she did or said only enhanced her charm. He studied her gauche gestures as if they were the graceful move- ments of a ballerina, and he listened with enraptured attention to her banal views and silly jokes." Later, at home in bed with his wife, Clare, mother of their two children, he decides not to make love to her but to remember his lunch with Jilly. "She was, after all, more like the girl he had married than was the woman lying at his side."

Jilly is simply amused, and when she thoughtlessly betrays John, the author makes it clear he is getting exactly what he de- served for being a mid-life fool. In fact, most of our literature, both fictional and professional, tends to be judgmental about these sexual flings. We understand the reasons behind the action, but the action is still condemned. The attitude appears to be that a forty-year-old should understand himself better than that, or if not, then perhaps he should go into therapy.

In fact, psychotherapy can help. Its dictum, Think, don't simply act, can help turn a mid-life crisis toward creative growth. Sex therapy, if the problem is rooted in marital sexual dissatisfaction, may be appropriate.

But sexual flings aren't necessarily destructive. As we suggested in the chapter on extramarital sex, they can sometimes help. One man in the midst of a mid-life-crisis affair, who saw us without his wife, found that sex *was* more satisfying with his lover and he still felt only lukewarm desire for his wife, but he eventually decided that what he had with his wife was precious and unique and not worth risking, even for fantastic sex. Having made that decision, he was then surprised and pleased to find that sex with his wife improved. He had obviously come to terms with his own priorities and with the realities of his marriage.

At mid-life, there is a potential for a deepened intimacy in marriage, an acceptance of sex for what it actually offers rather then for what we once imagined it could or should be. Many couples at forty or forty-five have lived through enough and learned enough to achieve this. And then, ironically, along come the changes of menopause, which can prove to be as much of a sexual turning point for the husband as for the wife.

Husbands' Reactions to Menopause

Menopause is a biological event for a female, but it is a psychological event for a couple. Some recent research correlating hormonal shifts in one spouse with similar shifts in the other spouse suggests that a wife's menopause may even have some biological significance for her husband. Husbands react to the fact of menopause. It is a symbolic turning point for them, too. And when a wife has scanty vaginal lubrication or seems to have lost her former zest for sex, it is likely to become a major sexual turning point for both spouses.

When we looked at the records of fifty couples who came to us for sex therapy within three to seven years of the wife's menopause, we found that forty-one of the women (none of whom were on hormone-replacement therapy) had a sexual problem. There was also a high incidence of sexual problems among the husbands.

Thirty-nine had a dysfunction, and in twenty-nine cases, it appeared that the wife's menopausal symptoms had played an important role in triggering the husband's dysfunction.

Jean and Roy P. are a good example of the complex interaction of biological and emotional reactions that can make menopause a sexual turning point for both husband and wife. Jean came for help in her mid-fifties, not for a sexual problem but for hot flashes and fatigue. She didn't mention a sexual problem until she was asked about sex. Then she said, "Well, that's more or less in the past for me and my husband. About two years ago (one year after her last period), I had gall bladder surgery and complications set in. I was in the hospital for a few weeks and really weak for a long time after it. Sex had gotten not so satisfying between us, anyway, what with my dryness and all, so we didn't have any sex for quite a while, I suppose maybe three months or more. And when we finally tried, it hurt me a real lot. Roy tried to be gentle, but even so, well, we just couldn't do it." When asked if she and her husband wanted to try to do something about their sex life, she answered, "Frankly, I'm not sure. We've made a kind of adjustment. He's not complaining, and I know he doesn't go elsewhere for it. Right now I just want to get feeling better myself." She was started on hormone-replacement therapy (HRT).

At her return visit, Jean spontaneously brought up the subject of sex. This time she added the information that she thought her husband was impotent. "When we tried sex again after my operation, he'd usually lose his erection. We don't talk about it, but I think that was the final straw, you know, the reason we just gave up trying and maybe why he didn't push me to go to a doctor." Jean decided she would bring up the subject with Roy to see if he wanted to try to change things.

At her next visit, she said sheepishly, "I just couldn't talk to Roy about it. I'd get right up to it and then back down." Jean decided that she wasn't ready to think about resuming sex until she was sure her vagina could be penetrated without pain. At her first visit, the gynecological examination had shown shrinkage of the vagina with a small, tight entrance. Jean had flinched at any approach to the vaginal area. Now, with HRT, the appearance of her genital area had changed. She could see the difference in a mirror and could be more relaxed about penetration. It was decided that she would begin to use vaginal dilators to reassure and relax herself about vaginal penetration.

At the next visit, Roy came along with Jean. He talked about his reactions to the events of the last few years. "Even before Jeannie's gall bladder operation, things weren't right. She had always been the eager type, wet right away. I had never had to think about whether it was okay with her. But it changed. I can't say when exactly, but I just sometimes got the idea may she didn't really want me to. It was the fact she wasn't always wet, yes. I just didn't get the same green light signals I used to get.

"I blamed myself. I thought I should be more romantic or something. I took her away for a weekend to a hotel, but it was a flop. I didn't know what was going on. I was confused. I think I felt hurt—you know, like she didn't want me sexually anymore. I was angry, too. I mean, I was trying my best. I felt she wasn't meeting me halfway. I even thought there could be another guy."

Jean looked shocked when Roy said that. She said, "You never said that to me. Don't you remember my telling you it was because of hormone changes in me and we'd have to try to make it through this menopause time together?" Roy answered. "Yeah, I guess so, but frankly I never understood what it was all about. Maybe I should have talked to your doctor back then."

Roy went on to describe the time after Jean's gall-bladder surgery. "During her time in the hospital, I was so tired and worried I didn't even think about sex. Once she got home, I was afraid to push it, but finally I did and then it was like coming up against a wall. I never did like the idea of pushing her. I really couldn't stand to see how it hurt her, but she'd sort of grit her teeth and try to relax and open up for me. I'd just shrivel up myself, you know, lose the erection.

"Yes, I still had sexual feelings. But I'm not one to masturbate, never was since I was a teenager. I just told myself to forget it, but I did feel like something was missing, and I'd be angry and resentful at times, but I love Jeannie so I'd stifle my feelings." Jean asked if he'd thought about sex with another woman. She said, "Roy, many times I wanted to tell you to go out and do it. I felt so bad about what I was doing to you."

"Ha," Roy responded. "Some other woman's the last thing I'd think about. I'd probably be no good at all. Just what I'd need, some fiasco scene. Besides, you've been my only woman for thirty-two years and I don't want anybody else."

We asked Jean and Roy if they had considered continuing to relate sexually but just not including intercourse. Jean said, "I think I would have done that but I always felt Roy didn't want to." Roy said, "I just couldn't see the point of starting anything if it led nowhere."

Jean and Roy continued with sex counseling. At first Roy had some difficulty becoming erect, but gradually this improved. Jean's HRT had helped the hot flashes, the fatigue, and the vaginal dryness and atrophy. She felt much more confident about herself and, in particular, about her vagina. After about two months of counseling, they were able to have intercourse comfortably and with pleasure. Roy even came around to the idea that sex didn't have to lead to any particular conclusion.

Physiological Changes of Aging

Some years ago, a very attractive silver-haired woman in her early sixties came to ask if we could help her. Three years earlier her husband, then sixty, had suddenly announced that their sex life was over. "We're past that stage now," was all he would say. He insisted that they get twin beds. She was confused and hurt. For a while, she suspected there was another woman in his life or perhaps he had some medical condition he wanted to hide from her. They were a couple who didn't "make scenes." In the tradition of their marriage, she expressed her hurt and disappointment very gingerly. He seemed unmovable. Seduction didn't work.

We told her we didn't see how we could be helpful without talking to her husband. Somehow she persuaded him to see Phil alone. In the first few minutes, the mystery was solved. One night three years before, he and his wife had had intercourse after a party. It was, he recalled, particularly exciting sex although he was tired, perhaps because he'd had several drinks. Then something unprecedented in his experience happened—or rather, didn't happen. He didn't ejaculate. No matter how vigorously he thrust and fantasized, he couldn't come. To save face, he pretended to come. After his wife fell asleep, he lay in bed in a cold sweat of panic. He told himself that he must be over the hill—that his failure to ejaculate was a warning sign of inevitable decline that would soon mean total impotence. Rather than face the pain and humiliation of complete sexual failure, he decided it would be better simply to end sex now, while the memories were happy and his sexual image was intact. And so he told his wife, "We're past that stage now." He didn't want to hurt her. He honestly believed that what he was doing was the kindest alternative.

We remember this story vividly because it was such a poignant and telling example of ignorance about sex leading to completely unnecessary pain. He didn't know that it is perfectly normal for a man not to ejaculate sometimes—particularly when he is tired, a bit drunk, and sixty years old. His belief in the myth of going over the hill caused him to misinterpret a normal variation as the harbinger of the death of sex for him.

ERECTION

The young man responds very quickly to a wide variety of turn-ons. One glance, one thought, one fleeting touch, and almost instantly an erection begins—in ten to thirty seconds, to be precise. Very, very gradually aging changes this. "Mere" psychic stimulation may be less likely to produce a response, and direct touching of the body or penis may be needed. The physiology of erection slows, so it may take a while—a minute or two or three—before the penis shows signs of filling.

A wife may think, "He used to get hard just seeing me take off my blouse; now I have to work to get the same result. It's much less spontaneous. Maybe he's not attracted by me anymore." The man may feel that he's losing his sexual vigor, that his potency is threatened. If he begins to worry about becoming erect and focuses his attention on how his penis is performing rather than focusing on pleasure, he may well disrupt the erection process and start a vicious cycle of worry/dysfunction/more worry, and so on.

Kinsey reported that as men age, the length of time they can remain erect changes. After age seventy, some men may sustain an erection for just a few minutes. Aging also makes it more difficult for the erection to return once it goes down. The men we have talked to who are in their sixties and seventies have expressed concern about their ability to please their partner. One man, whose wife was sixty and had symptoms of low estrogen, put his dilemma this way: "Now, just when she's at an age where it takes her a lot longer to lubricate and more stimulation to get her ready, I worry I'll never keep it up long enough for her." His wife described her futile attempts to hurry her own responses. She said, "For thirty years and more we took all this for granted. We didn't have to *think* about it. Now we're both trying to make it work out right, but the harder we try, the worse it goes."

One factor in the older man's loss of erection may be the position in which he has intercourse. The male-above position, probably the commonest position for couples over fifty in our culture, has a distinct drawback in that it requires a great deal of activity in the gluteal muscles (the muscles in the buttocks). The blood supply to these muscles comes in a branch off the pudendal artery, just above the branch to the penile artery. If too much blood is demanded by the gluteal muscles, there may not be sufficient blood flow to the penis to maintain erection. By simply lying on his side or his back and letting his partner do more of the active thrusting, an older man will often find that his erection maintains itself.

There is one other change in erection that sometimes concerns older men or their partners—that the erection may be somewhat less firm. A man can become so self-conscious about the extent and hardness of erection that he constantly monitors his penis. One man talked in terms of a 70 percent or a 90 percent erection, so obsessively was he measuring its firmness. For him, nothing less than 100 percent was a "real" erection. There are physiological changes that do tend to decrease erectile firmness as men get older. Particularly after age seventy, arteriosclerotic changes are likely to affect the filling pressure of the blood flowing into the penis.

This requires some adaptation, particularly a change in attitude. Full erection is not necessary for satisfying sex, neither for the man nor the woman. One man of seventy-three who was having a difficult time accepting this idea was lucky enough to overhear a conversation between two elderly women as the women were finishing a round of golf. One complained to the other that her husband "just isn't the same as he used to be—not as hard," and it was causing problems. The other, apparently a widow with wordly experience, said, "Oh, lots of men at our age have that problem; all you have to do is sort of stuff it in. It's just fine."

Usually, once a man stops worrying about the firmness of his erection, he finds that it is a bit firmer. His anxiety only compounds the problem.

Even the total absence of erection doesn't have to spell the end of sex so long as we don't define sex in a narrow, stereotyped way. Lovemaking is all the erotic looking, touching, holding, and talking that a couple does together. A woman whose husband was in his mid-seventies, a severe diabetic and taking antihyptertensive medication (both of which can affect potency) told us, "Fairly often when we make love, he can't get an erection but we can still do *something*. I find just being together and touching is very satisfying. I don't always need intercourse or even an orgasm. I *think* I'm finally persuading him to see things my way, thank goodness."

CHANGES IN EJACULATION

Ejaculation has a very special meaning for men. Often it is *the* fact of sex, the event that *is* sex. Perhaps that is why so many men interchange the words *erection* and *ejaculation*. Why does ejaculation equal sex in men's minds? It may be because ejaculation is needed for fertility. It may also relate to the experience of the adolescent. The boy has been having erections for years, probably even occasional dry orgasms. And then one day or night, he ejaculates for the first time. "Aha, so this is what it's all about. Now I'm a real man." Almost immediately, most boys begin a regular pattern of wet dreams and/or masturbation. At this age and for years to come, sexual arousal is connected with a strong sense of needing to "come," and whether in masturbation or intercourse, the young man will almost invariably ejaculate, sometimes more than once.

As the decades pass, the strong need to ejaculate diminishes. It is less intense and less frequent. More stimulation is needed before ejaculation takes place. For the man with premature ejaculation, it can be a plus. The adolescent hair-trigger response is gone, and he can enjoy more prolonged stimulation.

Other men miss that feeling of need, of urgency. "It was a damned nuisance when I was seventeen and wanting to come off a few times a day. I could hardly think about anything else when that need was there and I sometimes cursed the body that seemed to take over my will. Now that I don't have the feeling, I do miss it. It makes me aware of being old. Some special kick is gone from my life for good. Now sex is more something I decide to do, and sometimes I worry whether I'll get into the feelings or not." In fact, this man became anxious and depressed over what he perceived to be a waning of his life forces. His anxiety tended to put him off sex for a week or two at a stretch. He may have gotten into a vicious circle, perhaps even influencing his own testosterone level. There is some evidence that after ejaculation, there is a rise in testosterone. His periods of abstinence may thus have lowered his usual hormone levels, which in turn may have affected his loss of sexual urgency.

In the so-called plateau stage, before ejaculation, the Cowper's glands secrete a slippery fluid, some of which usually seeps from the penis. This fluid coats the urethra and may serve some function in protecting sperm and/or the urethra. In older men, this secretion gradually diminishes and may disappear. Some men then complain that the ejaculate causes a stinging sensation as it moves through the penis during ejaculation. This is due to the alkaline seminal fluid coming into direct contact with the walls of the urethra without the protective coating of the Cowper's glands secretion.

The actual process of ejaculation and the associated sensations change with age. The quantity of seminal fluid diminishes, as does the force with which it is expelled. In some men, the ejaculate simply spills out. In younger men, ejaculation has two distinct phases. First there is the filling of a sac at the base of the penis (the prostatic utricle), which gives the man the feeling that he is about to come. Then, in stage two, the prostatic utricle contracts rhythmically and the semen spurts from the penis.

In men over sixty, the sensation of stage one, the feeling of impending ejaculation, become less and less distinct and may disappear altogether. One man took this as a sign from his body that he should stop having sex. He thought his body was telling him, "Sex is more than you can handle now. It's not good for your health." His anxiety was really caused by the death of a close friend from a heart attack suffered during intercourse. The change in ejaculatory sensation served as a lightning rod for his fears of death.

We began this section on the physiological changes of aging with a description of a man who became convinced that he was over the hill when he failed to ejaculate. The occasional failure to ejaculate despite continued arousal and stimulation is a fact of sex in aging men. The so-called refractory period, the length of time after an ejaculation before a man can next ejaculate, gets longer as a man gets older. This may mean, for example, that at age seventy-two, he and his partner make love (perhaps including intercourse) three times in ten days but he only ejaculates once or twice. If either the man or his partner feels that sex is incomplete or a failure unless he ejaculates, they are in for disappointment and trouble.

SHIFTS IN MALE HORMONES

If there is controversy and a need for more data about female menopause, there is total nonagreement and almost no reliable data about a possible male equivalent—a cluster of symptoms caused by declining levels of male hormones. Starting in the 1940s, a number of writers began describing a syndrome of psychological and physical complaints experienced by some men that is similar to some of the symptoms of women with decreased estrogen production. In men, the symptoms are usually said to include some combination of listlessness, weight loss and/or poor appetite, decreased sexual interest and potency, difficulty in concentrating, weakness and fatigue, and irritability. Some men describe what sounds like hot flashes.

At the 1981 meeting of the International Congress on the Menopause, a West German, H. Schmidt, summarized the research findings on this topic. He believes that the research to date shows that there is no male "menopause," although there is a very gradual and continuous increase in so-called psychovegetative problems, including fatigue and loss of appetite, as men grow older. Schmidt's opinion was not unanimously accepted by the experts attending this congress. The dissenters believe that perhaps 15 percent of men have a male "menopause."

There is no doubt that there are sex-related changes among men after age fifty. Unlike women, whose fertility simply ends at menopause, male fertility declines very gradually and may continue into a man's nineties. There is also a gradual decline in "free" testosterone (the amount of this hormone available for tissue uptake) from about age fifty onward. But there is no simple and clear correlation between declining testosterone and declining sexual function, and, in fact, most men with a somewhat lowered testosterone level are still potent. However, men who are having problems with erection should always have a full medical checkup, including hormone evaluation.

What, then, can men expect to happen to them sexually as they age? The answer is: it depends. It depends on a man's lifelong experience of sex, his innate "drive," and his attitudes. It depends on his health and psychological well-being. It depends on whether he has a regular partner and, if so, on her health, her menopausal symptoms or lack of symptoms, and her attitudes toward sex. It depends on the feelings in that relationship and on his (and her) feelings about growing older. It depends, too, upon how much he knows about what to expect and how he copes with the changes and hurdles he encounters. For some men, it depends on the quality of professional help they receive when a problem surfaces.

There is reason to believe that the majority of men and women can adapt to aging, maintain an interest in sex, and continue to find it a source of satisfaction. Sexual behavior may become less frequent, sexual awareness less intense and pervasive, sexual responses altered, and yet, according to Brecher's 1982 study for *Consumer Report* magazine, almost none of the 4,246 respondents aged forty to ninety-two was totally sexually inactive, although for many, masturbation was the only sexual practice. It must be added that these 4,246 people are a self-selected group; they chose to respond to the questionnaire. One can speculate that they may not be representative of all men and women their age, but, even with this caveat, this survey suggests, as Brecher says, that the sexual interest and activity of older persons is one of the best-kept secrets in America.

22

Medical Problems

ILLNESS, surgery, and medical treatment are facts of life for most of us at some time in our lives. Usually we cope. We get through the illness, we recover from the surgery, and life goes on more or less unchanged. We may even feel psychologically strengthened for having weathered a storm and possess a renewed appreciation of life. But sometimes the illness turns out to be chronic, the surgery alters some important structure or function, or we have to take medications that produce negative side effects. Sexual functioning can be drastically or subtly affected, either directly—through impairment of perception, blood flow, or muscle tension—or indirectly—through the psychological impact on us and our spouse. In sex therapy work, it becomes clear that serious illness is often a sexual turning point.

Some illnesses, surgical procedures, or medications directly impair the physiology of sexual response. For example, diabetes often affects potency, prostatic surgery can alter ejaculation, some antihypertensive medications impair potency, and some drugs that are used to treat psychiatric illness can affect libido and arousal in both men and women. Some conditions may limit bodily movement or leave a person too chronically fatigued to enjoy sex.

Illness or surgery can be as much a psychological as a physical blow—sometimes more so. Most of us react intensely simply to the fact of being ill. There is also the stress caused by pain, disfigurement, loss of bodily functions or parts.

The experiences surrounding illness or surgery can be psychologically battering—the fear or humiliation of various tests and procedures; the coldness of some health-care personnel; the dehumanizing, depressing experience of the hospital; the awk-wardness of friends or relatives. Illness confronts us with our vulnerability, helplessness, dependence, and mortality; it tends to make us less confident and more anxious; it can trigger serious depression. Our psychological defense mechanisms begin to work overtime. We "deny" the severity of our illness; we deal with the facts but not our feelings; we may believe we are being punished.

The spouse or sexual partner feels the emotional impact, too, but has less social sanction for displays of intense feelings or "falling apart." He or she is usually expected to be strong and supportive to the one who is ill. There can be anger at the sick person, and ordinarily that anger has no outlet, because how can you get angry at someone who is sick?

Sexuality is not separate from the rest of us. A blow to our self-confidence is also a blow to our sexual functioning. Depression, fear, disappointment, and anger affect sexual desire and response. Ignorance and fear about the effects of illness on our sex lives can be disastrous. The man with a prostatic condition "knows" he will lose his potency, and it then becomes a self-fulfilling prophecy. The woman who has a breast removed "knows" that no man will ever be sexually attracted to her again, so she retreats into self-enforced celibacy.

Unfortunately, health-care practitioners are not always as helpful as they could be. They may be embarrassed or hesitant to talk about sex and so say nothing. Their silence can be interpreted as an ominous sign. They may make a remark in passing without realizing the devastating effect it can have, echoing for years in a patient's mind. Luckily most young doctors and nurses are now taking courses in human sexuality and should be able to talk sympathetically and informatively about the effects of illness and drugs on sex and about people's fears or problems.

When we understand what is happening to our bodies and what to expect, we can usually manage to adapt. Even catastrophic illnesses don't have to mean the end of sex. All that's needed are knowledge, flexibility, and the will to continue being sexual.

It is impossible to be comprehensive on so large a subject as medical conditions and their impact on sexuality. We would like to let people's real experiences tell the story of illness as a sexual turning point.

Bryan T. was a vigorous sixty-nine-year-old man for whom a bout of serious pneumonia proved to be a sexual stumbling block, largely because it shattered his self-image and the image his wife had of him.

Bryan T. prided himself on two things—his health and his robust sexuality. His sex life had begun at age twelve, in sexual play with a fourteen-year-old girl, and had continued as an uninterrupted source of pleasure all his life. He had weathered financial troubles, the death of a son, a mid-life divorce and remarriage without so much as a sexual hiccup. He couldn't remember even one occasion when sex had presented any real problems. He counted on his body, and it never failed him.

At sixty-nine, he was still a marathon runner. One winter morning, in spite of sleet and wind, he ran two miles and came down with viral pneumonia the next day. He ignored the fever and chest pains until he had trouble breathing. He was rushed to the hospital and put in an oxygen tent in intensive care for five days. He almost died.

His wife, Margaret, was at first simply annoyed with him for running in such terrible weather. When the doctor told her Bryan might die, she was stunned. She has thought of him as invulnerable, her protector. Her first husband had died when she was fifty-five, and she never wanted to go through that again.

Bryan came home from the hospital probably earlier than he should have because he couldn't bear being dependent and idle. Ten days later, although he was still weak, he initiated sex. During intercourse, he became acutely short of breath. Margaret told us later, "I felt terrified and then angry. I don't know why. Anyway, I just started to push him off me." Bryan immediately lost his erection. They stopped everything and went to sleep without talking. They never did discuss it.

Ten days later, Bryan seemed healthier. Partly out of guilt for the way she had treated him, Margaret initiated sex. This time Bryan was unable to get an erection, probably due to a combination of lingering fatigue from his illness, anger at Margaret for pushing him off the last time, and—a first for Bryan—anxiety about his own sexual functioning. Margaret felt insulted and angry. She assumed that desire produced erection; lack of erection must mean sexual rejection. On a deeper level, Bryan's sexual failure was another blow to her idealized image of Bryan, in which she so desperately needed to believe.

The subject was too uncomfortable for them to discuss, and neither dared to initiate sex again. Six months later, Bryan tried to have intercourse with another woman but couldn't get an erection with her. Margaret discovered what she assumed had been a consummated affair. He was too ashamed to tell her he had been impotent with the other woman, too.

At Margaret's insistence, they went to a marital therapist who saw them for a few sessions and then referred them for sex therapy. The therapy focused on the fear of death and infirmity and how *not* to use sex as a test of health and self-esteem. In fact, Bryan had no physical impairment of sexual functioning, and they were able to have intercourse more or less as they had before Bryan's pneumonia. What they found, interestingly, was that they began to have sex less often but enjoyed it more. Bryan said, "I think I needed to have regular sex almost in the same way I needed to run—to prove I was not just okay but superokay. This way I have less riding on it—no pun intended—it's more enjoyable."

What happened to Norman and Charlotte after his heart attack illustrates an iatrogenic (doctor-caused) problem, but more important, it shows how a couple can adapt to sexual limitations when they know what they are dealing with.

Norman, an insurance salesman, collapsed in his office two weeks before his fifty-ninth birthday. He was rushed to the hospital, where it was discovered that he had had a massive myocardial infarction—a heart attack. The course of his illness and recuperation were normal. The day before Norman left the hospital, the doctor spoke to his wife, Charlotte. One of the things he told her was, "Sex may be fine, but don't get him too excited."

Charlotte translated this as, "Sex could kill him unless it's very bland." Charlotte had always been a highly responsive woman who often initiated sex. She had usually had three or four orgasms when they made love. Now she was afraid to have her usual intense orgasms. They did resume sex, but only for a month or so. Norman couldn't figure out what was wrong. Charlotte just wasn't enjoying sex the way she used to. When he asked her about it, she shrugged and said maybe it was her hormones.

Norman had been brought up to believe that a gentleman never "uses" a woman. Sex had to be equal or it was selfish, wrong. Norman reacted to Charlotte's suppression of her own responses by becoming impotent. Charlotte thought perhaps it was just as well; at least she wouldn't have to worry about killing him.

Three years later, Norman had a second heart attack. This time the doctor talked with both of them. He warned them that the medications Norman would have to take from now on might affect his potency. In the ensuing discussion, the whole story emerged. The doctor was very upset to learn the effect his words had had. Norman and Charlotte went home and cried.

Then they decided to try to salvage whatever they could of their sex life. They came for sex therapy. During the time in therapy, Norman and Charlotte became closer than they had ever been before. Charlotte gradually regained her old spontaneity and sexual pleasure. But Norman never had more than a partial erection. His cardiologist changed his medications but still felt that Norman's potency was probably compromised by the combination of medications he was taking to lower his blood pressure and control his cholesterol level.

Norman decided to have his erections evaluated in a sleep laboratory. This is now a common procedure that helps differentiate biological from psychological impotence, although the results are not foolproof. Men normally have erections periodically in sleep, during the phase of sleep called the REM (rapid eye movement) phase. An instrument attached to the penis will record whether or not erection is taking place during sleep. Norman had no nocturnal erections, which tended to confirm that his problem was biological.

Norman and Charlotte knew that he could have a prosthetic device implanted in his penis that would either give him a permanent erection or allow him to become erect at will, but they weren't interested in that option. Charlotte said, "What we have now between us is so lovely. It's tender and warm. I still have my orgasms, and Norman sometimes thinks he has an orgasm, too. Maybe it's just his imagination, but who cares? It's certainly a lot more than we had after his first heart attack." Norman added, "For me, what has happened feels not bad but good because our love for each other is restored and to me sex was always a way of loving. It still is."

Angela is a young woman for whom cancer of the cervix, although it was easily cured, had a devastating effect on her sexuality. It completely altered her perception of her own genitals and made her fearful of vaginal penetration.

At age forty-two, when her children were nine and five, Angela was found to have an abnormal Pap smear (cancer test). Her doctor reexamined her the next month and repeated the Pap. It remained abnormal. He finally decided to operate to remove a segment of the cervix, a minor surgical procedure. Angela had always been somewhat afraid of examinations, and now, because she was so tense, the vaginal examinations were painful and frightening.

There was a checkup six weeks after surgery, and the examination hurt again. Angela began to feel that her vagina had been radically changed in some way, but she couldn't bring herself to tell her feelings to the doctor. Her husband, Peter, also had anxieties about the surgery. He wasn't at all sure just what had been cut out, although the doctor was very reassuring about all the cancer cells being gone.

Both Peter and Angela were frightened that sex would hurt her. Peter even had some thoughts that he knew were irrational about catching cancer from Angela's vagina. When they attempted intercourse, it *was* very painful for Angela, and she was so tight that Peter, upon entering her, ejaculated immediately. This pattern continued for several months until Angela told a friend about it. Her friend suggested that she and Peter seek professional help.

Angela's problem was fairly severe vaginismus. Underlying her involuntary muscle spasms was a vague sense of dread about her genitals. When we asked Angela to draw a person, we could see her anxiety on paper. The woman was complete except that there was a big, blank space between the upper thighs. Emotionally Angela had blanked out that part of her body because it was too frightening for her to contemplate. The starting point for Angela and Peter was a gentle physical examination in which Angela was told she *must* say if anything hurt. If it did, the examination would stop until she was comfortable. She and Peter were able to see her cervix and could then voice all their questions and fears. Once they could come to terms with the reality of the situation and dispel the demons of their imaginings, therapy could progress fairly easily.

Because somewhere between one- to two-thirds of diabetic men have problems getting or maintaining an erection, we have seen many men with diabetes. The diabetes often creates a situation in which erection is simply more vulnerable to other influences such as fatigue, alcohol, or negative feelings.

One man with late-onset mild diabetes was convinced he was now permanently and totally dysfunctional because he had been losing his erection regularly over the past six months. In counseling, it became clear that as long as he and his wife could keep their lines of communication open and avoid a buildup of unspoken anger and resentment, he could get and keep an erection. As soon as there arose what he called evil vibes between them, he lost his erection. The diabetes had made his penis a more sensitive barometer of emotional weather than it had been before.

Once he had regained confidence in his erections, a new problem developed. He still couldn't manage to perform to his own standards. He and his wife had almost always had simultaneous orgasms. Now he found that he couldn't maintain his erection quite long enough for her to have an orgasm, and that upset him. It took all our persuasive powers to convince him that if he insisted on striving for that particular goal, he might find it made things worse by increasing performance anxiety for both of them. It turned out to be one of those times when the therapists were proved wrong. His wife found a way to speed up her orgasms, and once more, they were able to climax simultaneously.

Men with diabetes do seem to be particularly vulnerable to performance anxiety. One of our patients, a sixty-year-old doctor who had been diabetic for three years, could trace his erection problems to the day he sat in his office leafing through the schedule for a medical conference he was thinking of attending. He noticed the heading for a symposium—"Diabetic Impotence"—and he felt himself break out in a cold sweat. He had known that in some diabetic men, erection may become impaired, but seeing it in print triggered his latent fears. For several weeks, he avoided sex, trying to overcome what seemed to him to be irrational fears. When he and his wife did begin to make love, the result was entirely predictable—no erection. They sought help immediately, and it wasn't very difficult for them to overcome this problem.

Not all women with breast cancer have a mastectomy (removal of the breast), but those who do face considerable physical and psychological stress, and there are usually repercussions in the woman's sexual life. In Western society, breasts are synonymous with female sexuality and sex appeal. We are almost fetishistic about breasts. Is it any wonder, then, that surgical removal of one or both breasts tends to be sexually traumatic for a woman and her sexual partner?

Florence was forty-two when her gynecologist felt a lump in her right breast. She was admitted to the hospital and signed a form that granted the surgeon permission to remove her breast if the lump was found to be malignant. When she woke up, she knew from the look on her husband's face that her breast was gone. During the next four days in the hospital, Stuart was solicitous and loving. He brought flowers every day. But whenever the doctors or nurses came to change her dressing, he excused himself to have a cigarette in the hall. Florence didn't blame him. She didn't look at herself until the fourth day, and then she felt a strange sense of unreality and mild nausea.

There was no thought of sex for weeks after she got home. Radiotherapy exhausted her, and she began to feel the psychological impact of the diagnosis. Somehow the weeks turned into months. Stuart was still a loving husband. They snuggled, he kissed her face and her hair, and then he went to sleep. Florence was feeling generally asexual and wondered if Stuart felt that way, too. Or was he feeling desire—only not for her?

One afternoon, reading a sexy novel, she suddenly felt very aroused. She masturbated to an orgasm in about two minutes. It was as if a switch had been turned back on. Now she thought about initiating sex but felt shy. She wanted desperately to know that Stuart didn't find her repulsive. She realized with a sinking feeling that he hadn't seen her naked since before the mastectomy.

Florence began giving hints and signals. Maybe she got through to him, because a week or so later, Stuart kissed her with some passion and said he'd like to make love. It wasn't very pleasurable for Florence. All she could think was, "My God, he's avoiding my breast altogether." Her nightgown never came off.

Over the next four months, they had intercourse about six times, less than half as often as before the mastectomy. Florence had an orgasm only once, while in the past, she had had orgasms easily. One difference in their sex life was the fact that they didn't use the woman-above position, which had been Florence's favorite. Now that Florence had gotten up the courage to remove her own nightgown, she felt too exposed to Stuart's eyes when she was above him.

One night Stuart walked in on her as she was standing in front of the mirror, looking at herself naked and crying. She said, "I feel that you hate my body now." He answered, "I don't hate your body, but to tell the truth, I am having some problems. I just don't feel the old spontaneity between us sexually." That night they decided to seek help. Her gynecologist suggested they talk to us.

Rather than explain how Florence and Stuart dealt with their particular situation, it seems more important to talk about what can be done to help prevent the sort of problems they encountered. Professionals who have studied the impact of mastectomy on couples have concluded that there are some important steps to be taken as preventive medicine. These are: (1) the husband should participate in the decision-making process before surgery; (2) he should visit his wife in the hospital frequently; (3) both the woman and her husband should view the operative site very early in the hospital stay, and they should help with dressing changes; (4) sex should be resumed quickly (one sex therapist advocates giving the couple privacy while the woman is still in the hospital and encouraging lovemaking to whatever extent the couple feels inclined); (5) it can help to talk with couples who have been through a similar ordeal. Organizations such as Reach For Recovery can help.

In recent years, reconstructive surgery has become quite common. Some surgeons prefer to wait until six months after the mastectomy before constructing a new breast. Others will do reconstruction at the time of the mastectomy so that the woman never faces the flat operative site. Although the nipple may be left, its nerve supply will be absent or, if the nipple is removed, a circle of brown-pigmented tissue can be created by using a skin graft from the woman's vulva. Although reconstruction may sound like the perfect solution to many of the psychological and sexual problems associated with mastectomy, it is important to realize that some men and women possess a very negative attitude toward breast reconstruction. Partners need to explore and share their feelings.

Ava, a forty-three-year-old woman who had a colostomy (creation of an opening in the abdomen for emptying the intestinal contents) because of severe ulcerative colitis, had feelings similar to Florence's. She was sure that her lover, Albert, would be repulsed by the sight of and odor from the ostomy opening. Unlike Florence, she dealt with it by talking to Al and to her doctors and to the nurses and other patients. She seemed to feel that if enough words were spoken, everything would be all right.

In the hospital, Al did look at the ostomy site and seemed to be reasonably comfortable about it. He said, "It's not gorgeous but it's not terrible either. It doesn't change *you* at all—not for me." Ava seemed less frantic after this, but the very next day her sister totally sabotaged Ava's progress by telling her, "You'd better not let Al slip through your fingers now. Imagine having to deal with this with some new guy."

Ava now became convinced that Al had been sweet-talking her but actually found both the ostomy and her repulsive. On her doctor's recommendation, she entered psychotherapy. Over the course of the next four months, Ava wouldn't do more than kiss Al. He said he loved her and would wait for her to believe him.

In her therapy, it became clear that Ava's problem was her own repulsion toward the ostomy. She hated the ostomy and she hated her body, which had betrayed her. How could she believe anyone loved her when she felt so unlovable? A subtheme in the therapy was her relationship with her sister, who had always tried to make Ava feel inferior.

When Ava came to terms with her illness and her body, she could let Al love her.

Enlargement of the prostate gland (a plum-size internal genital gland at the base of the penis that produces part of the seminal fluid) is a very common condition in aging men. The incidence increases with age—30 percent of men between forty-one and fifty have this condition, 75 percent of men over eighty.

Prostatic surgery has a bad reputation; men generally assume that it will make them permanently impotent. In fact, with the exception of one particular surgical approach (the perineal), surgery for benign prostatic enlargement does not interfere with nerve or blood-vessel supply to the penis. In the small number of cases of postoperative erectile problems (about 5 to 10%), the cause is almost certainly psychological.

There is, however, quite likely to be one major effect on male sexual response. Between 75 and 90 percent of men will have "retrograde ejaculation." This means that at the time of orgasm, the seminal fluid is not expelled through the urethra and out the tip of the penis. Instead, the seminal fluid enters the bladder and later leaves the body mixed with urine. Retrograde ejaculation is not painful; neither is it harmful.

The 5 or 10 percent of men who do develop erectile problems after surgery for an enlarged prostate may be reacting to the fact of retrograde ejaculation, which is, after all, a marked change from the man's prior experience. But there is evidence that the most important factors are ignorance, myth, and fears. If the doctor has a full, frank, and factual discussion with the man and his partner before the surgery, there is much less likelihood of postoperative sexual problems.

The story of prostatectomy for cancer of the prostate is, unfortunately, not the same. Virtually all men who undergo this radical surgical procedure will be unable to have erections. But that need not mean the end of sex. There is certainly much more to sex than an erect penis.

Lewis is an example of a man who reacted to prostatic surgery with erectile problems because his doctor had not fully prepared him for the change to retrograde ejaculation, or perhaps in his anxiety, he never really heard the doctor's explanation. What he did remember quite clearly was signing a medical release form the day before surgery. He was a cautious man who always read the fine print, and he found that he was swearing not to hold his doctor responsible for possible impairment of potency.

In the weeks after his surgery, he was delighted to find that there was no impairment of potency. The erections he had when he touched himself experimentally seemed as firm as ever. Then he decided to go ahead and masturbate to orgasm, and it was then that he was taken by surprise. The lack of ejaculatory fluid stunned and frightened him. He vaguely recalled the doctor saying something. Maybe this was what they meant by "impairment of potency." After that, Lewis became so extremely anxious about his penis that he stopped having erections until, six months later, he talked to his doctor about it. By now, simple reassurance from his doctor wasn't enough to overcome his anxiety, so he sought sex counseling. After three sessions of counseling, he was once again able to have erections and was beginning to accept the idea of retrograde ejaculation.

If there is a common theme in the experiences of all the people we have described, it is the importance of knowing what to expect from an illness or surgical procedure. If time and medical condition allow, reading reliable sources, talking to doctors and nurses who are knowledgeable about the psychosexual meanings of illness, and sharing concerns with others who have successfully come through a similar experience can help prevent problems. Of course, asking about the sexual implications of a medical condition can seem daunting. We tend to be afraid that others will be shocked or embarrassed if we bring up *that* subject when we "should" be concentrating on our health and well-being (as though sex weren't a natural part of well-being!). Luckily, an increasing number of people, professional and otherwise, will usually respond to a direct question or a simple expression of anxiety about sexual function without embarrassment or shock. It really is worth the risk. The alternative—ignorance and anxiety—can be so destructive to sexuality. Illness is an inescapable fact of life, but we can escape much of its potential sexual damage simply by caring enough to protect ourselves.

23

Widowhood

THE SINGLE most common reason for women over the age of sixty to report that they no longer have sexual intercourse is *not* symptoms of menopause; neither is it due to a partner's sexual problem: It is that they are widowed and do not have a sexual partner. One reason they don't have a new sexual partner is simply demographics. On the average, women now live ten years longer than men. Over the age of eighty-five, women outnumber men two to one. In retirement communities, the ratio is often eight or ten single women for every single man. In addition it is still less socially acceptable for an older woman to seek a new partner unless there is at least the *possibility* of marriage. Many older women eventually resign themselves to not having a sexual partner.

Widowers are often confronted with the opposite situation—too many women wanting sex and/or companionship and/or marriage. They may revel in it, or they may find it confusing and overwhelming.

Widows and widowers cope with their situations in many ways. Here is a small sample of what we have heard from some of them, explaining what sex means to them at this point in their lives.

Widows. "I was fifty-six when my husband died. I wanted to get married again but I knew the odds were against me. I had never enjoyed sex all that much. I mean it was okay, but more for my husband than for me. I made up my mind I wouldn't hold back sexually with men I met. Some people would say I was wrong to do what I did—you might even say promiscuous. But I found my second husband and I don't regret it."

"I always looked at the women in their sixties, after they were widowed, going through all these gyrations to look good—dieting, coloring their hair, buying new clothes, and then taking trips to meet men, or even, one woman I knew, going to the opera even though she didn't like opera because she wanted to meet so-called cultured men. I swore I'd never do that and I haven't. I've been a widow for seven years now and I've met a few men, mostly through my work, but nothing has come of it. I finally had to admit to myself that I wasn't all that motivated to meet men. I miss the companionship and sharing a bed. Sometimes I do feel sexual interest, usually because I've seen a film that's a good love story— old-fashioned romantic more than the almost 'X' stuff you get so much of today. I do masturbate but not very often."

"A very unusual thing happened to me about six months after my husband went into a nursing home. He had Alzheimer's disease, and by then he didn't even know who I was. You can imagine what a hard time this was for me, and to top it off, I had just recently had my menopause. I went to stay with a dear friend, Rhea, I had known most of my life. She's a 'bohemian' type, lives in a trailer in New Mexico. Anyway, we've always been very loving and affectionate, but this time we actually got into a sexual relationship. I hadn't experienced anything sexual with another female since I was thirteen, with my best friend. The amazing thing with Rhea, though, was how different and intense my sexual feelings were. I actually experienced that gushing I've been reading about—what I think they're calling a kind of female ejaculation. At first, I thought I was urinating. It happened every time I had an orgasm with her. I wondered if she was touching someplace special and I asked her, but she wasn't sure. Now, at this stage of my life, it's silly, but I'm wondering, like an adolescent, if I want women or men or both. I may decide to live with Rhea, but I don't really take to her life-style. I'm not anxious about the future. I feel very open to new experiences and I'm sure I'll have them."

"I don't like being alone but at least I don't have to put up with sex anymore."

"I've been widowed twice and I know I don't want to marry again. I just wish there were more men around who were decent lovers."

"I feel cheated. My husband and I had a very good sex life, which actually got better for me over the years. He died last year when I was sixty-one. I don't feel old at all. We were looking forward to enjoying retirement and each other, including sex, but now I have nothing to look forward to. I find the sexual frustration really terrible. Masturbation just isn't enough for me. I feel very preoccupied with sex thoughts and then I feel ashamed of myself. Sometimes I envy my friends who seem to have no interest in men and sex, but I do like being sexually alive. What a Catch 22!"

Widowers. "I think of my sex life with Margaret, who was my wife for forty-seven years, as ideal and I think I'll never have that again. It makes me sad and I also tend to avoid women."

"My wife died a year ago. There are a lot of people who want to introduce me to women, but I'm seventy and over the hill sexually and I feel I don't have anything to offer—no money, either. I don't want to just be a taker. I still see the man as the one who should be strong—the giver."

"I was only sixty-three when I lost my second wife. This may sound immodest, but I was, I think, the kind of man a lot of women are attracted to. You know, I had that distinguished Cary Grant sort of look and I knew my way around in life. I can honestly say I lost track of the number of women I went to bed with. Mostly they sought me out. My body sometimes astonished me— like four or five times in one night—like a teenager. After a year or so of this, I got a little bored. Probably I was proving something to myself and maybe I was running away from my feelings. I had an unexpected spell of depression. Suddenly, for no reason, I'd start to cry. I started to brood about my wife—my second wife. We had a stormy relationship, and I'd rehash old scenes between us. I was dreaming about her. Gradually I pulled out of it—the depression. Now I don't see so many women and I'm not hopping into bed all the time. I'd like to find one special woman. I think I probably will."

"I remarried very quickly after my wife died. I was sixty-eight and not used to being alone. I knew I needed someone. Really, the loneliness was unbearable. Sexually, well, I never believed a grown man should masturbate and I'm the type who doesn't go for casual sex, so that was another reason to find a wife. I had some trouble with my erection for a while with my new wife—I mean when we first started seeing each other. Now it's okay. We have sex maybe once a week."

Widowers' Syndrome

The last vignette, in which a sixty-eight-year-old man reports having some difficulties with erection with a new partner in the months following his wife's death, may represent an instance of so-called widowers' syndrome.

Starting in 1980, the professional literature began mentioning this *widowers' syndrome*, a pattern of erectile problems seen in some men over age fifty who have been widowed. The typical scenario involved the wife's prolonged illness, during which there was little or no sexual interaction, followed by further abstinence during a mourning period, and, finally, an attempt at intercourse that fails due to lack of erection.

Originally it was speculated that the widower's sexual dysfunction was due entirely to psychological factors—grief, guilt, hostility over the wife's death, and performance anxieties. Recently the question has been asked whether or not biological factors may be involved. It is known that recent widowers are more vulnerable to depression and to cardiovascular disease. Alterations in hormonal and cardiovascular systems may impair erection. Widowers are also more likely to increase alcohol and tobacco use, and these, in turn, may affect erections.

Whatever its cause, the widowers' syndrome is certainly not uncommon and it is very distressing. Just when a man thinks he has begun to move out of the shadow of illness, loss, and pain, he encounters an unexpected problem, one that threatens his self-esteem and the future of his sex life. The story of Eric N. is typical.

Eric N.'s wife had a rare, progressively degenerative disease. After three years of deteriorating health, she died one night, at home, in his arms. Eric was sixty-eight, at the top of his business career, a handsome and vigorous man. He and his wife had enjoyed a reasonably good sex life in their forty-one years of marriage. Eric described it as "very tender and caring . . . pretty much the same every time . . . not extremely exciting, but special, I guess because she was my wife." He added, "I was raised in the days of good girls and bad ones. Really lusty sex was reserved for—well, certainly not for a wife. So once in a while, I'd go to a prostitute, have a girl to my hotel room when I was out of town, or even have a brief, just physical affair. I never told Ginger [his wife] about these episodes and I don't think she suspected. They never meant much to me anyway."

During the last eighteen months of Ginger's illness, there was no sexual intercourse, although they did continue to hug and kiss. Eric rarely masturbated. His sexual abstinence continued for seven months after her death. Then he met a very nice woman in her early fifties while on vacation in Bermuda. At first, he thought this would be just like his previous casual affairs, but he found himself torn. Part of him couldn't help thinking about her more seriously, even as a possible future wife. As Eric told us, "Suddenly there was a lot more on the line for me. If my penis didn't perform or I couldn't satisfy her, it would *mean* something. I didn't want her for just one time. I didn't want her to reject me." Probably Eric's self-imposed performance demands contributed to his failure to get an erection.

For the next few months, he retreated from sexual encounters, although he spent time with several different women. "Quite a few women called me up or rang my doorbell. In one way it was nice—flattering—and I got some bonuses like home-cooked meals. One woman friend who was recently widowed was great to talk to. Actually we spent one evening crying together. The bad part was, I started to mistrust women. Were they after me for marriage or my body? Well, I just pulled back."

A few months later, he went to lunch with his firm's director of public relations, an attractive woman of sixty who was a widow. There was a strong attraction between Eric and Lenore. He liked her quick wit and her pale blue eyes.

Lenore had been a widow for five years. During that time, she had had two sexual relationships that were not very satisfying to her. She had never thought of herself as particularly sexy. In her life, the order of priorities had been career, children, home, community, and then husband. Even with her husband, companionship and responsibility were more important than sex. He had not hidden the fact that he had had affairs. Lenore had accepted it because she thought of herself as "undersexed" and too passive in bed. She believed that men had different needs from women.

She had been secretly attracted to Eric for a long time. After his wife died, she had wanted to spend time with him but pride wouldn't let her make the first move. She later told Eric that she just couldn't be the one to initiate things between them. She envied younger women who could assert themselves with men. She could be very strong in her work, but was "old-fashioned" when it came to men.

Lenore's menopause had been late, occurring at age fifty-four. She underwent hormone-replacement therapy for two years for hot flashes. She had stopped taking hormones to see if the hot flashes would recur. When they didn't, she decided to continue without hormone replacement. She was aware of changes in her body—urge incontinence, irritation around her vaginal opening, and very dry skin. She masturbated very rarely, but when she did she seemed to feel different—not as easily responsive as she remembered being in the past. She vaguely felt that her body wasn't attractive now—too "lumpy and droopy."

She and Eric began to spend a lot of time together. One night, at his house, they began kissing and touching in the kitchen. He suggested that they move to the bedroom, but when they got there, he stared at the bed and said, "I can't—not here; it reminds me too much of Ginger." He later told us that he also felt very panicky about his ability to perform. His concept of the male role in lovemaking was oriented toward achieving certain goals, particularly if you were *making love*, not just screwing. He felt he would have to "give" Lenore an orgasm, preferably with his penis. At this point, he wasn't at all confident that he could live up to these expectations.

A week later, this time at her house, they went to bed together. He felt very warm and tender toward her. He did have a partial erection but lost it. Lenore seemed different to him from Ginger. She was shy about him seeing her body. She was passive. When he asked her to show him how to touch her genitals, she didn't respond. He thought maybe his touching hurt her.

After another half-dozen occasions very like the first, Eric came to see us. Basically he told us the story as we have described it here. On his second visit, he brought Lenore with him. We saw them, usually together, over about a two-month period. Lenore was found to have changes in her vagina that would have made penetration uncomfortable. She used vaginal cream containing estrogen to treat the vagina and showed very prompt improvement. Eric had no apparent physical or hormonal problems.

Eric did have a problem separating emotionally from memories of Ginger. He often called Lenore Ginger, and he was impatient when Lenore's reactions made him realize how different she was from Ginger (or at least from his memory of Ginger). Lenore, too, had some unresolved feelings about her husband's extramarital sex. She was surprised to discover that beneath her apparent acceptance lay not so much anger as contemptuous rejection of male sexual feelings.

Both Lenore and Eric had to take a close look at their own and each other's sexual values and attitudes. Eric had to become less focused on performance and "giving" satisfaction and more focused on relaxed, sensual pleasure for its own sake. He began to take tremendous pleasure in Lenore's body, and that helped her feel more at ease with her "lumps and droops." She told him that her idea of satisfaction didn't mean she had to have an orgasm. She never had had orgasms with much regularity. She said, "If every time we make love, I have to think will I or won't I, I'd rather not even start." She made it a condition of continuing in therapy that he not make her orgasms a goal. He reluctantly agreed and then discovered that it liberated him.

As Eric's potency returned, he discovered that he craved sex more often than Lenore did. She struggled with her feelings that when he was horny, he was "like a dirty old man or an animal—degraded, somehow."

It was wonderful to see Eric and Lenore working through to such pleasure in sex and in each other. They had to struggle with both old and new issues raised by their unique relationship, but it was well worth the struggle.

A Widow's Story

There is no professional literature describing a widow's syndrome, but it is not unreasonable to assume that many widows also suffer from a combination of psychological trauma, sexual performance anxiety, and possible physical changes that may impair sexual function.

One fact of life that is more true for widows than widowers is that many fewer will remarry. This shouldn't have to mean the end of an active sex life, even if that sex life consists largely of fantasy and masturbation. But many widows do turn off their own sexual feelings. It may not be a conscious decision, but as the months of active mourning pass and they face the reality of their life situation, they may find no sexual situation that meets their emotional needs. Then gradually, imperceptibly, sexual interest and awareness decline until, as one fifty-two-year-old woman told us, "I was sure that part of me was simply dead and gone forever."

This woman, a nurse at the top of her profession, had been widowed for five years. During those years, all her emotional and physical energy had gone into her work, because she was dedicated and ambitious and because she was putting a son through dental school and a daughter through college.

"I didn't have time for men, and for me, sex had only been with a man I loved. I had almost never masturbated. It just didn't interest me. So when there were no men, there was no sex. I mean, it just was a blank space where once there had been something. I can't even say I missed it. I was too busy to think about it. I think I also got into thinking I should be faithful to my husband's memory—as if it would suggest we had had less between us if I could find that again with another man.

"One evening my daughter started to talk to me about sex. She was very open—more open than I had ever been with her, I have to admit. Anyway, she asked why such a pretty and sexy woman should be a social recluse. I was amazed to hear myself referred to in those words—and pleased. She asked if I masturbated, and when I said no, she said I should. Her timing was right, I guess. I had just started on hormone replacement therapy for menopausal symptoms and the money pressures had eased because both kids had finished school. I was ready for something new in my life.

"I must have been giving off vibes or something, because a few men asked me out all in the space of a month and I went out with two of them. No intercourse or anything, but I did sort of neck with one of them. I didn't even have an orgasm, but it reassured me to find my clitoris still responded. I even began having sexual dreams.

"After that time in my life—that was a year ago—I found that I felt reborn sexually. That part of me wasn't dead after all. I've seen a few men and one of them is pretty special, but I don't know if I'll want to have sex or not. Maybe I will never have sex again; maybe I will. But, in any case, I know that I like having the sense that I am sexual—I mean in myself."

Losing a spouse is considered one of life's most stressful experiences, and it is certainly a major sexual turning point. Since it is most likely to occur at a later age, it can be complicated by the physical and psychological effects of aging. Of all the turning points, it is the one most likely to bring an end to sexual behavior and even sexual interest, but as we have seen, it need not. There can be a continuity of sexual expression. There can even be a new beginning.

Afterword

Sex is inseparable from all human relationships. As infants, we learn to relate through being touched, held, loved, talked to, and fed. Infants who are not held and touched enough may actually die. In these earliest interactions, the core of our personality, including our sexuality, is formed. Our adult sexual experiences reconnect us with this early core in ourselves. As Heinz Lichtenstein, a neo-Freudian psychoanalyst, wrote, "Sexuality is the most archaic mode . . . and therefore is uniquely capable of conveying the emotional truth of personal existence."

Sex therapists and educators are sometimes criticized for overemphasizing the important of sex. In the mid-1970s, at a conference on sexuality and religion held in St. Louis, Dr. William Masters referred to sex as an "ultimate experience." One of the later speakers, a prominent theologian, gently chided him from the podium: "Dr. Masters, are you telling *us* about 'ultimates'?" Everyone laughed. He had a point. Given a theological point of view or even a secular scientific view, sex is not "ultimate." It is true that sex can be meaningless, trivial, or ludicrous. That, however, is a very narrow point of view in which the act of intercourse is viewed in isolation. If sex were really an isolated biological event such as sneezing, for example (an event to which orgasm is often compared), we would be neither as fascinated nor as troubled by it as we are. There is no escaping the fact that sex is an important part of the fabric of our lives.

Like everything else, sex presents us with challenges and perplexities. It won't stay put or be still or well behaved. Society tries to tame and rationalize sex through laws, moral judgments, religious prohibitions, and concepts of normality. As individuals, we struggle to understand the meaning of sex in our lives and to deal with our unruly feelings. We are endlessly curious to know how others deal with *their* sexuality.

Someone once said that human beings have a major design flaw: If sex is so important, it should have been made much, much simpler. It is hard to imagine what our lives would be like then. Boring, perhaps—and somehow less fully human. And yet as professionals in the field of sexuality, we could appear to be aiming at such utter simplicity, to be trying to turn sex into something that functions as automatically and flawlessly as a perfectly performing machine. That isn't our goal and, in fact, it is surely impossible. No amount of social engineering, sex education, or therapy can ever make sex completely problem free.

Even if there can never be a sexual utopia, we can all strive to know a bit more about sex—the biology and the psychology of it— to understand our own attitudes and feelings and those of others. It is a display of human strength to try to improve our lot in life; surely sex ought not to be exempted.

The central theme of this book has been that our sexuality grows, changes, and shifts as long as we live, and that it is challenged and stressed continually by life events and biological changes. We need to be prepared for these changes and understand what is happening, or we will waste a great deal of energy on anxiety and unhappiness. Perhaps the concept of sex education needs to be revised radically or at least expanded. It isn't only children and adolescents who need to learn about their sexuality. Learning about sex needs to be lifelong.

Bibliography

Bancroft, John. *Human Sexuality and Its Problems*. London and New York: Churchill Livingstone, 1983.

Barbach, Lonnie. *For Yourself: The Fulfillment of Female Sexuality*. New York: Doubleday and Company, Inc., 1975.

———. *Women Discover Orgasm*. New York: The Free Press, Macmillan, 1980.

Berne, Eric. *Sex in Human Loving*. New York: Simon and Schuster, 1970.

Brecher, Edward. *Love, Sex and Aging*. Boston: Little, Brown and Company, 1984.

Coleman, Arthur, and Coleman, Libby. *Earth Father, Sky Father*. Englewood Cliffs, N.J.: Prentice-Hall, 1981.

Cooper, Wendy. *No Change*. London: Arrow Books, 1975; revised 1983.

Ephron, Nora. *Crazy Salad*. New York: Alfred A. Knopf, Inc., 1975.

Eysenck, Hans, and Wilson, Glenn. *The Psychology of Sex*. London: J. M. Dent and Sons, 1979.

Francoeur, Robert. *Becoming a Sexual Person*. New York: John Wiley and Sons, 1982.

Francoeur, Robert, and Francoeur, Anna. *Hot and Cool Sex*. New York: Harcourt Brace Jovanovich, Inc., 1974.

Franks, Helen. *Prime Time*. London and Sydney: Pan Books, 1981.

Galenson, Eleanor, and Roiphe, Herman. "Some Suggested Revisions Concerning Early Female Development," in *Women's Sexual Development*. Edited by Martha Kirkpatrick. New York and Toronto: Plenum Press, 1980.

Hallstrom, T. "Sexuality in the Climacteric." *Clin. Obstet. Cynecol.: The Menopause*. Edited by Greenblatt, R. B., and Studd, J. London: Saunders, 1977, vol. 4.

Hariton, E. B., and Singer, Jerome. "Women's Fantasies During Sexual Intercourse: Normative and Theoretical Implications." *Journal of Consulting and Clinical Psychology*, vol. 42, pp. 313–322, 1974.

Hepworth, M. "Sociological Aspects of Mid-Life," in *The Controversial Climacteric*. Edited by Van Keep, P. A.; Utian, W. H.; and Vermeulen, A. Lancaster, Boston, and The Hague: M.T.P. Press Limited, 1981.

Kinsey, Alfred C., et al. *Sexual Behavior in the Human Female*. Philadelphia: W. B. Saunders Co., 1953.

———. *Sexual Behavior in the Human Male*. Philadelphia: W. B. Saunders Co., 1948.

Kolodny, Robert; Masters, William; and Johnson, Virginia. *Textbook of Sexual Medicine*. Boston: Little, Brown and Company, 1979.

Krebs, Richard. *Alone Again*. Edinburgh: Saint Andrew Press, 1978.

Lessing, Doris. *The Summer Before the Dark*. New York: Penguin Books, 1975.

Levinson, Daniel J. *The Seasons of a Man's Life*. New York: Alfred A. Knopf, Inc., 1978.

Lichtenstein, Heinz. "Identity and Sexuality: A Study of Their Inter-relationship in Man." *Journal of the American Psychoanalytic Association*, vol. 9, pp. 179–260, 1961.

Marshall, Donald, and Suggs, Robert. *Human Sexual Behavior*. New York and London: Basic Books, Inc., 1971.

Masters, William, and Johnson, Virginia. *Homosexuality in Perspective*. Boston: Little, Brown and Company, 1979.

———. *Human Sexual Inadequacy*. Boston: Little, Brown and Company, 1970.

———. *Human Sexual Response*. Boston: Little, Brown and Company, 1966.

Mayle, Peter. *Divorce Can Happen to the Nicest People*. London: W. H. Allen and Company, Ltd., 1979.

Naeye, Richard. "Coitus and Associated Amniotic Fluid Infection." *New England Journal of Medicine*, vol. 301, p. 198, November, 1979.

Neugarten, Bernice. *Middle Age and Aging*. Chicago: University of Chicago Press, 1968.

O'Neill, Nena, and O'Neill, George. *Open Marriage*. New York: Avon Books, 1972.

Pfeiffer, Eric, and Davis, G. "Determinants of Sexual Behavior in Middle and Old Age." *Journal of the American Geriatrics Society*, vol. 20, pp. 151–158, 1972.

Project on Human Sexual Development: *Family Life and Sexual Learning*, (Vol. I: A Summary Report), Population Education, Inc., 1978.

Read, Piers Paul. *A Married Man*. New York: Harper and Row, 1980.

Reitz, Rosetta. *Menopause, A Positive Approach*. London: Univan Paperbacks, 1977.

Rimmer, Robert. *The Harrad Experiment*. New York: New American Library, 1977.

Rogers, Carl. *Becoming Partners*. New York: Delacorte Press, 1972.

Sarrel, Lorna, and Sarrel, Philip. *Sexual Unfolding*. Boston: Little, Brown and Company, 1979.

Sarrel, Philip, and Masters, William. "Sexual Molestation of Men by Women." *Archives of Sexual Behavior*, vol. 11, no. 2, 1982.

Sarrel, Philip, and Sarrel, Lorna. "The Redbook Report on Sexual Relationships." *Redbook*, October, 1980.

———. "Using the Draw-A-Person (DEP) Test in Sex Therapy." *Journal of Sex and Marital Therapy*, vol. 7, no. 3, 1981.

Sheehy, Gail. *Passages*. New York: E. P. Dutton and Company, Inc., 1974.

"The Tampax Report." Research and Forecasts, Inc., New York, 1981.

Tennov, Dorothy. *Love and Limerence*. New York: Stein and Day, 1981.

Van De Velde, Theodor. *Ideal Marriage*. New York: Random House, 1965.

Van Keep, P. A.; Utian, W. H.; and Vermeulen, A. *The Controversial Climacteric*. Lancaster, Boston, and the Hague: M.T.P. Press Limited, 1982.

Weis, David. "Affective Reactions of Women to Their Initial Experience of Coitus." *Journal of Sex Research*, vol. 19, August, 1983.

Weldon, Fay. *Female Friends*. London: Picador, 1975.

Index

marital sex vs., 162, 233
mid-life crisis and, 270–271
between older men and younger
   women, 164–165
potency regained by, 165–166,
   167–168
sexual reawakening through, 160

fallopian tubes, 135
   ligation of, 212–214
fantasies, sexual:
   communication of, 247
   content of, 128–130
   homosexual, 129
   incestuous, 203
   of males vs. females, 52–53
   masturbation and, 22–23, 52
   of rape, 129
   sexual orientation and, 30
fatigue:
   among dual-career couples, 101
   ejaculations and, 274–275
   erections and, 283, 287
   menopausal, 256, 259, 272, 274
   postpartum, 194
fellatio:
   ejaculation with, 53
   erections attained by, 96, 119
   fear of, 35–36
female-above position:
   for first intercourse, 40
   vaginal containment and, 155
feminism. *See* women's movement
fetus:
   sexual development of, 64–65
   sexual intercourse and, 181, 183,
      186, 187, 189
fidelity, 72–73, 117
   communicating expectations of,
      100–101
   See also extramarital sex
foreplay, vaginal lubrication and, 132
foreskin, 65
formication, 258
For Yourself (Barbach), 131, 226
Francoeur, Robert, 168
frenulum, 37
Freud, Sigmund, 49, 125, 203

Freudian analysis, 221
friction, overemphasis on, 118

Galenson, Eleanor, 205
gall stones, hormone-replacement
   therapy and, 266
gay movement, 33
Glamour, 15
gluteal muscles, 276
gonorrhea, 135
G spot, 126
guilt feelings:
   commitment prevented by, 69
   contraception and, 48–49
   first intercourse and, 38, 41
   living together and, 58–59
   masturbation and, 21, 23–25, 70
   plunging into sex and, 25–26, 38
   about promiscuity, 175–176
   of rape victims, 26–27
   about sex as indulgence, 101
gynecological examinations:
   for cervical cancer, 285–286
   before first intercourse, 138
   partner's participation in, 66, 135,
      146–147
   in sex therapy, 66, 146–147, 286
   vaginismus and, 133–134

habituation, 110–112
hair distribution, 10, 12, 209
handicaps, physical, 240–241
Hariton, Barbara, 129
Harrod Experiment, The (Rimmer), 168
heart attacks, sex after, 284–285
herpes, genital, 136
high-risk pregnancies, 187
Hoffman, Dustin, 269
homosexuality:
   case history of, 33–34
   children's same-sex sexual experi-
      ences and, 30, 31, 70, 209
   in extramarital sex, 162–163
   fantasies of, 129
   fear of, 30–32, 70, 87
   myths of, 33
   shades of, 32–33

menarche, 16–18, 75
average age at, 13, 16–17
defined, 8
semenarche vs., 18–19, 20
menopause, 249–267
attitudes on, 251–252
average age at, 252
contraception and, 253
effect of, on sexuality, 239,
251–256, 261–264
emotions associated with, 253–254
estrogen levels in, 249, 250, 255,
263
family relations during, 255
female sexual response and, 267
feminist perspective on, 259
hormonal changes leading to, 249,
252, 253, 255, 258
hormone-replacement therapy in,
250, 256, 257, 258, 259, 260,
261–262, 264–266
husband's reactions to, 271–274
male, 279–280
novelty effect and, 267
orgasms and, 255–256, 264
pregnancy sought in, 254
sexual activity during, 260
sexual desire and, 255–256,
263–264
sexual dysfunction and, 271–274
surgically induced, 214, 216
symptoms of, 250, 252, 254–264
vaginal changes during, 260,
261–262
Menopause: A Positive Approach (Reitz),
259
menstrual cycle:
anovulatory, 253
irregular, 252–253
orgasms and, 128
pain and, 132
sexual interest affected by, 178
menstruation:
first. *See* menarche
learning about, 16, 204, 209
resumption of, after abortion, 75
symptoms before, 253
tampon use during, 17, 18

mid-life, 239–248
crisis in, for men, 268–271
extramarital sex in, 270–271
group therapy in, 244, 245–247
intimacy in, 271
job pressures in, 251
psychotherapy in, 271
sexual desire in, 242, 255–256,
263–264
See also aging; menopause
Mid-Summer Night's Sex Comedy, A, 72
miscarriage, 181
missionary (male-above) position, 40,
276
molestation:
reverse, 234–236
See also rape
monilial infections, 134–135, 136,
193
multiple orgasms:
female, 128, 184
male, 116–117
muscle pain, menopausal, 258–259

Naeye, Richard, 189–190
nerve impulses, estrogen levels and,
260
New England Journal of Medicine,
189–190
nipples:
erotic sensitivity of, 16
after mastectomy, 289
milk leaking from, 194, 195
pain in, during pregnancy, 183
novelty effect, 267

obesity, estrogen levels and, 255, 265
odors:
children's attitudes toward, 204, 205
colostomy and, 290
urge incontinence and, 263
vaginal, 178
O'Neill, George, 168
O'Neill, Nena, 168
open marriage, 73
Open Marriage (O'Neill and O'Neill),
168

penis:
  as aggressive tool, 186
  blood supply for, 276
  clitoris vs., 64–65
  curvature in, 12
  development of, fetal, 65
  development of, pubescent, 10, 209
  foreskin of, 65
  hypospadias of, 64
  prosthetic implants in, 285
  vaginal containment of, 155–156
  See also erection, penile
penis size:
  apparent vs. real, 12
  locker room assessments of, 13
  masturbation and, 21
  nonerect vs. erect differences in,
    12–13
  women's orgasms and, 12
perineal prostatic surgery, 290
periods, menstrual. *See* menstrual
  cycle; menstruation
Pfeiffer, Eric, 263, 267
Pfeiffer, Jules, 100
physical handicaps, 240–241
pituitary gland, 18, 214
plateau phase, 151, 278
Polynesia, sexuality in, 20
positions. *See* sexual positions
postpartum period, 174, 192–196
  breast-feeding in, 15, 137, 192–194
  first intercourse in, 192–193
  physiological and psychological
    changes in, 113, 192–193,
    195–196
pregnancy, 173–191
  abstinence during, 181, 183–184,
    187
  "accidental," 177
  attempts at, 178–180
  deciding about, 173–181
  desire for, by man vs. woman,
    176–177
  desire for, in menopause, 254
  fear of, 71, 76, 117, 132, 194, 212
  first trimester of, 182–184
  high-risk, 187

husband's extramarital sex during,
    190–191
  prevention of. *See* contraception
  second trimester of, 184–186
  sexual disenchantment and,
    112–113
  sexual intercourse during, 181,
    182–185, 186–188, 189–190
  as "solution," 174–175
  third trimester of, 186–188, 189
  as trauma, 74
premature ejaculation, 40, 41, 115–117
  abstinence and, 98, 116, 194
  biological normalcy of, 115
  goal orientation and, 98
  in postpartum period, 194
  relativity of, 115
  tension and, 87
  vasectomy and, 214
premenstrual symptoms, 253
preorgasmic women, 130–131
primary emotional attachment, shifting of, from parents to peers,
  28–30, 47, 82–84, 241
privacy:
  of children, 200, 209
  parents' need for, 199–201
progesterone, 249, 253, 264
  cancer and, 265
progestin, 265, 266
promiscuity, guilt feelings about,
  175–176
prostate, 290–291
  cancer of, 291
  enlargement of, 290
  seminal fluid and, 290
prostatic surgery, 290–291
  ejaculation and, 281, 290–291
  erections and, 290, 291
prostatic utricle, 278
prostitution, 94, 241, 296–297
Proust, Marcel, 110
pubarche, 8
puberty:
  bodily changes in, 9–20, 22
  defined, 8
  girl-boy discrepancy in, 9–10